AF679999

By Antonio Escohotado

Reality and Substance (1986)

Philosophy and Methodology in the Sciences (1987)

The Spirit of Comedy (1991)

Whores and Wives (1993)

From Physis to Polis (1995)

The Question of Cannabis (1997)

Portrait of a Libertine (1998)

Chaos and Order (2000)

Learning About Drugs (2002)

Sixty Weeks in the Tropics (2003)

Elementary History of Drugs (2003)

Four Myths on Sex and Duty (2003)

The Enemies of Commerce (2008)

THE GENERAL HISTORY OF DRUGS

Volume Four Part One

Antonio Escohotado

translated and edited by
G. W. Robinette

GRAFFITI MILITANTE PRESS
Valparaiso, Chile
2024

Copyright 2024
Graffiti Militante Press
Valparaiso, Chile

All rights reserved
including the right of reproduction
in whole or in part in any form.

First English Edition

ISBN: 978-1-7357878-7-9

Cover: "*Chez la Marchande de Pavots* [At the Poppy Shop]." From *Le Bonheur du Jour, ou Les Graces à la Mode* [The Happiness of the Day, or Fashionable Graces], Plate # 8. Text and design by Georges Augustin Barbier (1882 – 1932), engraving by Henri Reidel. Paris: Chez Jules Meynial, 1924; illustration at Metropolitan Museum of Art, [metmuseum.org, hereinafter MMA].

For Albert Hofmann and Tom Szasz, who with their friendship and advice helped to distill the essence of this chronicle.

Note. – This endeavor to bring it about, that our own likes and dislikes should meet with universal approval, is really ambition ...; wherefore we see that every one by nature desires ... that the rest of mankind should live according to his own individual disposition: when such a desire is equally present in all, every one stands in every one else's way, and in wishing to be loved or praised by all, all become mutually hateful.[1]

-- Benedict de Spinoza (1632 – 1677)

I owe gratitude also to Pablo Fernandez-Florez who was always distrustful of the project even though he ended up writing various portions and contributed valuable documentation for the rest; to Luis Gil, who guided me decisively through Greco-Latin antiquity, moreover remediating some inappropriate remarks in the proofs; to Ramon Sala, for making accessible to me many sources about the contemporary period; and to Monica Bacazar, my wife, who stoically supported the birth of the whole book, collaborating also in the typewritten transcription. With their economic assistance, the Center for Sociological Investigations first, and later the Ministry of Culture, permitted an undivided attention to the work in its initial and final stages.

---

1 Improvement of the Understanding, Ethics and Correspondence, tr. R. H. M. Elwes. London: L. Beling Tetens, 1901 [archive.org, hereinafter AO], Part III. Origin and Nature of the Emotions, Proposition XXXI, p. 152; *Schol. Hic conatus efficiendi ... odio invicen sunt* (Benedicti de Spinoza. Opera, Vol. I. Lipsiae: Typis et Sumtibus Bernh. Tauchnitz Jun., 1843 AO, Pars Tertia De Origine et Natura Affectum, p. 294).

Author's Preface

It has not been very common to unite theory and practice in the matter of drugs, and this explains perhaps some adventures that accompanied the composition of *La historia general de las drogas*. In 1988 the criminal court of Palma condemned me (being then a professor of Sociology) to two years and a day of prison, having found me guilty of drug trafficking. The six year punishment requested by the prosecutor was reduced by two-thirds, because for one judge of the court the offence was found to be *en grado de tentativa imposible* [literally, a crime impossible to commit]. Effectively, those who were offering to sell and those who were offering to buy (by means of three interposed users, one of whom was myself) were agents of the police or their pawns. Just one week after this judgment, the criminal court of Cordoba declared a verdict of pure entrapment upon similar facts, whereupon they proceeded to annul all the charges, an interpretation that in time would become the accepted jurisprudence in Spain.

Apprehensive over what might end up happening on an appeal to the Supreme Court in a litigation where a certain citizen was alleging to have been blackmailed by the authorities, while they in turn were accusing him of being an opulent drug dealer who hid his criminal empire behind the lectern of the scholar, I preferred to serve the sentence without delay. As a then magistrate of the Supreme Court made clear, the matter was poisoned by the fact of my being a spokesperson for reform on the issue, already well-known since 1983. Given the facts of the case, to absolve without conditions would incriminate in some manner the incriminator, and would open a path toward a demand for a scandalous reparation.

After some inquiries, I discovered that, thanks to its understanding Director, the jail at Cuenca would concede me the three things necessary to take advantage of such a stay: a light switch inside the cell, an ancient PC, and isolation. During that fully-paid (albeit humble) vacation, four-fifths of this work was written. Naturally, I had entered into that establishment with no small number of kilos of index cards and notes, gathered during many long years. I had only to structure them, polishing the final exposition.

It could be added that I did not lose much time, and for this same reason neither was I downhearted. However, the conditions for bibliographic consultation are not ideal in a penitentiary and before I could abandon it this book began to be published,[1] so that it was dogged from the beginning by innumerable imprecisions, more than those which trouble any really extensive work. Some of them were remediated in the third edition, thanks above all to the effort of the chemist and ethnobotanist Jonathan Ott who tirelessly inserted the many changes and additions necessary, thoroughly revising the system of references and transforming entire sections of the text.

With this new English edition, the degree of precision demanded in a scientific work has been perfected once more, completed by a researcher who has been able to confirm and amplify my work making use of various libraries and the internet. As a result, the edition that the reader now holds in his hands not only suffers from far fewer errors and oversights, but also hopes to fulfill even closer the goal of an academic standard with regards to the precision of its information. No doubt, in twenty years this history will need to be revised again as new data becomes available. I look forward to reading that book.

La Navata
February 2021

---

[1] Volumes I and II in the *Alianza* edition.

Translator's Preface

This will be the third of his works posthumously published. I will miss our long, rambling midnight talks. The translation and research of Antonio's work is a graduate course encompassing history, sociology, psychology, literature, biology and chemistry among many other disciplines. To read him is to watch a great mind wrestle with an expansive subject. Though not many ever really learn from the past, for sure no one will ever learn if there is no past upon which to reflect. So far Escohotado has written the best history of drugs that exists.

This is the first part of the fourth volume, subtitled Volume Four, Part One. The second part of the third volume, subtitled Volume Three, Part Two, was published in 2023. I have issued these parts separately for the same reason that at my age I eat dessert first.

I implore you to read it in the original Spanish, just for his style if nothing else. This first English edition of the first half of the fourth volume has been annotated with many primary sources newly accessible online. These help illustrate the original themes with a deeper and more nuanced understanding of drugs and drug policy in the late nineteenth and early twentieth centuries. In a few instances the text has also been updated to reflect changes in fact and perspective over the last forty years.

E. H. Carr called history a dialogue between the present and the past. To paraphrase Dr. Johnson, when new facts emerge, I change my mind. What do you do? It's been a privilege to do my part to bring Escohotado's work to an English language audience. All errors are mine. Enjoy.

G. W. R.
Tecopa Hot Ditch
April 2024

P. S. This one is for solitude.

Contents

Chapter 22.	**Commerce, Colonies and Conscience**		**1509**
A.	The *Status Quo Ante*		1510
	1.	The *Pure Food and Drug Act*	1510
	2.	The Compromise of Autonomy	1513
B.	Early Far East Crusades		1520
	1.	The Philippines	1527
		a. The Spanish System	1531
		b. The American System	1534
	2.	The Philippine Opium Investigation Committee	1537
	3.	The International Opium Commission of 1909	1542
C.	The Debate Over the Foster Bills		1552
Chapter 23.	**Junkies and Juicers**		**1567**
A.	The Hague Conference		1568
	1.	Opium	1571
	2.	Other Drugs	1575
	3.	Details	1578
	4.	Signatures	1581
B.	The *Harrison Act*		1585
	1.	The Controversy Over Dispensing	1588
	2.	The Legal Nature of the Precept	1595
		a. The Medical and the Nonmedical	1599
		b. Possession and Dispensation	1604
	3.	Judicial Reservations	1607
C.	The *Volstead Act*		1618
		1. Alcohol and Heredity	1632
		2. The Therapeutic Estate	1636
		3. Crime	1640

Chapter 24. The Crusade Begins (I) **1651**
A. The Initial Dissidents 1655
1. The American System 1664
2. The British System 1671
B. Closing the Clinics 1677
1. Numbering the Addicts 1681
2. Changing Demographics 1687
C. Opening the Farms 1694
D. Medical, Legislative and Judicial Dissent 1702
E. Militant Prohibitionists React 1707

Chapter 25. The Crusade Begins (II) **1719**
A. The Re-legalization of Alcohol 1722
1. Possession and Trafficking 1727
2. The European View 1729
B. The Demonization of Cannabis 1733
1. Opposing Viewpoints 1741
2. The *Marihuana Tax Act* of 1937 1747
C. International Agreements 1754
1. The 1925 Geneva Conference 1755
2. The 1931 Geneva Conference 1764
3. The 1936 Geneva Conference 1768
D. Spain 1771
1. International Obligations 1774
2. Social Reality 1778

Bibliography **1779**

Index **1811**

Illustrations

Figure 293. The Devil's Weed xxi

Chapter 22. Commerce, Colonies and Conscience

Figure 294. William Howard Taft 1507
Figure 295. H. W. Wiley 1511
Figure 296. The Usual Irish Way of Doing Things 1516
Figure 297. Columbia – Hands off, gentlemen! 1519
Figure 298. Josiah Strong 1522
Figure 299. Theodore Roosevelt, Jr. 1526
Figure 300. The Battle of Manila Bay 1527
Figure 301. Opium den on Manila Street 1536
Figure 302. Bishop Brent 1541
Figure 303. Hamilton Kemp Wright 1547
Figure 304. David Johnson Foster 1551
Figure 305. This boy knows a good thing when he sees it 1563
Figure 306. Chamberlain's ... Remedy 1564
Figure 307. Directions for Using ... Diarrhoea Remedy 1564

Chapter 23. Junkies and Juicers

Figure 308. The Age of Drugs 1566
Figure 309. Henry J. Finger 1569
Figure 310. Interior, Collins Pharmacy 1574
Figure 311. Francis Burton Harrison 1586
Figure 312. Dean Roscoe Pound 1592

Figure 313. Dr. Lawrence Kolb 1598
Figure 314. Richmond Pearson Hobson 1602
Figure 315. Oliver Wendell Holmes, Jr. 1611
Figure 316. Andrew John Volstead 1619
Figure 317. Booker Taliaferro Washington 1624
Figure 318. William Ashley Sunday 1631
Figure 319. Dutch Schultz 1639
Figure 320. Jamaica Ginger 1643
Figure 321. Meyer Lansky 1646
Figure 322. Lucky Luciano 1647
Figure 323. Al Capone 1648

Chapter 24. The Crusade Begins (I)

Figure 324. *King of the Opium Ring* 1649
Figure 325. Dr. Ernest Simons Bishop 1654
Figure 326. Dr. Willis Pollard Butler 1660
Figure 327. Dr. and Mrs. Willis P. Butler 1663
Figure 328. Lexington, Kentucky PHS Hospital 1669
Figure 329. Sir Humphry Davy Rolleston 1670
Figure 330. Stephen Geyer Porter 1680
Figure 331. While the morphine 1685
Figure 332. Here, reclining 1686
Figure 333. *Narcotic* (1933) 1692
Figure 334. Andrew W. Mellon 1693
Figure 335. Levi G. Nutt 1697
Figure 336. Lester David Volk 1701
Figure 337. *Narcotic* (1933) 1706
Figure 338. Harry Jacob Anslinger 1713
Figure 339. William Seward Burroughs 1716

Chapter 25. The Crusade Begins (II)

Figure 340. Cocaine Lil 1717
Figure 341. Agents Pour Alcohol into Sewer 1721
Figure 342. Liquor Raid at Luigi's 1721
Figure 343. Representative La Guardia pours beer 1725
Figure 344. Anti-prohibition parade 1726
Figure 345. Parade for Repeal 1726
Figure 346. Speakeasy 1728
Figure 347. Assassin of Youth 1732
Figure 348. Marihuana 1735
Figure 349. Injecting Marihuana 1740
Figure 350. Beware! 1745
Figure 351. Dr. Walter Lewis Treadway 1746
Figure 352. Dr. William Creighton Woodward 1748
Figure 353. The Sweet Pill 1750
Figure 354. Alfonso XIII 1770
Figure 355. Advertisement for Bonald Laboratories 1773
Figure 356. Juan Carlos Usó Arnal 1777
Figure 357. Carlos Esplá Rizo 1781
Figure 358. Severiano Martinez Anido 1784
Figure 359. Miguel de Unamuno 1788

Introduction

The first half of Volume Four covers the early twentieth century. Chapter 22 reviews the *status quo ante* of nineteenth century *laissez faire* drug policy gradually succumbing to a growing Welfare State, the discovery of new psychopharmaceuticals, a newly industrialized society, the aspirations of the medical establishment, pressures from the prohibitionist movement, and a social tension connected to the influx of minorities, immigrants and the marginalized. John Fiske argues for Manifest Destiny, Josiah Strong extols WASP ideals, Roosevelt's Big Stick upends the Monroe Doctrine, Wilbur Crafts wants to civilize child races, the US confronts opium-smoking Filipinos, moral entrepreneurs gain influence, Harvey Washington Wiley promotes the *Pure Food and Drug Act*, physicians compromise their autonomy to monopolize prescribing privileges, an international opium commission meets, and the Foster Bills fail.

In Chapter 23 the 1912 Hague Conference agrees to not export opium to where it is prohibited and to only use morphine and cocaine for medical and legitimate purposes. World War One effectively nullifies the agreement which is then piggybacked into the Versailles Treaty. The US passes in 1914 the *Harrison Act* which on its face is little more than a licensing and taxing measure but was intended to be a criminal statute, initially judges refuse to enforce it except very narrowly, Hobson compares junkies to lepers, and possession becomes a crime. By the end of the decade, the judges begin to enforce it as a criminal statute, maintaining addicts is now criminalized, and doctors who do so should be boiled in oil. The *Volstead Act* criminalizes the manufacture and sale of alcohol, dry zones are instituted around military bases, and Billy Sunday holds a mock funeral for John Barleycorn.

In Chapter 24 Dr. Ernest S. Bishop advocates for maintenance therapy and sees addiction as disease, is attacked by the Narcotic Division but defended by the AMA. Dr. Willis Pollard Butler operates a clinic in New Orleans until it is shut down. Some physicians observe that prohibition causes drug addiction. Others see it as vice. Towns makes junkies vomit but few are cured. In England Rolleston recommends maintenance doses, a system that lasts forty years. Kolb finds maintenance permits addicts to live normal healthy lives. The Narcotics Division closes the rest of the clinics. Politicians exaggerate the number of addicts, prohibition changes demographics, narcotic farms are opened, narcotic agents entrap doctors, the Supreme Court upholds maintenance prescriptions, prohibitionists argue for stricter enforcement and then the Supreme Court outlaws maintenance prescribing. Anslinger takes over the Federal Bureau of Narcotics.

Chapter 25 describes the US re-legalization of alcohol due to astonishing corruption, injustice, hypocrisy and the creation of huge numbers of new delinquents. The Eighteenth Amendment is repealed by the Twenty-First. Anslinger demonizes cannabis as addictive and the cause of absenteeism, crime, impotence and insanity, worse than a fictional movie monster. Studies in the Canal Zone, at Bellevue, in the military, and in New York all find cannabis to be not addictive or the cause of crime. Congressional hearings in 1937 ignore the testimony of Drs. Treadway and Woodward and criminalize it anyway. Internationally, cannabis becomes a so-called controlled substance in 1925 at Geneva at the behest of both Britain and Egypt but the US delegation walks out. Two further agreements expand the reach of international prohibition. In Spain, the penal code of 1870 fines those not authorized to fabricate harmful substances but Bayer sells heroin and Merck cocaine, no prescription needed. A royal decree in 1918 changes that and drugs quickly become expensive and adulterated. Unamuno is exiled.

The Genesis of the Crusade

Figure 293 (previous page). "The Devil's Weed." Film poster, 1949. Re-release of "She Shoulda Said 'No'!" aka "The Story of Lila Leeds and Her Exposé of the Marijuana Racket," directed by Sam Newfield (Sherman Scott), distributed by producer Howard W. 'Kroger' Babb (1906 – 1980).

Figure 294. "William Howard Taft." Painting, oil on canvas, c. 1911. Zorn, Anders (1860 – 1920). White House, Washington DC.

22

Commerce, Colonies and Conscience

Often the remedy causes the disease ....[1]
-- Balthasar Gracián y Morales (1601 – 1658)

A. The *Status Quo Ante*
  1. The *Pure Food and Drug Act*
  2. The Compromise of Autonomy
B. Early Far East Crusades
  1. The Philippines
    a. The Spanish System
    b. The American System
  2. The Philippine Opium Investigation Committee
  3. The International Opium Commission of 1909
C. The Debate Over the Foster Bills

---

[1] The Art of Worldly Wisdom, tr. Joseph Jacobs. London: Macmillan and Co., 1892 AO, CXXI, p. 71; *Muchas vezes haze la enfermedad el mismo remedio* ... (Oráculo Manual y Arte de Prudencia. Huesca, ES: Juan Nogues, 1647 [cervantesvirtual.com, hereinafter CV], Maxim CXXI, unpaged).

When examining the fundamentals of the Northamerican reaction to nineteenth century *laissez faire* drug policy, we had occasion to allude to a complex of initially autonomous factors which fit together like cogs in a single machine. Generically, the causes are the substitution of the Minimal State by the Welfare State, the discovery of new psychopharmaceuticals thanks to progress in the chemical techniques of analysis, and the basic anxiety inherent in contemporary, industrial society. Among the specific causes one can count the aspirations of the medical establishment, pressures from the prohibitionist movement, and a social tension connected to the influx of minorities, immigrants and the marginalized.

A. The *Status Quo Ante*

All these factors were already present in the last third of the nineteenth century. The connections between them, however, are speedily strengthened with the ascent of the United States to the status of a great world power. Eventually this confluence of motives will provoke a call for both an internal and an external crusade.

1. The *Pure Food and Drug Act*

The *Pure Food and Drug Act* [PFDA] of 1906 did not satisfy the expectations of that branch of medicine with an institutional vocation nor those of the so-called toadstool millionaires. Based on the principle of truth-in-advertising,[2] the PFDA demanded a drug manufacturer detail exactly the composition of each drug, analytically decipherable by chemists like Harvey Washington Wiley (1844 – 1930).

---

[2] For a more in-depth discussion, see GHDV3P2, Chapter 18. The Anti-Liberal Reaction, B. 3. The Principle of Truth-in-Advertising, pp. 1278-1287.

Figure 295. "H. W. Wiley – working in the U. S. Department of Agriculture's Bureau of Chemistry laboratory." B&W film negative, c. 1907. Library of Congress Prints and Photographs Division, Washington, DC LG.

Although this doubtlessly benefitted the public it did not cease to be prejudicial to the interests of many manufacturers. At the same time, it was irritating to those prohibitionists concerned with non-alcoholic drugs, who attributed to them intrinsic powers of trickery. So long as these were not accompanied with restrictive laws, the war between the Hippocratics and the so-called quacks would remain indecisive on a crucial battlefield, that of the control of substances with an influence over the soul.

In fact, like Gaul the medical estate in the United States (as in Europe) was divided into three zones of influence, corresponding to the three professional branches in play: the manufacturers, the pharmacists and the physicians. To purchase morphine, heroin or cocaine wholesale was as difficult then as obtaining ether or pure alcohol in large quantities today, because these alkaloids were shipped from the manufacturers directly to the pharmacies, and to obtain them not in their habitual doses (vials, capsules, envelopes, pills, etc.) it was necessary to physically go to the laboratory where they were being prepared. Some manufacturers offered to send them through the mail, avoiding the mediation of middlemen, but they were then obliged to risk the inconvenience of a bad reputation, because the pharmacists responded to the attempt to evade their intervention by recommending to their clientele that they should only trust so-called respectable brands. On the other hand, the wholesaler of these products never saw either the pharmacies or the drugstores as competition, because thanks to these intermediaries the drugs were sold to the public in small doses according to weight (as had been traditional with the herbalists), enjoying a completely different economic regimen. On their side, the herbalists continued selling very cheap drugs like cannabis, poppies, solanaceas, datura, peyote and even homemade opium.

However, the doctors felt defenseless before this intrusion. Their economic condition was many times more modest than it is today, due to the lack of rigor in the prerequisites for a diploma exhibited by a large number of practicing physicians; to avoid this required a long academic career which excluded those wanting or needing to earn a living quickly. As urgent or even more so was the need to establish an influence on the other two professional branches of the medical estate.

As the founders of the American Medical Association [AMA] clearly foresaw, the latter depended on the power to determine which medicines were admissible, as well as the power to decide who could administer them. Something accepted as so natural today was unthinkable in the past, and was little more than a simple hope then. For this hope to be converted into reality, it was necessary for doctors to accept the premises of an institutional state medicine, renouncing part of their ancient independence (some feared all of their independence would be lost), and even then it would be necessary to gather additional support, both inside and outside the therapeutic trade.

2. The Compromise of Autonomy

Inside would not be easy, because the power to decide which medicines were admissible and which inadmissible affected the prerogatives of the manufacturers, physicians and pharmacists, promoting disputes among them for more than a decade. As for the doctors, their agreement with the standard of Hippocratic principles was more apparent than real. At the beginning of the century, only some thirty percent of professional doctors were members of the AMA. The American Pharmaceutical Association [APhA] in turn flatly opposed any collaboration so long as physicians could operate as pharmacists and turn their consulting rooms into actual pharmacies, establishing a direct relationship with both the manufacturers and the clients. Since renouncing this would mean a considerable economic loss (which many doctors would reject), the atmosphere then between the two associations was one of mutual distrust and suspicion.

On a professional level however there was perfect complementarity. This was not only because both the doctors and pharmacists were united in the struggle of so-called scientific medicine against traditional therapies, but also because the constitutions of both associations demanded a monopoly on public health. Similar by-laws called for people capable of administering trusted medicines with skill to each particular patient no less than persons capable of controlling their production and distribution. Yet, we will see that at the moment of establishing a system for dispensing pharmaceuticals, here and there the accord will be broken.

With regards to outside support, nothing compared to the strength of the prohibitionist movement. Divided during the nineteenth century into a multitude of sects, the prohibitionists did not always coordinate their actions, but one could say that from around 1900 this attitude ceded to a larger self-consciousness. The goal was to illegalize any unnatural appetite, and by such they meant ebriety in any form. If they were more worried about alcohol and tobacco, it was because more people used them, not because other substances with euphoric action on the soul merited anything other than unconditional reproach; except for coffee and tea (which some religious sects and feminist leagues also condemned), every vehicle of ebriety then known constituted signs of criminal depravity. In this sense it is important to understand that the very rigor of the prohibitionist creed forbade any expectation of a practical victory, among other things because its naive formulation not only stumbled up against the drug consumer but also the medical class as a whole. Some doctors had already contributed their voices to raising the alarm of the fundamentalists regarding certain alkaloids,[3] but while there was not a true understanding between the leaders of the medical estate (incarnated in the colleges of medicine and pharmacy) and the leaders of the prohibitionist movements, there was lacking the minimum conditions to produce legislative change.

The conditions of such a pact were simple: doctors and pharmacists could continue to prescribe alcoholic drinks as part of their professional treatments in case a Dry Law was established, and they would receive a rigorously exclusive system for dispensing cocaine, opiates and any other drug that merited, in their opinion, such control. In exchange for this, the AMA and the APhA would support the basic positions of the Prohibition Party, presenting the consumption of psychopharmaceuticals as a subtle and violent epidemic, foreign to American souls, and rapidly capable of being abolished with measures of sufficient force.

In the first decades of the twentieth century, both doctors and pharmacists began singing from the same prohibitionist hymnbook. At their fifty-first annual meeting in 1903 the chairman of the APhA compared drugs to murder: "A murderer who destroys a man's body is an angel beside one who destroys that man's soul and lets the body live for crime."[4] The president-elect of the AMA argued in 1919 for an internal housecleaning and cooperation with legislators:

---

[3] See for example GHDV3P2, Chapter 18. The Anti-Liberal Reaction, B. 4. The Battle Over Psychotropic Drugs, p. 1292.

[4] Eberle, E. G., chairman and Frederick T. Gordon. "Report of the Committee on the Acquirement of Drug Habits," Proceedings of the American Pharmaceutical Association. Baltimore, MD: Published by the American Pharmaceutical Association, 1903 [archive.org, hereinafter AO], p. 477.

THE USUAL IRISH WAY OF DOING THINGS.

Figure 296. "The Usual Irish Way of Doing Things." Thomas Nast (1840 – 1902). Wood engraving on paper. *Harper's Weekly*, Volume XV, No. 766, Saturday, 2 September 1871 AO, p. 824.

> The responsibility of the medical profession is becoming greater and greater to see to it that some action should be taken against a few renegade and depraved members of the profession who, joining the criminal class, make it possible to continue the evil and illicit drug trade. For any complete control of the situation, the medical profession must work in harmony with the state and federal governments.[5]

While in 1924 one of the most pre-eminent physicians in Europe opined that morphine was a curse unless first blessed by the hands of a physician: "In morphia are combined a blessing and a curse. If it is dispensed by the hand of a physician its power is divine."[6]

Along with this grab bag of extremist dichotomies it is important to take into consideration the prejudices that connect one or another social and racial minority with this or that drug, within a scheme of circular reasoning. On the one hand, the fact of disparaging a minority group leads to disparaging the vehicles of cure and recreation most used by its members, which are invested with the features of perversity or inconvenience appropriate to the group itself. On the other hand, the fact of using this or that substance permits one to include a certain social group in one category or another, justifying the attribution of those very features of perversity or inconvenience. This model obviously marks each drug that is considered dangerous. With alcohol, for example, identical reasoning identified the Irish, who already in the times of Cromwell had been sold as slaves in the markets

---

[5] Lambert, Alexander. "Address of the President Elect," The Journal of the American Medical Association, Volume 72, No. 24, June 14. Chicago, IL: The American Medical Association, 1919 AO, p. 1767.

[6] Lewin, Louis. Phantastica: Narcotic and Stimulating Drugs, Their Use and Abuse, tr. P. H. A. Wirth. NY: E. P. Dutton & Company, 1964 AO, pp. 69-70; *Segen und Fluch verknüpft sich ... den nur die Hand des Arztes spenden soll* (*Phantastica: die betäubenden und Erregenden Genussmittel Für Ärzte und Nichtärzte*. Berlin: Verlag Von Georg Stilke, 1924 AO, 5. Die Hilfe gegen den wachsenden Morphinismus, p. 62); see also GHDV3P2, Chapter 18, p. 1292.

of Virginia, and later the Jews and Italians; they are depreciated because they drink wine or liquor, but they drink wine and liquor because they are depreciable.

With opium, the same thing occurs, though the group in question is now the Chinese, which for the unions have the additional vice of working more for less money. In the case of cocaine, it is the Negroes, who seek equality with Whites, and with cannabis it will be the Mexicans, against whom will be felt analogous resentments as those centered on the Irish, Jews, Italians, Chinese and Negroes. Really devastating drugs which millions of persons consume, like barbiturates, are not symbols of despised minorities and remain simple medicines for more than half a century, free from any social and legal stigma.

In large part, these are the conditions at the beginning of the twentieth century in the United States. In the judgment of the Special Committee of Congress on the Acquisition of the Drug Habit there are in 1902 supposedly some 200,000 persons dependent on opium, opiates and cocaine in the country, as well as an uncalculable number of episodic users: "From the reports made ... we believe it is quite safe to estimate that at least five different unfortunates of this class are known to every pharmacist, making at least 200,000 in this country, or about three to every 1,000 of our population."[7] This is the moment when a number of moral entrepreneurs appear, whose energy and influence will make decisive changes.

---

[7] Hynson, Henry B. "Report of the Committee on Acquirement of the Drug Habit," Proceedings of the American Pharmaceutical Association at the Fiftieth Annual Meeting held at Philadelphia, PA, September, 1902. Baltimore, MD: Published by the APhA, 1902 AO, Minutes of the Section on Education and Legislation, p. 570.

Figure 297. "Columbia – Hands off, gentlemen! America means Fair Play for All Men." Thomas Nast (1840 – 1902). Wood engraving on paper. *Harper's Weekly*, Volume XV, No. 738, 18 February 1871 AO, p. 149.

B. Early Far East Crusades

According to an historian of the diplomatic corps, "It was the American missionaries in the Far East ... who played the greatest part in inducing the United States to take the lead in the movement against the [opium] traffic."[8] Moreover, it can be said that the initiative to put an end to similar vices keeps a strict relationship with the doctrine of Manifest Destiny, which justifies American intervention in the Atlantic and Pacific. As early as 1885, an article with the same name appeared in *Harper's*, predicting the global hegemony of the United States and approving the necessity of war to achieve it:

> War, as we have seen, is with barbarous races both a necessity and a favorite occupation; as long as civilization comes in contact with barbarism it remains a too frequent necessity .... I believe that the time will come when such a state of things will exist upon the earth, when it will be possible ... to speak of the United States as stretching from pole to pole, or with Tennyson to celebrate the 'parliament of man and the federation of the world [quotation marks original].'[9]

Political and commercial goals were inextricably linked with missionary pretensions by the Reverend Josiah Strong (1847 – 1916) in a work which sold 170,000 copies (an uncommon amount then) and underpins the already circulating doctrine of manifest destiny with racial dreams and WASP ideals:

---

[8] Taylor, Arnold H. American Diplomacy and the Narcotics Traffic, 1900 – 1939: A Study in International Humanitarian Reform. Durham, NC: Duke University Press, 1969 AO, p. 29.

[9] Fiske, John. "Manifest Destiny," *Harper's New Monthly Magazine*, Volume LXX, No. CCCCXVIII, March 1885 AO, pp. 588, 590.

Is there room for reasonable doubt that this race ... is destined to dispossess many weaker races, assimilate others, and mold the remainder, until, in a very true and important sense, it has Anglo-Saxonized mankind? ... Is it manifest that the Anglo-Saxon holds in his hands the destinies of mankind for ages to come? Is it evident that the United States is to be the home of this race, the principal seat of his power, the great center of his influence?[10]

Strong was the General Secretary (1886 – 1898) of the Evangelical Alliance for the United States (established 1867), previously a coalition of Protestant groups, today the Federal Council of Churches. The American Home Missionary Society (established 1826) published his most famous book from which the previous quote is taken. Both organizations had national reach and a prohibitionist orientation. Many years later, after the assassination of William McKinley (1843 – 1901) makes Theodore Roosevelt Jr. (1858 – 1919) president, Strong's book, as well as those of Rear Admiral Alfred Thayer Mahan (1840 – 1914)[11] and the so-called father of American political scientists John William Burgess (1844 – 1931),[12] will find an

---

[10] Strong, Josiah. Our Country: Its Possible Future and its Present Crisis. NY: The American Home Missionary Society, 1885 AO, Ch. XIII The Anglo-Saxon and the World's Future, pp. 178, 179.

[11] "The condition of these people is not that of sheep to be owned, although in some respects it much resembles that of sheep without a shepherd; for ... much of the force of the Asiatic is expended in maintaining a dogged stationariness of development, which has settled at last into an apparent impotency for self-regeneration, whether of social institutions or of government" (Mahan, A. T. The Problem of Asia and Its Effect upon International Policies. Boston, MA: Little, Brown, and Company, 1900 AO, p. 87).

[12] "There is a population ... in Sweden, Norway, Denmark and the Netherlands, which ... is probably the purest Teutonic stock, and the best stock, in Europe. I mean to include them ... among the Germans, Britons and North Americans in the great work of the world's civilization" (Burgess, J. W. "Germany, Great Britain and

Figure 298. "Josiah Strong." Portrait with added signature, prior to 1893. Wannamaker, John. Book News: A Monthly Survey of General Literature, Volume XI, September 1892 to August 1893. Philadelphia, PA: John Wannamaker, 1893 AO, p. 517.

---

the United States," *Political Science Quarterly*, Volume XIX, No. 1, March 1904 AO, p. 2).

echo in the Roosevelt corollary to the Monroe Doctrine, which in practice meant declaring the right to intervene militarily in any state in Latin America or the Pacific which might show so-called impotence:

If a nation shows that it knows how to act with reasonable efficiency and decency in social and political matters, if it keeps order and pays its obligations, it need fear no interference from the United States. Chronic wrongdoing, or an impotence which results in a general loosening of the ties of civilized society, may in America, as elsewhere, ultimately require intervention by some civilized nation, and in the Western Hemisphere the adherence of the Untied States to the Monroe Doctrine may force the United States, however reluctantly, in flagrant cases of such wrongdoing or impotence, to the exercise of an international police power.[13]

The Monroe Doctrine on the other hand had been influenced by the letters of Thomas Jefferson (1743 – 1826) to his faithful disciple and friend James Monroe (1758 – 1831), who had solicited his advice for his annual message to Congress:

our first and fundamental maxim should be, never to entangle ourselves in the broils of Europe; our 2d never to suffer Europe to intermeddle in Cis-Atlantic affairs. American, North & South, has a set of interests distinct from those of Europe, and peculiarly her own. she should therefore have a system of her own, separate and apart from that of Europe. while the last is laboring to become the domicil of despotism, our endeavor should surely be to make our hemisphere that of freedom. ... But we have first to ask ourselves a question. do we wish to acquire to our own Confederacy any one or more of the Spanish provinces? I candidly confess that I have ever looked on Cuba as the most interesting addition which could ever be made to our system of states. ... yet, as I am sensible that this can never be obtained ... but

[13] Roosevelt, Theodore. "Theodore Roosevelt's Annual Message to Congress for 1904," Records of the U.S. House of Representatives, National Archives [catalog.archives.gov, hereinafter CAG], House Records HR 58A-K2; see also "Policy toward other nations of western hemisphere," Congressional Record, Senate, 6 Dec 1904 [govinfo.gov, hereinafter GIG], p. 19.

by war ... I have no hesitation in abandoning my first wish to future chances .... I could honestly therefore join in the declaration proposed that we aim not at the acquisition of any of those possessions, that we will not stand in the way of any amicable arrangement between them and the mother country: but that we will oppose, in all our means, the forcible interposition of any other power, either as auxiliary, stipendiary, or under any other form or pretext, and most especially their transfer to any power, by conquest, cession, or acquisition in any other way.[14]

The Monroe Doctrine was based on libertarian, anticlerical and noninterference principles:

We owe it, therefore, to candor and to the amicable relations existing between the United States and those [European] Powers, to declare, that we should consider any attempt on their part to extend their system to any portion of this hemisphere, as dangerous to our peace and safety. ... [W]e could not view any interposition for the purpose of oppressing them [former colonies], or controlling, in any other manner, their destiny, by any European Power, in any other light than as the manifestation of an unfriendly disposition towards the United States.[15]

In his corollary, Roosevelt's Big Stick foreign policy expresses the exact opposite.

The combination of imperial ambition and missionary zeal which characterizes American policy in this era can best be exemplified in the writings of the director of the International Reform Bureau (established 1895), Wilbur F. Crafts (1850 – 1922). In 1900 Crafts published under the auspices of his organization a curious book in which he declared:

---

[14] Thomas Jefferson to James Monroe, 24 October 1823, Monticello, Oct. 24. 23. Papers of James Monroe, Founders Online [founders.archives.gov, hereinafter FO]).

[15] Monroe, James. "Message to Congress," December 1823, Annals of Congress, 18th Congress, 1st Session, Senate Journal, 12-19, Library of Congress, "A Century of Lawmaking" [memory.loc.gov, MLG], p. 22.

No Christian celebration of the completion of nineteen Christian centuries has yet been arranged. Could there be a fitter one than the general adoption, by separate and joint action of the great nations of the world, of the new policy of civilization, in which Great Britain is leading, the policy of prohibition for native races, in the interest of commerce as well as conscience, since the liquor traffic among child races, even more manifestly than in civilized lands, injures all other trades by producing poverty, disease and death. Our object, more profoundly viewed, is *to create a more favorable environment for the child races that civilized nations are essaying to civilize and Christianize* [italics original].[16]

From his position as a cleric and public figure, Crafts neatly expresses the concepts in play. Inextricably fused, both moral and commercial motives counsel a policy of prohibition for the child races, a policy that will crown twenty centuries of Christian history. Using England as a guide (because now that the Chinese have returned to cultivating opium, the British do not want to enforce its importation but rather prohibit its exportation to other countries), Western nations must impose their own culture and faith upon others. Fundamentally, this describes a Christian enterprise and only, secondarily, a profitable business.

[16] Crafts, Dr. & Mrs. Wilbur F. and Misses Mary & Margaret W. Leitch. Intoxicating Drinks & Drugs in All Lands and Times: A Twentieth Century Survey of Intemperance, Based on a Symposium of Testimony from One Hundred Missionaries and Travelers, Revised Eleventh Edition. Washington, DC: The International Reform Bureau, 1911 AO, p. 14.

Figure 299. Theodore Roosevelt, Jr. (c. 1903). Oil on canvas by John Singer Sargent (1886 – 1925). White House, Washington, DC.

Figure 300. "The Battle of Manila Bay." Undated. Black and white print. Library of Congress Prints and Photographs Division, Washington, DC.

1. The Philippines

The war with Spain (even more so than the seizure by gunboat of the Kingdom of Hawaii) marks the beginning of the overseas expansion of the American Empire. Action in the Philippines begins on the morning of 1 May 1898 when Commodore George A. Dewey commanding nine warships "steamed into Manila Bay ... and almost casually destroyed a Spanish fleet defending what was then a colony of Spain."[17] For a modest initial casualty list,[18] the Spanish-American War

---

[17] Pomeroy, William J. The Philippines: Colonialism, Collaboration, and Resistance! NY: International Publishers, 1992, I. Suppressing a Nation, p. 1.

[18] For example: "At the cost of just 121 casualties in a single day of sporadic fighting, the United States had become ... an imperial power (McCoy, Alfred W. Policing America's Empire: The United States, the Philippines, and the Rise of the Surveillance State. Madison, WI: University of Wisconsin Press, 2009, Chapter 1 Capillaries of Empire, p. 15).

bestows upon the conquerors Puerto Rico, Guam, the Philippines and absolute control over Cuba (coveted, as we have just seen, since the Jefferson administration).

In the beginning, many Filipinos saw Americans as an ally in their struggle for independence against the Spanish colonists. But at the termination of Spanish domination, their new ally declared that their new country was not ready for self-government. Then began a long and hard war which could only be won by bribing the local oligarchy:

> That war, which lasted on a large scale from 1899 to 1902 and in sporadic guerrilla form until 1912, was conducted in the most ruthless, savage fashion by U.S. forces. No mercy was shown to Filipinos who resisted .... Conservative estimates are that over 200,000 Filipinos died as a direct result of U.S. military conquest; other figures of direct and indirect deaths reach up to one million.[19]

The American command oversaw an army of 120,000 soldiers[20] who comported themselves with unusual cruelty. The proportion of dead to wounded Filipinos is eloquent testimony. In recent wars the

---

[19] Pomeroy, 1992, p. 2.

[20] *Teniendo en cuenta que en la guerra se emplearon hasta 125,000 soldados norteamericanos* (Gamella, Juan F. and Elisa Martin. "*Las Rentas de Anfion: El Monopolio Español del Opio en Filipinas (1844 – 1898) y su Rechazo por la Administracion Norteamericana* [The Profits of Opium: The Spanish Opium Monopoly in the Philippines (1844 – 1898) and its Rejection by the Northamerican Administration]," *Revista de Indias*, Volumen LII, número 194, 1992 Consejo Superior de Investigaciones Científicas [revistadeindias.revistas.csic.es, hereinafter CSIC], p. 86); "It took over 120,000 American troops, first and last, to put down the struggle of the Filipinos for independence" (Blount, James M. The American Occupation of the Philippines 1898-1912. NY: G. P. Putnam's Sons, 1913, Chapter XIV The Taft Commission, p. 316).

ratio of wounded to dead had been five to one, while here the reverse happened:

> In 1900 a War Department official reported that to date 14,643 Filipinos had been killed and 3,297 wounded. The strange ratio of nearly five to one – reversing the figures of the Civil War and the current Boer War – was remarked upon by Mr. Atkinson and drew a deadpan rejoinder from General MacArthur: "It arises from the fact that our soldiers are trained in what we call 'fire discipline'; that is, target practice. In other words, they know how to shoot [quotation marks original]."[21]

When hostilities ended, the consumption of opium (before the war limited to the Chinese colony) shot up among all ethnic and social groups:

> When in 1898 the United States snatched from Spain the control of the Philippines, there was residing in the archipelago a considerable population of Chinese, among whom the custom of smoking opium was very extensive. ... However, a few days after landing in Manila, the Northamerican military command put an end to the Spanish system, instituted a tax on the sale of opium and prohibited public smoking establishments. In part as a result of this measure, and also because of the social and economic crisis that shook the islands during the military occupation and the brutal war against the Filipinos fighting for independence (1899 – 1902), the use of opium spread throughout the indigenous population to an alarming degree [tr. gwr] ....[22]

In Manila there were 190 public establishments dedicated to selling opium; now not only Filipino men consumed it, but also women and teenagers. After the terrible epidemic of cholera that

---

21 Wolff, Leon. Little Brown Brother: How the United States Purchased and Pacified the Philippine Islands at the Century's Turn. NY: History Book Club, 2006 (reprint) AO, Ch. 12 Exit Otis, p. 306.

22 *Cuando en 1898 ... la población indígena de forma tan alarmante ...* (Gamella and Martin, 1992, p. 61).

devastated the islands in 1902, the astringent qualities of opium practically demanded its use.[23] Moreover, one of every three American soldiers regularly used the drug, as affirmed by various testimonies from the era.[24] Adding up the one to the other, the atrocities and the demoralization of its army, this war was clearly the antecedent of American involvement in Vietnam.[25]

A little before the great epidemic swept the islands, Charles Henry Brent (1862 – 1929) arrived to take command of the Episcopalian Diocese of Manila, a man animated by the goal of defeating the opium scourge throughout Asia. Brent, like Crafts, saw in opium a fundamentally moral subject. Agreeing completely was another Northamerican, Homer Clyde Stuntz (1858 – 1924), a Methodist Episcopal Bishop and Superintendent of Missions to the Philippines (1901 – 1907). Together they influenced in a decisive manner subsequent events, beginning when the then civilian governor of the Philippines (1901 – 1904), future President and later Chief Justice of the United States William Howard Taft (1857 – 1930), was named Chairman of the Second Philippine Commission (aka the Taft Commission) to study the subject of opium in the Philippines.

---

[23] *en 1903 había en Manila 190 tiendas que dispensaban opio ... no sólo para combatir sus síntomas, sino para prevenirlos* (Gamella and Martin, 1992, p. 85).

[24] *Así se ha llegado a una situación en la que probablemente unos tres soldados americanos por compañía se habituaron al opio* [italics original] (Gamella and Martin, 1992, p. 86, quoting a letter from George A. Zeller, an Illinois physician who served three years in the Philippines, to Mrs. Hamilton Wright who led a three month long commission of inquiry sponsored by the Bureau of Narcotics, found in Taylor, 1969, Ch. 10 American cooperation with the League on the Far Eastern problem and illicit traffic, pp. 273-274).

[25] *En éste como en muchos otros aspectos, esa guerra fue un claro antecedente de futuras aventuras diplomáticas y militares americanas en Asia, especialmente de la guerra del Vietnam* (Gamella and Martin, 1992, p. 86).

a. The Spanish System

The permanent Chinese colony in the archipelago (which dated to the fifteenth century at least)[26] was never well thought of by the Spanish, probably due to its prosperity and the independence of its customs, as well as to the rancor often produced in less hardworking and more improvident peoples than the diligent Chinese. The last great outrage suffered by the Chinese at the hands of the Spanish administration occurred in 1814 when a governor prohibited the importation and sale of opium in the islands, envisaging six years in prison for contraband and up to four years for a reincidence of consumption.[27] It appears the law was supremely disobeyed:

> Also, they are aficionados of smoking opium, and as this was not permitted in the colony until the establishment of smoking places, in order to do so they used to rent the lower floor of a house of some influential or privileged person, whose protection sheltered them from the inquiries of the mayors [tr. gwr].[28]

---

26 "There were traders of the country of Mo-yi ... carrying valuable merchandise to the coast of Canton (for sale) in the seventh year of Tai-ping-shing-kuo (of Sung dynasty, that is 982 A.D. ... It is often loosely stated that the Chinese have lived in the South Seas for many centuries, and a distinction is rarely drawn between trading visits and permanent settlement. ... So the mass immigration of the South Seas was very late, beginning in the Ming dynasty .... The first cause of this migration ... was the influence of Cheng Ho's expeditions .... A great Chinese fleet ... under the command of the famous admiral Cheng Ho, visited Lingayen, Manila Bay, Mindoro and Sulu in 1405-6, 1408-10, and 1417 .... In 1405 a Chinese governor ... was appointed to the island of Luzon" (Ching-hong, Wu. A Study of References to the Philippines in Chinese Sources from Earliest Times to the Ming Dynasty. Quezon City, PI: University of the Philippines, 1959 pp. 75, 119, 120, 123).

27 *cuando el enérgico gobernador ... de prisión por consumo* (Gamella and Martin, 1992, p. 64).

28 *Tambien son aficionados ... de los alcaldes* (Buzeta, E. Manuel and Fr. Felipe Bravo. *Diccionario geografico, estadistico e historico de las Islas Filipinas*, Vol. 2 D-Z. Madrid: Imp.

By 1828 a royal ordinance re-authorized the cultivation of poppy for export.[29]

But the normalization of consumption only happened after the Treaty of Nanking (1843), which put an end to the First Anglo-Chinese War. That same year an official Spanish opium commission appointed to study the issue consulted the diplomat, adventurer, poet, early photographer and lead sinologist of the time, Sinibaldo de Mas y Sanz (1809 – 1868), who responded that, from his own experience, the Chinese who smoked opium worked more than those who were abstemious.[30] With these arguments, the commissioners advised a policy of legalization under a regimen of state controlled opium shops, stating concretely that:

1. It was not scientifically proven that opium causes physical harm and, in any case, the harm would not be more than that caused by tobacco and alcohol;
2. Prohibition would not be respected by the Chinese population of the Philippines. Its imposition would only result in an increase in crime, and more expenses for the judicial system and the police. Experience demonstrated that smuggling was impossible to stamp out in an archipelago of more than seven thousand islands;
3. A monopoly on opium would bring in money for the public treasury, with which the control of the use of opium would convert an expense into an income; and,
4. To persecute the Chinese for its use of opium would prejudice the foreign relations of Spain with the Celestial Empire, more and more commercially important for the colony [tr. gwr].[31]

---

de D. José C. de la Peña, 1850-1851 [ustdigitallibrary.contentdm.oclc.org, hereinafter UST], p. 246).

[29] *una real ordenanza ... para su exportación* (Gamella and Martin, 1992, p. 66).

[30] *los chinos que fumaban opio trabajaban tanto o más que los abstemios* (Gamella and Martin, 1992, p. 67).

[31] *Con estos argumentos a su favor ... para la colonia* (Gamella and Martin, 1992, pp. 67-68).

These recommendations were accepted, an opium monopoly was established in 1844,[32] and by 1867 there were some 478 public smoking establishments.[33] The tendency of the almost 15,000 users[34] was basically moderation (with an individual median of around three grams a day),[35] which would only be modified at the beginning of the wars between the Spanish and the Northamericans. In principle, sales were restricted to the Chinese.

---

32 "[T]he opium monopoly ... was established in Filipinas on Jan. 1, 1844, and later confirmed by the Spanish government, after much discussion and controversy" (Blair, Emma Helen and James Alexander Robertson, trs., eds. The Philippine Islands, 1493-1898, Vol. 52: 1841-1898. Cleveland, OH: Arthur Clark Co., 1907 AO, p. 318, fn 244).

33 *la existencia de 478 fumaderos en todo el país* (Gamella and Martin, 1992, p. 78); "but Jagor found that, besides the 478 public opium-joints – which were 'actual hotbeds of immorality, and always full of Chinese' – hundreds of individuals were allowed, contrary to the law and to the intentions of the government, to smoke opium in their own houses" (Blair, et al, 1907, p. 318, fn 244); *ausser den 478 öffentlichen Opiumläden (Fumaderos) «wahren Heerden der Immoralität und immer mit Chinesen angefüllt», Hunderten von chinesischen Privaten die Erlaubniss verkauft ...* (Jagor, Andreas Fedor. *Reisen in den Philippinen* [Travels in the Philippines]. Berlin: Weidmannsche Buchhandlung, 1873 AO, Anhang, Einführung der Opium-Regie, p. 310).

34 *unos quince mil usuarios de opio* (Gamella and Martin, 1992, p. 78, citing E. B. Wickberg's The Chinese in Philippine Life, 1850-1898. New Haven, CN: Yale University Press, p. 118).

35 *de unos 3,1 gramos por día* (Gamella and Martin, 1992, p. 78).

b. The American System

The new colonial power perceived, after some delay, that the use of opium was growing at a high rate, and Governor Taft drew up a pragmatic legal framework, thinking to halt the expansion of use among Filipinos as well as the sudden increase in smuggling. It authorized a state monopoly "to import and sell opium to Chinese persons of the full blood over the age of twenty-one"[36] through contracts on which only Chinese businesses could bid. But smoking establishments would remain prohibited, and consumption would have to be done in private, under penalty of large fines. The income resulting from the state monopoly would be destined for public education and health. Except for the provision against public smoking, this was very nearly the Spanish system.

The project was ready to be sent to Congress when, in the words of the Reverend Crafts, "(t)his national disgrace was thus electrocuted by Presidential lightning that had been called out by a telegraphic vote of Christian citizens."[37] The director of the International Reform Bureau printed off a pamphlet in which he declared himself scandalized before the "piratical sale of enslaving intoxicants and opium to aboriginal races, civilized and uncivilized."[38] He certainly did not learn of the Taft proposal by chance but through the Bishops Brent and Stuntz, who in collaboration with Crafts were also trying very hard to summon both American and English prohibitionist societies to bombard the White House with letters and

[36] Stuntz, Homer C. The Philippines and the Far East. Cincinnati, OH: Jennings and Pye, 1904 AO, pp. 276-277.

[37] Crafts et al, 1911, Appendix, p. 220.

[38] Crafts, W. F. Memorandum concerning Concerted International Restraint of the Traffic in Intoxicants and Opium Among Aboriginal Races. NY: Press of the Reliance Trading Company, 1906 AO, p. 3.

telegrams. Brent crossed letters in the post with Roosevelt, among which was one in which he said:

> The opium traffic stands in the category of crime except so far as it is imported for purely medicinal purposes. It cannot be ranked with the liquor trade, for, as every temperate man acknowledges, in this latter there is a legitimate consumption as a beverage, however much the liberty may be abused, whereas there is no unvicious use of opium or its immediate products as a foodstuff or a beverage. The consumption of opium is not merely a personal weakness; it is a social vice, i.e., a crime.[39]

But now the issue threatened President Roosevelt, because, according to Stuntz: "There is in the United States an electorate of no less than thirty millions ... who are opposed unalterably to the basic principle of this decree and all its details [tr. gwr]."[40] This prompted a cablegram from Secretary of War Elihu Root to Governor Taft: "Hold opium monopoly bill. Further investigation. Many protests."[41]

The further investigation would be a debate between Taft and his lay collaborators on the one side, and Brent and Stuntz on the other.[42] Stuntz admitted that a few members of the Chinese Chamber of Commerce wanted to defeat the bill in part so as to protect "their importations of opium. This was a total of five men out of more than two hundred members."[43] Against this he claimed to have circulated a petition that had been

---

[39] Zabriskie, Alexander C. Bishop Brent: Crusader for Christian Unity. Philadelphia, PA: The Westminster Press, 1948 AO, Ch. 7 An American Statesman *Opium in the Philippines*, 6 July 1903 Submission to the Commissioner of Education, p. 98.

[40] *hay en los Estados Unidos ... a todos sus detalles* (Gamella and Martin, 1992, p. 88).

[41] Crafts et al, 1911, Appendix, p. 221.

[42] Taylor, 1969, pp. 37-38.

[43] Stuntz, 1904, p. 277.

signed by seven thousand in Manila, and was only in circulation a few days. Taft attempted to discredit the petition by alleging that an expert had discovered that one of the names on the petition was that of a famous Chinese general who had been dead three hundred years. The governor should have reflected that no small number of George Washingtons and U. S. Grants can be found in almost any ward or township in our own country. ... Another charge he brought was, that the petition contained the name of a monkey-god of China. But why not? Is he not familiar with the custom of placing infants under the protection of idols by giving them the name of the idol? The petition was said to contain the same name several times. Again, why not? Are our own people quite free from duplicate names in the Smith and Jones and Brown families? Would it be possible to secure a petition anywhere signed by seven thousand that did not contain duplicates? ... The fact is that the sturdy good sense of the mass of Manila Chinese saw in the Bill the most serious menace to the morals and efficiency of their countrymen, and rose to make what was perhaps the first protest that was ever listened to from them in all the centuries of nominal Christian rule.[44]

Figure 301. "Opium den on Manila Street." Circa 1924. Black and white photo print. Library of Congress Prints and Photographs Division, Washington, DC.

[44] Stuntz, 1904, pp. 277-278.

2. The Philippine Opium Investigation Committee

Regardless, Taft saw that he was risking his reputation before American public opinion and ceded to a political move, proposing to postpone legislation in the Philippines until a commission of which Brent would be a member could investigate the legal status of opium in the Far East. Though the results of that investigation would not support his point of view,[45] Brent proposed to Roosevelt an "America bringing to colonialism a new attitude and competence that would improve on English methods and on the laissez-faire style of the French administrators."[46] In plain words, he wanted a law that would prohibit all non-medical use of opium in the Philippines beginning in 1908.

The Philippine Opium Investigation Committee in 1903 would consist of two physicians and Reverend Brent.[47] The three visited nine different localities in the Far East and in a 1905 report made thirteen recommendations, including a "strict government monopoly," imports after three years "for medical purposes only," licenses for "habitual users of opium," free hospital "treatment for the opium habit" for the indigent, and that the "cultivation of the poppy ... shall be made

---

45 In the Far East colonies, the systems then in place ranged from the laissez faire of Persia with neither monopoly nor restrictive laws, a strict government monopoly over the distribution of opium as in French Indochina and Dutch Java, to private contracts (opium farms) as in Hong Kong, Formosa, Ceylon and Malaysia (Carter, Edward C., Chairman, et al. Report of the Committee Appointed by the Philippine Commission to Investigate the Use of Opium and the Traffic Therein. Washington, DC: Bureau of Insular Affairs, War Department, 1905 AO, pp. 5, 29, 38, 28, 84, 29).

46 Musto, David F. The American Disease: Origins of Narcotic Control, Third Edition. NY: Oxford University Press, 1999 AA, p. 26.

47 Carter, 1905, p. 49.

illegal."[48] Their sixth recommendation was to remove the voting rights of opium users and their right to hold political office: "That no person who is known to be an habitual user of opium shall be authorized to exercise the franchise or hold office under the Government of the Philippine Islands."[49] The committee added as general principles regarding the physiology of the inveterate habitué the "impossibility of obtaining a spontaneous cure" and the "fatal tendency of passing from the use to the abuse of opium."[50]

Those opposed to the recommendations denied these points, alleging a lack of knowledge of the facts (both clinical and historical, beginning with the success of the Spanish system) while affirming that any prohibition would foment smuggling and corrupt the constabulary, already under enormous temptation. What is true is that a group of Chinese businessmen contracted an American lawyer in order to be represented in the struggle against the projected law. In his testimony before the Commission, the attorney admitted that "his clients really wanted the licensing of opium dens, but that they would prefer prohibition to the contract system because prohibition could be more easily evaded."[51]

In order to prepare the local population for the coming prohibition, the authorities would send out between 1906 and 1907 some 12,700 opium user identification cards to whom free treatment would be offered. But how many of the Chinese in Manila would be voluntarily willing to go without opium? Of all those eligible for the free treatment, the commission admitted that the "total number of applicants has been 10. It is to be feared that this indicates that the

---

[48] Carter et al, 1905, pp. 47-48.

[49] Carter et al, 1905, p. 47.

[50] Carter et al, 1905, p. 44.

[51] Taylor, 1969, p. 37.

victims of the habit continue to get the drug without great difficulty."[52] For comparison, the Japanese in Formosa experienced a similar fiasco when in 1929 they offered free treatment to all non-registered addicts, and found that of the 25,000 users calculated to exist on the island, only thirty arrived to be treated.[53]

One of the favorite therapies then was opiate substitution, with morphine alone or in combination with other ingredients taken in the famous anti-opium pill, with heroin substitution for the newly acquired morphine addiction.[54] Some did go along with the abstinence

---

[52] Garfield, James Rudolph, Secretary of the Interior. Eighth Annual Report of the Philippine Commission to the Secretary of War, Part 2. Washington, DC: Government Printing Office, 1908 [National Library of the Philippines, nlpdl.nlp.gov.ph, hereinafter NLP], Report of the Secretary of the Interior, "Treatment of Opium Patients," p. 18.

[53] *Los japoneses en Formosa experimentaron un fiasco semejante, cuando en 1929 ofrecieron tratamiento gratuito a todos los opiómanos no registrados y se encontraron que, de unos 25.000 usuarios que se calculaba existían en la isla, sólo treinta acudieron a tratarse* (Gamella y Martin, 1992, 5. La Prohibicion, p. 100, fn. 132).

[54] "Heroin is held to be of much value ... and to be preferable to morphine ... because it does not disturb digestion or produce a habit readily. ... [I]t is also used as a mild anodyne and as a substitute for morphine in combatting the morphine habit" (Weicker, Theodore, President. Squibb's Materia Medica, Part II. NY: E. R. Squibb & Sons, 1906 AO, p. 310); "That heroine will take the place of morphine without its disagreeable qualities I am convinced, as I have repeatedly quieted morphinomaniacs whose cravings were awful ..." (Ahlborn, Maurice B. "Heroine in the Morphine Habit," The New York Medical Journal, Volume LXXIV, July to December, 1901, Inclusive. NY: A. R. Elliott Publishing Company, 1901 AO, p. 235); "[A]lthough the Chinese Government had issued regulations in which it was distinctly laid down that anti-opium pills should not consist of opium or morphia, it was well known that pills containing a large proportion of the forbidden drugs were being sold broadcast in China" (Brent, Charles H., President. Report of the International Opium Commission, Shanghai, China, February 1 to February 26, 1909, Volume I. Report of the Proceedings. Shanghai: North-China Daily News & Herald Ltd., 1909 AO,

treatment (gradual or brusque), others tried the miraculous anti-opium pills, and others still abetted the growth of smuggling. In the late 1920s, there was cheap opium and police corruption in the Philippines,[55] as there had been in 1839. In 1959 opium was easy to find but was expensive and adulterated.[56]

Summing up the evidence one historian remarked: "On no issue did the missionaries exercise greater influence in both public opinion and official policy than on the opium question."[57] The political missionary knew that the unbeliever did not know what was in his own best interests, and this attitude accompanies the American expansion to its new territories. A planetary crusade for mental and moral health from now on will be the symbol of its penetration in the world. Greece exported philosophy, Rome law; the United States will export prohibition under the guise of health.

Minutes of the Ninth Session, 19 February 1909, Sir Cecil Smith, p. 37).

55 "Illegal opium is coming into the Islands in such quantities as to make smoking opium procurable freely at very low prices .... [I]t will be no surprise to learn that prohibition of opium smoking in the Philippines does not in fact prohibit. Any one who wishes to buy prepared opium can buy it at a moderate price .... Evidence was also found pointing to a large trade in morphia pills ..." (May, Herbert L. Survey of Smoking Opium Conditions in the Far East: *A Report to the Executive Board of the Foreign Policy Association*. NY: Opium Research Committee of the Foreign Policy Association, 1927 AO, pp. 15, 21, 23); see also Taylor, 1969, pp. 272, 274.

56 Zarco, R. M. "A Short Study of Narcotic Drug Addiction in the Philippines 1521-1959," *Historical Bulletin of the Philippines* III, 4, 1959, *Journal of the Philippine Historical Association*.

57 Taylor, 1969, pp. 29-30.

Figure 302. "Bishop Brent." Photograph by Brown Bros., prior to 1918. Powell, Lyman P. and Gertrude W. The Spirit of Democracy. New York: Rand McNally and Company, 1918 AO, Comrades in a Common Cause, p. 207.

3. The International Opium Commission of 1909

It is curious and generally little understood that the American prohibition with respect to opium in the Philippines should be (as Spanish policy had been) directly linked to the purpose of gaining access to the immense Chinese market. For this we must ask what had happened between the United States and China during this era of bad feelings. After a period of continuous provocations and violence from both ordinary people and labor unions, some complaining that the Chinese lived in foul smelling opium dens and were corrupting America, others inciting racial disturbances and lynchings in cities like San Francisco and New York, the tension between both countries reached a climax when the Northamerican Congress excluded Chinese laborers with the *Chinese Exclusion Act* [CEA]. The response of the Chinese business community to the riots, assassinations and the CEA was to decree a voluntary embargo of American goods.

In the face of this economic blockade, a number of Americans backpedaled. Roosevelt admitted:

> We have behaved scandalously toward Chinamen in this country. Some of the outrages by mobs which have resulted in the deaths of Chinamen were almost as bad as anything that occurred at the hands of the Chinamen themselves in the Boxer outbreak. The Germans and English may have taken advantage of the boycott, but the boycott itself is due to our own misdeeds and folly.[58]

Businessmen like the financier and president of the Great Northern Railroad James J. Hill (1838 – 1916) opposed the new act:

---

[58] Beale, Howard K. Theodore Roosevelt and the Rise of America to World Power. Baltimore, MD: The Johns Hopkins University Press, 1956 AO, p. 230.

> The Oriental trade will in time adjust itself, I hope. The people of this country will come after a while to know the Chinaman. We are unable to compete for business in the Orient now, excepting in raw material or some commodity with little work upon it, and the latter is soon copied by the Chinaman. The boycott is a serious matter, and I have no way of knowing whether it will be done away with or not.[59]

Then Secretary of War Taft had already given a commencement speech in 1905 in which he called for the continued exclusion of Chinese laborers but not trade, attributing the boycott of American goods to the *Chinese Exclusion Act*:

> One of the great commercial prizes of the world is the trade with the four hundred million Chinese. Ought we to throw away the advantage which we have by reason of Chinese natural friendship for us and continue to enforce an unjustly severe law, and thus create in the Chinese mind a disposition to boycott American trade and drive our merchants from Chinese shores simply because we are afraid that we may for the time lose the approval of certain unreasonable and extreme popular leaders of California and other coast states? ... We must continue to keep out the coolies, the laborers; but we should give the freest possible entry to merchants, travelers and students, and treat them with all courtesy and consideration.[60]

Brent had previously suggested an international opium commission to help China in its battle against opium, which would have also strengthened his own crusade in the Philippines. It was thus an opportune moment to reduce the tension between the two

---

[59] Unknown writer. "J. J. Hill for Reciprocity: Too many Americans going to Canada – Chinese boycott serious," *New York Times*, Wednesday 10 January 1906 AO, p. 8, column 7.

[60] Taft, W. H. "The Baccalaureate Oration Delivered on the Occasion of the Eighty-first Annual Commencement of Miami University at Oxford, Ohio," *The Miami Bulletin*, Series IV, Number 9, November. Miami, OH: Published by Miami University, 1905 AO, pp. 9-10; see also Beale, 1956, p. 220.

countries, and the advisors to the President suggested that he should not pass up the occasion. The nexus between this so-called humanitarian initiative and American economic interests did not go unnoticed in Washington.

Roosevelt asked a small amount from Congress for a three member delegation to an International Opium Commission who would meet in Shanghai in February of 1909, investigate the problem and make recommendations. One was Dr. Hamilton Wright (1867 – 1917), a young and ambitious physician who wrote Secretary of State Knox in late 1909:

> Our move to help China in her opium reform gave us more prestige in China than any of our recent friendly acts toward her. If we continue and press steadily for the Conference, China will recognize that we are sincere in her behalf, and the whole business may be used as oil to smooth the troubled waters of an aggressive commercial policy there.[61]

Another was the diplomat, educator and Chinese missionary Charles Daniel Tenney (1857 – 1930). The third was Bishop Brent himself, Chief Commissioner to the American delegation. This time the clerics found themselves in a voting majority.

As soon as he received his appointment, the politically experienced Wright broached the necessity of also having repressive national legislation to save face at the meeting. It is not strange that he would come to be considered the father of American laws on stupefacients. With the promise from Congress to carefully study the problem, the three commissioners began also planning a repressive federal law on opium (which in principle exceeded their authority and would require an amendment to the Constitution, a titanic task in administrative terms), and set off to Shanghai to meet with the other

[61] Musto, 1999, Chapter 2 Diplomats and Reformers, p. 39.

international invitees. They carried in their briefcases the proposal of Brent to outlaw all non-medical use of opium.

The thirteen countries who ultimately met did not include the major opium exporting nation of Turkey,[62] while the other major exporter Persia sent a merchant denoted the official agent of H. M. the Shah of Persia. The other delegations demonstrated an academic but distant interest in the proposals:

> Most nations were mildly interested in the subject but unwilling to exert much effort for non-medical prohibition as proposed by the United States; it was impossible to get general agreement that the use of opium for other than medicinal purposes was evil and immoral.[63]

His Excellency Tuan Fang, Viceroy of Liangkiang, welcomed the delegations on 1 February 1909 with an elaborate list of exaggerated claims, promises kept and great hopes for the future:

> On the 20th of September, 1906, an Imperial Edict was issued prohibiting the cultivation and use of opium throughout the Empire within the period of ten years. As a matter of fact, the area where the poppy has been cultivated in the Kiangnan portion of Kiangsu province, has been now reduced by eighty *per cent*, while it is on record that from the six provinces of Shansi, Yunnan, Fukien, Anhui, Honan and Heilungkiang, or Northern Manchuria, memorials have been presented to the Throne reporting that the cultivation of the poppy will be entirely stopped by the winter of the present year. Even more than that, the gentry and merchants of the various provinces of the Empire have everywhere started societies to exhort and assist opium smokers to get rid of the baneful habit. For instance, we have an Association in Fukien province known as the "Anti-Poison Society" which has been making considerable progress in its campaign against the drug. Indeed, ... there are great

---

[62] Brent, 1909, List of Delegations and Representatives, pp. 3-6.

[63] Musto, 1999, p. 36.

hopes that the consumption of opium can be stopped in its entirety before the end of the prescribed limit of ten years [italics, quotation marks original].[64]

But at the Sixth Session on 12 February, Sir Alexander Hosie of the British delegation took issue with the information and the numbers in the Chinese report:

Mr. T'ang might have informed the Commission with equal truth that it was impossible to furnish an official reliable return of the production of opium in China .... [A]s regards the inland provinces – the greatest opium producing districts in China, where the taxation is irregular and for the most part evaded, and where public or official returns are practically unknown – the estimate is merely patchwork. Attempts have also been made to arrive at the number of smokers ... but, based as they are on figures admittedly unreliable, the result is necessarily of inconsiderable value. ... [T]he question of opium production in China ... is admitted to be altogether unsatisfactory and untrustworthy .... [I]t is stated that the cultivation of the poppy has been entirely suppressed in Fengtien, the southern province of Manchuria. Since when? ... It is simply an instance illustrating the difficulties with which the High Provincial Authorities in China have to contend, and the laxity that prevails in accepting statements as facts ... based on by no means accurate or reliable data. ... So much for production. I come now to the question of consumption. Opium smokers have not yet been registered throughout the Empire and their number is unknown ... but actual percentages will remain unknown quantities until China is able to produce reliable information regarding production, or better still the numbers of smokers registered under the regulations.[65]

---

64 Brent, 1909, "Report of the Proceedings," p. 9.

65 Brent, 1909, "Minutes of the Sixth Session," pp. 27-30.

Figure 303. "Hamilton Kemp Wright." Photograph by Bain News Service, 20 August 1909. Library of Congress Photographs and Prints Division, George Grantham Bain Collection, Washington, DC.

To the suggestion from Germany that the United States should pass its own domestic measures if it felt itself ready to do so,[66] Wright expressed the position

> that no Government represented may by its National Laws wholly solve its own opium problem without the conjoint aid of all those Governments concerned in the production and manufacture of opium, its alkaloids, derivatives and preparations. ... [T]o take our own case, we are not able and will not be able to make the law effective unless we have assistance. I think everybody recognizes that. We frankly acknowledge in this resolution that our Government cannot solve its opium problem by its own national law, and think that the other Governments ought to help us; and I think the same remark applies to other countries.[67]

The debates were polite but vehement. In fact, the positions of the delegations were far from clear or, at least, from being transmitted in clear concepts. Brent, Tenney and Wright maintained an emotional accord over the sinister powers of opium, while behind the idea of restricting it to medical use lay the proposition of eventually illegalizing pure and simple this malign substance one day. But such a thing was not expressable in technical terms, nor was it opportune to do so in a forum where the majority of those present spoke from a lay perspective, with commercial and pharmacological notions in place of moral or fundamentally theological ones.[68]

Moreover China, the country which they were pretending to help, had resolved the problem of civil disobedience and corruption

---

[66] "Yet here was one more instance in which enactment of exemplary domestic laws became necessary in order to avoid international embarrassment" (Musto, 1999, Chapter 2 Diplomats and Reformers, p. 51).

[67] Brent, 1909, pp. 48, 53.

[68] A member of the British delegation objected that "the Commission was not appointed with a scientific basis" (Brent, 1909, 19 February 1909, Cecil Clementi Smith, Minutes of the Ninth Session, p. 37).

motivated by the politics of prohibition; they feared justifiably a resurgence of secret societies if opium returned to the black market, and even stroked the perspective of relieving British India of its role as almost exclusive provider of opium in the larger Asiatic market. The English had punished the Chinese return to cultivation by planting huge acreages of tea in Ceylon and in the Hindostan peninsula, whereas before from 1700 they had been importing this plant almost exclusively from China, and the most important economic benefit derived from it could only be compensated by substituting one crop for another. As this threat to export opium set off alarm bells in the United States and England, the Chinese delegations limited themselves during the meetings to appeasing everyone, while extra-officially listening to the commercial proposals of the Americans and Europeans.

After four weeks of meetings (which Wright considered disappointing in private, and a great success when he informed Congress), the commission formulated a number of resolutions which were in fact "merely recommendations as they would never be submitted for ratification to the governments represented."[69] Only two satisfied some of the hopes of Brent and his colleagues. Resolution 2 requested "each Delegation concerned move its own Government to take measures for the gradual suppression of the practice of Opium smoking in its own territories and possessions ...."[70]

Resolution 4 stated that no country should export opium to any country that had prohibited it:

[69] Musto, 1999, p. 37.

[70] Brent, 1909, p. 84.

> [I]n the judgment of the International Opium Commission it is also the duty of all countries to adopt reasonable measures to prevent at ports of departure the Shipment of Opium, its alkaloids, derivatives and preparatives, to any country which prohibits the entry of any Opium, its alkaloids, derivatives and preparations.[71]

Coming after a century of decline in the Qing dynasty (when the prevalence of opium there was neither more nor less than that of alcohol in any European country undergoing similar prohibitions, revolutions, invasions and wars), it remains inexcusably ironic that the former opium smugglers (Holland, France, Britain, and the United States chiefly) should now sit around a table to recommend something so completely obvious and straightforward as a matter of international law.

Indeed, that sordid history lingered in many minds, especially that of Chairman Brent as he set an ahistoric tone for the first session on 1 February 1909, suggesting they all simply ignore what he termed useless historical questions:

> But, if I may be permitted to make a suggestion to this assembly, it seems to me that it would be extremely wise if we were to rule out of our deliberations what might be termed useless historical questions beneath which a great deal of controversy lies hidden, and which would only tend to fog the issue. The one way to reach a satisfactory solution of a grave problem is to simplify, as far as possible, the elements of that problem, and I believe that history bears me out when I say that no great question has ever been satisfactorily settled until men have come to a realization of the fact that purely side issues, and controversial matters which do not touch the main question, must be set aside and ignored. They may be of interest, but they are of no practical importance and, indeed, are impediments in the actual working out of the main question.[72]

---

[71] Brent, 1909, p. 84.

[72] Brent, 1909, "Minutes of the First Session," p. 11.

Wright was even more adamant, declaring: "That the Government of the United States had not actually engaged in the opium trade in the Far East; that it ... from early days discouraged the opium trade in the Far East ... that it had ... endeavoured to prevent its citizens from pushing the trade on unprotected people."[73] No doubt Forbes had simply been unaware.

Figure 304. "David Johnson Foster." Photograph by Harris & Ewing. Library of Congress Photographs and Prints Division, Harris & Ewing Collection, Washington, DC.

[73] Brent, 1909, Eleventh Session, 23 February 1909, pp. 43-44.

C. The Debate Over the Foster Bills

In spite of the reverses suffered in his first two experiences, Brent had won new backing for his cause with the accession of President Taft.[74] Taft was a personal friend and had also decided to back the untiring activity of Wright. While continuing to espouse an international reunion, Wright also worked to get a new federal law against opium, and believed he had found a way around the Constitution using the tributary prerogatives of Washington.

The first thing needed was to get a sponsor in Congress. At that moment no one seemed more appropriate than James Robert Mann (Rep. IL, 1856 – 1922), best known for responding to a manufactured hysteria with the twisted law known as the Mann Act (White-Slave Traffic Act of 1910) which prohibited both interstate and foreign transportation of "any woman or girl for the purpose of prostitution or debauchery, or for any other immoral purpose."[75]

---

[74] Taft is worthy of a brief mention. Vicepresident duting the second term of Roosevelt, he won the next election with votes from the Eastern states. However, he exhibited such a mix of incompetence and laxity before the abuses of Big Business, and a striking inability to fulfill his own campaign promises, that Roosevelt felt it was time to return to politics in order to block his reelection. Of course, Roosevelt was obliged to create his own party, as Taft and his friends controlled the machinery of the Republicans. Up to what point the citizens were disappointed with Taft is proved by the fact that Roosevelt was able to do better with his own improvised political organization. What he could not achieve was to defeat the Democratic candidate Woodrow Wilson, President of Princeton University and Governor of New Jersey.

[75] Knox, Philander Chase, Director. The Statutes at Large of the United States from March, 1909, to March, 1911, Volume XXXVI, Part I. Washington, DC: Government Printing Office, 1911 AO, Sixty-First Congress, Session II, Chapter 395, Section 2, p. 825; strikingly, the color of the female being trafficked was completely relevant while males of any race were not included.

Mann had previously sponsored the *Pure Food and Drug Act* of 1906, which invoked the Constitution's commerce clause to regulate the interstate shipment of food and medicine, shifting the balance of power away from the states and toward the federal government to regulate business. Mann presented a proposal based on the regulation of interstate commerce which was quickly shot down by a combination of objections from the Department of Agriculture, drug manufacturers and pharmacists.

Two years later a representative from Vermont, David Johnson Foster (Rep. VT, 1857 – 1912) presented to Congress four bills:

> Gentlemen, several bills have been introduced here having in view the regulating of the manufacture of smoking opium within the United States, the prohibition of the importation and use of opium for other than medicinal purposes; and regulating the production, manufacture, and distribution of certain habit-forming drugs. These bills were all introduced by Mr. Foster and bear the following numbers, 25240, 25241, 25242, and 28971.[76]

Even before the efforts of Wright had convoked an international conference on opium to be celebrated at The Hague in 1911-1912, President Taft had personally directed to Congress a special message (edited in good measure by Wright) in which he declared that passing the Foster Bills was a pressing necessity:

---

[76] Unknown compiler. Importation and Use of Opium Hearings before the Committee on Ways and Means of the House of Representatives, 61st Congress, 3d Session. Washington, DC: Government Printing Office, 1911 AO, "Wednesday, 14 December 1910," p. 65.

I transmit herewith a communication form the Secretary of State transmitting a report on the International Opium Commission and on the opium problem as seen within the United States and its possessions, prepared by Mr. Hamilton Wright on behalf of the American delegates to the said commission, held at Shanghai in February, 1909. ... I commend to the Congress with my approval and the request that action should be taken accordingly.[77]

Not quite two years later, he would reiterate his call for domestic legislation: "In view of the fact that there is now sitting at The Hague so important a conference ... it seems to me essential that the Congress should take immediate action on the antinarcotic legislation to which I have already called attention by a special message."[78]

The Foster Bills would prohibit all traffic and use not strictly medical of opiates, cocaine, chloral hydrate and cannabis, regardless how small the quantities. According to the draft, the violations would be castigated with no less than a year in prison and no more than five.[79] This implied quintupling the penalties foreseen in the *Pure Food and Drug Act* for adulterations.[80] As a result, during the third session of the sixty-first Congress, the Committee on Ways and Means of the House

---

[77] Peters, Gerhard and John T. Woolley, editors. William Howard Taft, Special Message Online, 21 February 1910, The American Presidency Project, University of California, Santa Barbara [thepresidency.ucsb.edu, hereinafter UCSB], unpaged.

[78] Unknown compiler. Congressional Record: Containing the Proceedings and Debates of the Sixty-Second Congress, Second Session, Volume XLVIII, Part I. Washington, DC: Government Printing Office, 1912 [govinfo.gov, hereinafter GIG], Congressional Record – Senate, Thursday, 7 December 1911, p. 74, column 2.

[79] For example, H. R. Bill 25242, Section 3 provided penalties for importing smoking opium of "not less than one year nor more than five years, or both" (Importation, 1911, p. 104).

[80] Section 1 of the PFDA provided for a penalty of only one year for adulteration or misbranding (Greeley, Arthur P. The Pure Food and Drugs Act, June 30, 1906, A Study. Washington, DC: John Byrne & Company, 1907 AO, Appendix, p. 73).

of Representatives held two days of hearings on the subject of opium importation, with testimony not always too far from the hilarious.

The Foster Bills were supported by testimony from Wright, who presented doctors, pharmacists and nurses as basically unscrupulous persons who could not be trusted:

> I stated that 10 per cent of the retail druggists in this country were doing an illicit business. ... Quite so [agreeing with the estimate that two percent of physicians were victims of the morphine habit]; and in Maine, I know, and in rural communities in New York, the reports I have show that the country physician has been largely responsible for the spread of the morphine habit, especially in rural New England. ... Two or three summers ago, when I first undertook this investigation for the State Department, I saw a large wholesale and retailing store, with six stage coaches drawn up in front, each coming there to get its supply of morphine.[81]

As for cocaine (which was still not classified as a narcotic), Wright assured the committee (without original sin) that the direct connection between cocaine and the crime of rape of white women by Negroes in the South had been clearly demonstrated: "The cocaine habit is greatly increasing in the South. ... I have most reliable evidence that the crime of rape has largely been caused by the use of cocaine among the Negroes in the South in the last 10 or 15 years."[82] Wright had hardly mentioned this drug in his writings and speeches, but Foster and others thought that to bring there a cliché so commonplace in the South would serve to convince the democratic representatives of those states, so reactive always in the face of intrusions from the federal government. But the most interesting part

---

[81] Unknown compiler, Importation, 1911, "Additional Statement of Mr. Hamilton Wright," p. 84, "Further Statement of Mr. Hamilton Wright," p. 92.

[82] Unknown compiler, Importation, 1911, "Additional Statement of Dr. Hamilton Wright," pp. 82-83.

of Wright's testimony, all told, was where he recognized indirectly the true state of things: "[T]here is no attempt here to say that there shall be only a small amount of morphine manufactured or that there shall be only a certain amount of opium, but that all the opium imported and manufactured in this country shall be done in daylight."[83]

Charles A. West, the chairman of the legislative committee of the National Wholesale Druggists' Association (NWDA) complained that one of the bills was too complex, difficult to enforce and incorrect in what it included:

> [It] is altogether too great in its detail, and if enforced in its present position it would completely revolutionize the wholesale drug business. ... [W]e would also object to the articles coco [sic] leaves, alpha and beta, eucaine. [sic] chloral and cannabis being included, for the simple reason that coco leaves ... is [sic] an article of very small moment to the drug trade, except to the manufacturer. Alpha and beta and eucaine practically have no sale whatever. Chloral is an article which is rapidly decreasing in sale, and cannabis is not what may be called a habit-forming drug. ... [M]y idea is to have the bill as simple as possible and have it workable. Now, if you had merely opium. [sic] morphia, cocaine, their salts, derivatives, and preparations, it would be a much simpler bill to work and would accomplish all that is desired. ... [W]hat we want is a simple law, one that can be enforced and will not inflict too much of a hardship on the trade.[84]

Representative Francis Burton Harrison (Dem. NY, 1873 – 1957), who was later appointed Governor-General of the Philippines by President Wilson, interjected, asking West: "Is it not desirable, in your opinion, to include these habit-forming drugs with the others

---

[83] Unknown compiler, Importation, 1911, "Further Statement of Mr. Hamilton Wright, American Delegate to the International Opium Commission," p. 88.

[84] Unknown compiler, Importation, 1911, "Statement of Charles A. West, of Boston, Mass," Wednesday 11 January 1911, pp. 109, 110, 114.

against which this bill is aimed, Coca Cola and Pepsi Cola and all those things that are sold to Negroes all over the South?"[85]

Trying to cut through this dialog of the deaf, Chairman Sereno E. Payne (Rep. NY, 1843 – 1914) opined that "the most that that regulation would do would be to make it so unprofitable to sell the stuff that wholesale druggists might go out of that part of the business."[86]

Representative Henry Sherman Boutell (Rep. IL, 1856 – 1926), later appointed an envoy to Switzerland, asked West whether

> this legislation, or any legislation ... would be successful in preventing absolutely the sale of these drugs by reputable dealers, would stop appreciably the illegitimate use of these drugs? ... Would it not simply result in the importation or transfer in interstate commerce, and the peddling out in secret, under-handed ways, of these drugs to about the same extent? ... Any more than a prohibition law in a prohibition State prevents the drinking of anything that has alcohol in it.[87]

Harrison asked West: "But is it not true that if you make it more and more difficult to get those things, you lessen the number of the persons who acquire the habit in the first instance?"[88]

West responded: "That is an open question. I am not prepared to answer that. The hope is by this bill to control it in such a way that the habit will decrease; but I do not think it can be done by this bill."[89]

Then it was the turn of businessman William Jay Schlieffelin (1866 – 1955), president of Schlieffelin & Company and president of

---

[85] Unknown compiler, Importation, 1911, p. 115.

[86] Unknown compiler, Importation, 1911, p. 116.

[87] Unknown compiler, Importation, 1911, pp. 116-117.

[88] Unknown compiler, Importation, 1911, p. 117.

[89] Unknown compiler, Importation, 1911, p. 117.

the NWDA, to be questioned closely by James Beauchamp "Champ" Clark (Dem. MO, 1850 – 1921) who proposed an analogy between drinks and opiates:

Mr. Clark. Is it any worse to use these drugs than to use intoxicating liquors?
Mr. Schieffelin. Very much so.
Mr. Clark. Why?
Mr. Schieffelin. It probably means death; and almost certainly it means insanity.
Mr. Clark. The other means death and insanity too?
Mr. Schieffelin. Oh, no.[90]

On the subject of prohibition leading to increased smuggling, Mr. Schieffelin was perfectly happy to agree:

Mr. Clark. The more restrictions you put around it the more you drive it away from legitimate druggists into the hands of what you call bootleggers?
Mr. Schlieffelin. Absolutely. I would like to see it entirely driven into the hands of bootleggers.
Mr. Clark. That is where you want it driven?
Mr. Schlieffelin. Yes; the drug trade wants to handle these things with clean hands, and only sell them for legitimate medicinal purposes, and have nothing to do with supplying the victims of the habit.[91]

Charles Marius Woodruff (1851 – 1932), an attorney representing six prominent pharmaceutical manufacturers including Parke, Davis, denied the indifference of the pharmaceutical estate to the public health. On the contrary, its representatives had struggled indefatigably for the uprooting of the traffic in morphine and cocaine: "We have had a system for 28 years of trying to keep, so far as

---

[90] Unknown compiler, Importation, 1911, "Statement of Mr. William J. Schieffelin, President of the National Wholesale Druggists' Association," p. 120.
[91] Unknown compiler, Importation, 1911, p. 120.

possible, morphine, and later cocaine, out of the hands of even doctors, for there are some physicians scattered all over this country who have been destroyed by the habits."[92] He added: "The welfare of this country depends upon the welfare of the manufacturer."[93]

The next testimony came from the chairman of the legislative committee of the Kings County Pharmaceutical Society, Dr. William Edward Muir (1884 – 1951), who felt education would solve any problems, contrasting the dangers of cocaine with the benefits of opium:

> I think the majority of people to-day are strong and healthy. ... [J]ust go out into Central Park he would see the finest, strongest, most robust specimens of manhood ... anywhere in the world. I believe that this country is all right. Education has come along and we have found cocaine, which is a new thing. I admit the curse of cocaine ... but how many men understood it when it first came out? ... It was hailed as a great discovery of something to relieve pain. Now we have found that it is a bad thing. ... But look at the remedial effect of opium to relieve pain; look at the good side. It is wonderful what it has done for pain, to relieve it. Every doctor has it in his saddlebags or his hand bag.[94]

He added, using an argument[95] considered and rejected by the early church father and archbishop of Constantinople, John Chrysostom (c. 347 – 407):

---

[92] Unknown compiler, Importation, 1911, p. 122.

[93] Unknown compiler, Importation, 1911, pp. 122-123.

[94] Unknown compiler, Importation, 1911, "Statement of Dr. William Muir, of Brooklyn, N. Y.," p. 125.

[95] "What then? Is there no such thing as a good man becoming wicked? And the contrary again takes place, and life abounds with many such examples? But Christ saith not this ..." (Schaff, Philip, ed. A Select Library of the Nicene and Post-Nicene Fathers of the Christian Church, Volume X: Saint Chrysostom: Homilies on the Gospel of Saint Matthew. NY: The Christian Literature Company, 1888 AO, p.

> We admit there is wrong comes from good things. We admit there are a good many people killed by automobiles; but there is a good deal of pleasure gotten from them; and this idea of stamping this out and killing it is wrong, because you can not stamp it out with any such means as this.[96]

Muir ended by warning the committee that some five hundred pharmacists had just met with the goal of opposing the project should it ever be approved:

> We had a meeting yesterday afternoon of 500 of the best druggists in Brooklyn, at which we discussed this matter, and there were resolutions passed and we did not favor this. If you want to know the reason why we did not take action here, I will tell you we thought this bill would fall by its own weight. ... Now we are awake and now that the bill has a chance of passing, you will hear more from the retail trade than you ever did before.[97]

Charles Barnes Towns (1862 – 1947), of whom we will speak more later, owner of a prosperous private New York city clinic espousing cures for alcoholism and other addictions based on *Atropa belladonna* (deadly nightshade) and *Hyoscyamus niger* (henbane), and *Zanthoxylum americanum* (prickly ash)[98] demanded cannabis be included in the list of habit-forming drugs because of its pleasurable sensations:

---

164); see also biblehub.com.

[96] Unknown compiler, Importation, 1911, p. 125.

[97] Unknown compiler, Importation, 1911, p. 127.

[98] "The treatment ... was given to me by Mr. Charles B. Towns .... Briefly stated, it consists in the hourly dosage of a mixture of belladonna, hyosyamus and xanthoxylum. This mixture is given every hour, day and night, for about fifty hours" (Lambert, Alexander. "Care and Control of the Alcoholic," *The Boston Medical and Surgical Journal*, Volume CLXVI, January – June. Boston, MA: W. M. Leonard, 1912 AO, 25 April, p. 618).

> In the case of cannabis, to my mind it is inexcusable for a man to say there is no habit from the use of that drug. There is no drug in the Pharmacopoeia to-day that would produce the pleasurable sensations you would get from cannabis, not one – absolutely not a drug in the Pharmacopoeia to-day, and of all the drugs on earth I certainly would put that on the list.[99]

He also spoke of the horrors of addiction and the ease of acquiring drug habits:

> Once a patient becomes addicted to the use of opium or morphine, or any of these alkaloids, it is absolutely impossible for that man to rid himself of that habit. No amount of will power on earth can relieve him of that habit. ... I can speak as to how easily these people acquire this habit.[100]

He argued for an even stronger bill: "I think Dr. Wright, in the framing of this bill, is asking for what he thinks he can get. I do not think he is drawing a bill half strong enough."[101]

Albert Plaut (1857 – 1915) of Lehn & Fink of New York (import/export and wholesale druggists) quizzed Mr. Towns on the ease of acquiring such habits: "If the use of minute quantities of opium in compound preparations led to the effect you just described, would not every person in this room, including the gentlemen up there, now be morphine fiends?"[102] Mr. Towns seemed not to understand the question.

In the end victory was won by the National Wholesale Druggist's Association (NWDA), disposed to put up with in theory

---

[99] Unknown compiler, Importation, 1911, "Statement of Mr. Charles B. Towns, representing the Charles B. Towns hospital, 119 West Eighty-First Street, New York City," p. 140.

[100] Unknown compiler, Importation, 1911, p. 140.

[101] Unknown compiler, Importation, 1911, p. 140.

[102] Unknown compiler, Importation, 1911, p. 143.

(though not in practice) neither severe controls nor condemnations for pharmacists and large manufacturers. Its weekly, the *American Druggist and Pharmaceutical Record*, announced in large letters on the first page of the issue of 27 February 1911:

> Foster Bill Killed.
> The vigorous protest which was made by members of the drug trade, under the leadership of the AMERICAN DRUGGIST, with reference to one of the bills, convinced the more conservative members of the committee that it would be unwise to take any hasty action. ... [Democrats] take the ground that such legislation is properly passed, if at all, by the state, rather than the federal government, and that it is not wise to invade the field of state activity. ... The method proposed by the Foster bill was the requirement of a revenue stamp to be employed under certain conditions by all dealers in drugs [capitalization original].[103]

Doubtless, one of the other basic hurdles was that proprietary medicines or homemade drugs were already obligated by the 1906 Wiley law to declare their composition, denying now that they fell under the infamous label of narcotic. In the words of the chairman: "Most of the States have opium and cocaine laws now."[104]

Effectively, it was clear from the beginning that the majority opinion was not conscious of any evil, and that for this same reason it would not really feel inclined to annihilate it. Wright had tried in Washington, as he had at Shanghai, to manufacture public opinion. The user of narcotics was presented as an anti-American threat analogous to communists and anarchists, with features of ruin akin to sexual delinquents and intimations of racial cancer. Once again, there appeared in circulation (now promoted in the seat of the legislature) a

---

[103] Editorial Comment. "Foster Bill Killed," *American Druggist and Pharmaceutical Record*, January – June 1911, Volume 58, Issue 4 AO, p. 23.

[104] Unknown compiler, Importation, 1911, p. 118.

subject capable of including all of the so-called trash of a society. Thanks to Wright the good people of the United States could feel united in the pious task of decontaminating themselves by liquidating the life and liberty of a fellow citizen. Once again, the preference for a particular *pharmakon* meant rallying the mob for a *pharmakoi* elected as victim for a ritual sacrificial banquet.

Figure 305. "This boy knows a good thing when he sees it." Color chromolithograph, 1850 – 1900. Chamberlain's Cough Remedy. National Library of Medicine Digital Collections, Bethesda, MD. This cough remedy was said to contain no opium.[105]

105 "There is no opium ... in Chamberlain's Cough Remedy ..." (Brisbane *Telegraph*, Saturday 9 May 1903 [trove.nla.gov.au, hereinafter NLA], p. 7).

Figure 306. "Chamberlain's Colic, Cholera and Diarrhoea Remedy." Chamberlain Medicine Company, Des Moines, Iowa. Glass, paper, cork, 1882. Smithsonian, National Museum of American History [NMAH], G. E. Damon Collection, Washington, DC.

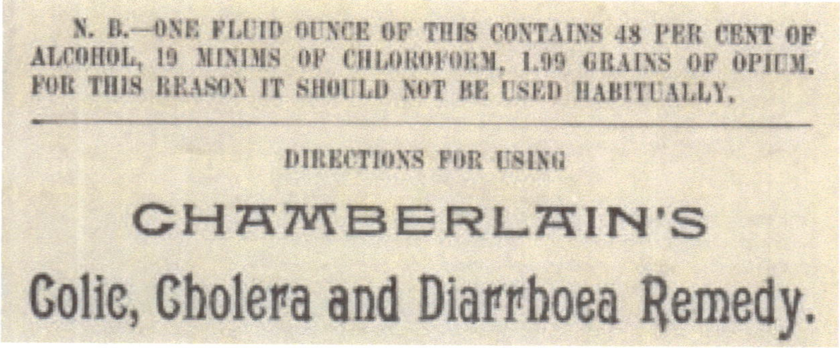

N. B.—ONE FLUID OUNCE OF THIS CONTAINS 48 PER CENT OF ALCOHOL, 19 MINIMS OF CHLOROFORM, 1.99 GRAINS OF OPIUM. FOR THIS REASON IT SHOULD NOT BE USED HABITUALLY.

DIRECTIONS FOR USING

CHAMBERLAIN'S

Colic, Cholera and Diarrhoea Remedy.

Figure 307. "Directions for Using Chamberlain's Colic, Cholera and Diarrhoea Remedy." Des Moines, Iowa: Chamberlain's Medicine Company, 1910-1915 National Library of Medicine, Bethesda, MD. The colic, cholera and diarrhea remedy contained alcohol, chloroform and opium.

THE AGE OF DRUGS.

SALOON KEEPER.—The kind of drunkard I make is going out of fashion. I can't begin to compete with this fellow.

Figure 308. "The Age of Drugs." Dalyrmple, Louis (1866 – 1905). NY: J. Ottman Lithograph Company, 1900. Library of Congress, Prints and Photographs Division, Washington, DC [loc.gov, hereinafter LG]; see also *Puck*, Volume XLVIII, No. 1231, 10 October 1900 AO, pp. 8, 9 of 16.

23
Junkies and Juicers

At times we ought to reach the point even of intoxication, not drowning ourselves in drink, yet succumbing to it; for it washes away troubles, and stirs the mind from its very depths and heals its sorrow just as it does certain illnesses of the body; and the inventor of wine is not called the Releaser [Liber, the Roman Bacchus] on account of the licence it gives to the tongue, but because it frees the mind from bondage to cares and emancipates it and gives it new life and makes it bolder in all that it attempts.[1]

-- Lucius Annaeus Seneca the Younger (4 BC – 65AD)

A. The Hague Conference

1. Opium

2. Other Drugs

3. Details

4. Signatures

B. The *Harrison Act*

1. The Controversy Over Dispensing

2. The Legal Nature of the Precept

a. The Medical and the Nonmedical

b. Possession and Dispensation

3. Judicial Reservations

C. The *Volstead Act*

1. Alcohol and Heredity

2. The Therapeutic Estate

3. Crime

---

[1] Seneca Moral Essays, Volume II, tr. John W. Basore. Cambridge, MA: Harvard University Press, 1932 [archive.org, hereinafter AO], Ad Serenum De Tranquillitate Animi, Liber IX, Chapter XVII, Section VIII, p. 283; *Non numquam et usque ad ebrietatum veniendum ... et audaciorum in omnis conatus facit* (Seneca, 1932, p. 282, esp. ftnt a); see also L. Annaeus Seneca Minor Dialogues Together with the Dialogue On Clemency, tr. Aubrey Stewart. London: George Bell and Sons, 1889, The Ninth Book of the Dialogues of L. Annaeus Seneca, addressed to Serenus, Of Peace of Mind, p. 286; as well see the volume at Perseus [perseus.tufts.edu, hereinafter PER].

In the first few decades of the twentieth century several drugs will be prohibited in the United States. But the legal regimen will look considerably different for each. One is a common medicine sometimes used habitually. Another is a common beverage sometimes used medicinally. Prescriptions will now be needed for both.

A. The Hague Conference

Though still without its own federal prohibitionist statute, the United States managed to convene a new international opium conference at Den Haag [The Hague, Netherlands]. Achieving even this much required laborious effort, feeding into the suspicions of Charles Henry Brent (1862 – 1929) and Hamilton Kemp Wright (1867 – 1917) that a planetary conspiracy opposed their American crusade. "To the Americans there appeared to be a conspiracy afoot to block the meeting."[2]

For the first time a retired apothecary and chemist would be part of the American delegation, one Henry James Finger (1853 – 1930).[3] Pharmacology had not been front and center in the efforts of the two crusaders, and the inclusion of a mere technician might have been thought to cause them to fear for the enterprise as a whole. But Finger, a member of the California State Board of Pharmacy, was the "author of California's pharm[acy] law, [an] act regulating sale of poisons, [an] act regulating itinerant vendors of drugs, and Calif[ornia]

---

[2] Taylor, Arnold H. American Diplomacy and the Narcotics Traffic, 1900 – 1939: *A study in international humanitarian reform*. Durham, NC: Duke University Press, 1969 AO, Chapter 4, p. 92; see also pages 93, 94 and ftnt 76, p. 106.

[3] Detwiler, Justice B., ed. Who's Who in California A Biographical Directory 1928-1929. San Francisco, CA: Who's Who Publishing Company, 1929 AO, p. 326, column 2.

laws relating to detention and cure of inebriates and drug victims,"[4] and like Wright was interested in including cannabis in any international restrictive agreements.[5] Even so, Wright was said to have "very much resented the appointment of the diplomatically inexperienced California pharmacist."[6]

HENRY J. FINGER

Figure 309. "Henry J. Finger." Downs, David. "The Grand, Racist, Hundred-Year History of Pot Prohibition in California," *East Bay Express*, 23 January 2013 [eastbayexpress.com, hereinafter EBX], unpaged.

---

[4] Detwiler, 1929, p. 326.

[5] Gieringer, Dale H. "The Forgotten Origins of Cannabis Prohibition in California," *Contemporary Drug Problems*, Volume 26, Number 2, Summer 1999, revised 2006 [researchgate.net, hereinafter RGN], pp. 17-18.

[6] Gieringer, 1999, p. 17.

The conference (which held its first session on 1 December 1911 and its twenty-sixth and last session on 23 January 1912)[7] did not completely satisfy the hopes of the American prohibitionists. In the first place, few nations bothered to send a delegation. As at the Shanghai conference Turkey declined to attend, and this time so did Austria-Hungary. "Thus, amongst the unrepresented Governments were Turkey, Austro-Hungary, and Spain; also Bulgaria, Bolivia, and Peru, as well as Guatemala, Cuba, and Costa Rica."[8] Secondarily, what began as an opium conference similar to the one held three years earlier in Shanghai quickly morphed into a conference on other drugs as well, setting up seemingly irresolvable conflicts among the participants.

---

[7] Smith, Cecil Clementi, et al. Report of the British Delegates to the International Opium Conference held at The Hague, December 1911 – January 1912. London: His Majesty's Stationery Office, 1912 AO, pp. 2, 22.

[8] Brent, Charles H., President. Report of the International Opium Commission Shanghai, China February 1 to February 26, 1909, Volume I. Shanghai, China: North China Daily News and Herald Ltd., 1909 AO, Report of the Proceedings, List of Delegations and Representatives, pp. 3-6; Unknown contributor. "The Proceedings of the International Opium Conference at The Hague," *The British Medical Journal*, Volume II, 14 September 1912 AO, Part II, Report of Redaction Committee, p. 637.

1. Opium

With regards to opium, the various nations who did attend often talked at cross-purposes. Portugal defended its inaction on the trade in prepared opium [for smoking] exported through Macao: "That further action in regard to the limitation of the number of ports from which raw and prepared opium could be exported ... could not be undertaken by Portugal, since Macao was already the only Portuguese port of export in the Far East."[9] Wright summarized Portugal's position on the issue: "Macau on the China-coast still continues to import large quantities of the drug, manufacture it into smoking opium, which is used locally, or exported for revenue purposes."[10]

Persia also defended its ancestral practices, little changed from three years earlier:

> The poppy is cultivated quite freely and there is no attempt by the Government to monopolize the manufacture and sale of opium. ... [I]t is estimated that from 200,000 to 300,000 pounds were consumed in Persia annually. The balance of the drug is exported to foreign countries, the high-grade opium going to Europe and America for medicinal purposes and the rest to Hongkong and the Straits Settlements to be manufactured into smoking opium. The Persian Government derives a large yearly income from an export duty on the drug. In 1901– 1904 the opium revenue amounted to about £350,000. Persia has no treaty relations with China ....[11]

---

[9] Smith, 1912, p. 22, paragraph 89 (2).

[10] Wright, Hamilton. "The International Opium Conference," The American Journal of International Law, Volume 6. New York: Baker, Voorhis & Company, 1912 AO, Number 4, October, p. 888.

[11] Wright, Hamilton. "The International Opium Commission (Part 1)" The American Journal of International Law, Volume 3. New York: Baker, Voorhis & Company, 1909 AO, Number 3, July, pp. 664-665; see also Wright, Hamilton. "Report to the Secretary of State on the Second International Opium Conference by

In Holland, besides the income it receives from thousands of tons of Javanese coca leaf,

a considerable revenue is derived by the Netherlands Indies Government from the importation, manufacture and distribution of opium for smoking purposes .... [M]any ordinances have been passed by the Batavia Government aimed to extend government control over the habit of opium smoking .... No doubt there will be many difficulties to meet, as the net revenue from the opium regié last year was in the neighborhood of eighteen million florins.[12]

France was torn between the loss of revenue from opium consumption in its colonies in Indochina and the fear of increased consumption at home:

In France there is no poppy culture for opium. ... Opium is imported into France chiefly from Turkey in the crude form for medicinal purposes only. ... In Paris, Toulon, and Bordeaux there is probably a large illicit use of morphine and considerable smoking of opium, but it seems to be confined to these few cities. In French Indo-China only a small amount of opium is produced .... The manufacture of smoking opium in French Indo-China is a Government monopoly or regie, with a single factory at Saigon .... The trade by land [with China] was allowed on payment of an export duty taels 20 per picul, but French merchants and persons under French protection were restricted as to the place of trade. There were also restrictions as to reimportation of Chinese opium by the coast ports.[13]

---

the American delegates: Hamilton Wright, Lloyd Bryce, Gerrit John Kollen (31 July 1913)," Papers Relating to the Foreign Relations of the United States, with the address of the President to Congress December 2, 1913, [history.state.gov, hereinafter HSG], Appendix I, "The International Opium Convention," p. 245.

[12] Wright, AJIL, Vol. 6, 1912, pp. 887-888.

[13] Wright, AJIL, Vol. 3, 1909, pp. 658-659; Wright, Papers, 1913, Appendix I, p. 242.

Russia "fortunately has no opium problem."[14] Indeed, there was "no evidence at hand that would show that Russia has an opium problem in her home territories. Amongst the Mohammedan population opium is used combined with tobacco, and in Siberia, where there are Chinese, opium smoking exists to some extent."[15]

As for Siam, the

> poppy is not grown in Siam. The crude drug is imported from India and was until recently manufactured and distributed through an opium farm which the Government sold to the highest bidder. For the last 20 years the importation or sale has been a Government monopoly. ... The Siamese Government derives a large part of its revenues from the manufacture and sale of smoking opium.[16]

Japan had no opium problem "except in the Island of Formosa, where an opium regié exists for the avowed purpose of finally suppressing the opium vice."[17] When Japan acquired the island it faced much the same problem as the United States had with the Philippines in that

> there were over 200,000 opium smokers in Formosa, and it appeared to the Japanese authorities that it would be difficult for the smokers to break off the habit at once. There was also a danger that the people would be alienated in the event of the Japanese applying their own strict home laws to the island. The Government therefore determined to put the importation, manufacture, and sale of smoking opium under Government control. ... Under the system of Government control licenses are granted to the Formosa Chinese, who are the only members of the population addicted to smoking.[18]

---

[14] Wright, AJIL, Vol. 6, 1912, p. 888.

[15] Wright, AJIL, Vol. 3, 1909, p. 666; Wright, Papers, 1913, Appendix I, p. 245.

[16] Wright, AJIL, Vol. 3, 1909, p. 667; Wright, Papers, 1913, Appendix I, p. 246.

[17] Wright, AJIL, Vol. 6, 1912, p. 888.

[18] Wright, AJIL, Vol. 3, 1909, pp. 663-664; Wright, Papers, 1913, Appendix I, p. 245.

Essentially, with regards to opium the Japanese recreated in Formosa what the Spanish had created in the Philippines, much the same system proposed by Governor William Howard Taft (1857 – 1930) before it provoked backlash from the missionaries.

Figure 310. "Interior, Collins Pharmacy, Islip, Long Island, New York." Ca. 1915. Library of Congress, Prints and Photographs Division, Washington, DC [loc.gov, hereinafter LG].

2. Other Drugs

Though officially titled an International Opium Conference, talk quickly shifted to other drugs. England for example only wanted to talk of morphine and cocaine, making it

> a *sine qua non* that their participation in the International Opium Conference would depend upon the willingness of the interested governments to pledge themselves to the same drastic legislation for the control of the production, manufacture, and trade in morphine and cocaine as in regard to opium ... [italics original].[19]

This expansion of subject matter was deemed essential:

> Our instructions emphasised the fact that His Majesty's Government held it essential that 'the conference should thoroughly and completely deal with the question of restricting the manufacture, sale, and distribution of morphia and cocaine' [quotation marks original].[20]

British concern over the traffic in morphine and cocaine had grown as a direct result of the enforcement of restrictive legislation which had subsequently encouraged their use as substitutes for the now banned opium: "[F]or, beginning with the suppression of the opium vice in China and other far eastern countries, a determined, and one almost might say a calculated, effort was made by the manufacturers of morphine and cocaine to introduce these drugs in

---

[19] Wright, Hamilton. "The International Opium Conference. Part II," The American Journal of International Law, Volume 7. New York: Baker, Voorhis & Company, 1913 AO, January, No. 1, p. 125

[20] Smith, 1912, p. 2, paragraph 4.

replacement of opium."[21] What was true in China was also true of British India:

> [I]t had been shown beyond a doubt that immense quantities of these drugs [morphine and cocaine] were being smuggled into British India to take the place of opium; also that in China they tended to supplant the use of opium which the British Government had agreed that India should soon cease to export, and the production and use of which China on her part had agreed to suppress.[22]

But this emphasis on morphine and cocaine offended Germany which protested "not because of any abuse of these drugs in German territory, but because of the large financial investment in their manufacture"[23] on the part of its powerful laboratories. It noted other countries [like Switzerland] were not present and would only take advantage of any new restrictions for their own benefit:

> [Germany had] a practical monopoly of cocaine production, and claimed to have a satisfactory system of domestic control, [so] her delegates were reluctant to embark on further measures that might sacrifice a lucrative German industry for the benefit of outside countries not represented at the conference.[24]

The head of the German delegation in turn attempted to embarrass the head of the American delegation by asking "what guarantee they could give to the other Powers that, after ratification, their Government would pass the legislation necessary to put the stipulations of the treaty in force."[25] Wright replied ahistorically that

---

[21] Wright, AJIL, Vol. 7, 1913, p. 126.

[22] Wright, AJIL, Vol. 6, 1912, p. 870.

[23] Wright, AJIL, Vol. 6, 1912, p. 887.

[24] Smith, 1912, p. 7, paragraph 35; Taylor, 1969, Chapter 4, p. 106.

[25] Unknown contributor, "The Proceedings," *BMJ*, 14 September 1912, p. 637.

the "United States could give a guarantee of one hundred and twenty-five years of national good faith."[26]

Italy sought to include cannabis in the proposed legislation. The "Italian Government ... proposed that the production and traffic in the Indian hemp drugs be included as part of the programme of the conference."[27] However, the Italian delegation only appeared at the first and the fourth day[28] of the conference as its head was "detained in Paris by reason of the labours of the International Sanitary Conference."[29] Also, "it appeared that the Italian delegation was not to present any specific proposal in regard to hemp drugs, but rather to leave it to the conference as a whole to take such measures in regard to these as it might deem expedient."[30] The Programme Committee referred the matter for further study.[31]

---

26 Unknown contributor, "The Proceedings," *BMJ*, 14 September 1912, p. 637.

27 Wright, AJIL, Vol. 6, 1912, p. 871.

28 Unknown author. International Opium Conference The Hague december 1, 1911 – january 23, 1912, Summary of the Minutes (Unofficial). The Hague, NL: National Printing Office, 1912 AO, pp. 1, 5, 10, 13, 18, 25, 32, 39, 48, 54, 61, 75, 81, 87, 94, 96, 102, 108, 113, 117, 122, 129, 137, 143, 147, 150.

29 Unknown author, International Opium Conference, Thirteenth Plenary Session, Thursday 21 December 1911, p. 81.

30 Smith, 1912, p. 14, paragraph 57.

31 Smith, 1912, p. 14, paragraph 58.

3. Details

As we have seen, the so-called International Opium Convention was only partly about opium. The first two chapters circumscribed the import and export of opium. Chapter I, Article 3 demanded that the signing countries "prevent the export of raw opium to countries that shall have prohibited its entry" and to "control the export of raw opium to countries which restrict its import."[32] Chapter II, Article 7 prohibited the import and export of prepared opium [for smoking], unless a nation was "not yet ready" in which case it should prohibit it "as soon as possible."[33] The recalitrant were required under Article 8 to restrict the number of ports from which it could be exported, prohibit the export to countries forbidding its import, limit consignment, mark each package and license exporters.[34]

The next chapter expanded that scope to apply regulations to other drugs as well, though at the risk of increasing obfuscation. Chapter III, Article 9 of the Convention limited morphine and cocaine to medical and legitimate purposes. "The contracting Powers shall enact pharmacy laws or regulations to confine to medical and legitimate purposes the manufacture, sale, and use of morphine, cocaine, and their respective salts ...."[35] The same article required the signatory parties "to co-operate with one another to prevent the use"

---

32 Bevans, Charles I., compiler. Treaties and Other International Agreements of the United States of America 1776 – 1949, Volume I Multilateral 1776 – 1917. Washington, DC: Department of State, Division of Publishing and Reproduction, 1968 LG, Suppression of Abuse of Opium and Other Drugs, p. 858; No. 222. The International Opium Convention, signed at The Hague, January 23, 1912, and subsequent papers. League of Nations Treaty Series, 1922, p. 193.

33 Bevans, 1968, p. 859; No. 222, International, 1922, p. 195.

34 Bevans, 1968, p. 859; No. 222, International, 1922, p. 195.

35 Bevans, 1968, p. 860; No. 222, International, 1922, p. 197.

of "morphine, cocaine and their respective salts" for "any other purpose" than "medical or legitimate."[36] This implied of course that there was some medical or legitimate use for these drugs.

Yet, while there was some general agreement as to the meaning of the word, medical (which would be quickly tested and found wanting), nowhere was there any definition of the word, legitimate. Wright clearly distinguished what he termed the "unnecessary production and vicious consumption of opium" from "legitimate opium."[37] Opium eating for example was more legitimate than opium smoking; the Indian government regarded "a certain amount of opium eating as legitimate" which did "not apply to the smoking habit."[38] Similarly, Wright felt that "morphine and cocaine ... may be imported" as long as the sellers "disposed of [them] ... in a legitimate manner."[39] Domestically, Wright noticed that "some 30 of the [US] states have improved the intrastate legislation aimed to confine narcotics to legitimate uses ...."[40] But he elaborated no further on the difference between vicious and legitimate consumption.

Chapter III, Article 14(d) further expanded the reach of the agreement beyond the newly enumerated drugs to new drugs not yet enumerated, requiring national pharmacy laws to apply broadly to "all new derivatives of morphine, or cocaine, or of their respective salts, and to every other alkaloid of opium, which may be shown by scientific research, generally recognised, to be liable to similar abuse and productive of like ill-effects."[41] Exempted under Article 14 were all preparations "(officinal and non-officinal, including the so-called

---

36 Bevans, 1968, p. 860; No. 222, International, 1922, p. 197.

37 Wright, "The International," AJIL, Vol. 6, 1912, October, No. 4, p. 867.

38 Wright, AJIL, Volume 6, 1912, p. 886.

39 Wright, AJIL, Volume 6, 1912, p. 889.

40 Wright, AJIL, Volume 7, 1913, p. 135.

41 Bevans, 1968, p. 861; No. 222, International, 1922, p. 199.

anti-opium remedies)"[42] containing less than 0.2 percent cocaine or less than 0.1 percent morphine, as well as those containing less than 0.1 percent of "heroin, its salts and preparations."[43] Heroin was defined in Chapter III as "Diacetyl-morphine, having the formula C21H23NO5."[44] Naturally, these percentages omitted products with notable psychoactivity. Possession was to be criminalized under Chapter V, Article 20: "The contracting Powers shall examine the possibility of enacting laws or regulations making it a penal offence to be in illegal possession of raw opium, prepared opium, morphine, cocaine, and their respective salts ...."[45]

The American delegation was satisfied with the first part of the accord. Strictly, the various nations signing the agreement only promised not to export these drugs to countries which had prohibited them by national legislation. But the Americans were completely opposed to the second part where the legislatures of each country were free to implement appropriate measures. The degree of internal control was a question reserved for each of the contracting Powers. For Wright and Brent, such a provision amounted to maintaining the *status quo ante*, while they believed it was necessary to establish international and not merely national restrictions.

---

[42] Bevans, 1968, p. 861; No. 222, International, 1922, p. 199.

[43] Bevans, 1968, p. 861; No. 222, International, 1922, p. 199.

[44] Bevans, 1968, p. 859; No. 222, International, 1922, p. 197.

[45] Bevans, 1968, p. 861; No. 222, International, 1922, p. 201.

4. Signatures

But perhaps the largest problem for the American delegation was its insistence on adopting not recommendations but resolutions:

> The International Opium Conference, composed of delegates with full powers, was a sequel of the International Opium Commission which met at Shanghai, China, February, 1909. That commission was, generally speaking, a commission of inquiry .... Its conclusions ... were on their face only moral in effect. ... [A] conference, composed of delegates with full powers ... [could] conventionalize the conclusions of the commission.[46]

This however raised the problem of how to bring the Convention into force due to the poor attendance:

> Only twelve nations were represented at the Conference. Others had been invited, but had not accepted the invitation, while yet others had not been invited to participate. Among the nations not represented were several which, either actually or prospectively, had an important stake in the decisions which might be arrived at. ... Clearly, for a few nations to bind themselves by a self-denying ordinance to restrict trade in opium, morphine, etc., while leaving others free to extend their commerce in the like commodities, or even to set up a trade which the more virtuous had either abandoned or severely limited, would be neither just nor politic – neither good business nor good law.[47]

Hamilton Wright and the other members of the disappointed US delegation to the twelve nation conference "were counseled to wait for adherence from the world's forty-six powers, particularly those involved in the opium and cocaine traffic, such as the absent Turkey,

---

[46] Wright, AJIL, Vol. 6, 1912, p. 867.

[47] Unknown contributor. "The Proceedings," *BMJ*, 14 September 1912, pp. 636-637.

Switzerland, Bolivia, and Peru."[48] The lack of signatures meant that the Convention remained in suspense, while a second conference was convoked in 1913[49] and a third in 1914[50] for the purpose of incorporating the signatures of more countries. But by the conclusion of the latter [25 June 1914], pressure from the Northamericans on Latin America and the rest of the world had resulted in the signatures of only some thirty nations.[51]

Three days later Archduke of Austria-Este Franz Ferdinand (1863 – 1914) was assassinated at Sarajevo, and the First World War exploded. "[A]s war enveloped Europe in 1914, very little progress in carrying out the international aspects of the Convention was possible anyway. ... The preoccupation of the powers with World War I hampered further action."[52] As a consequence, the agreement was suspended pending the signatures of other nations. By 1915 just five [the United States, China, the Netherlands, Honduras and Norway] had ratified it and intended to put it into operation.[53]

The ratification of the Convention would have had an unforeseeable fate had not a British diplomat suggested a clever strategem, to incorporate the Hague Agreement as Article 295[54] of the Treaty of Versailles [1919] which put an end to that conflict. This

---

[48] Musto, 1999, p. 51.

[49] Bevans, 1968, p. 869.

[50] Bevans, 1968, p. 873.

[51] Bevans, 1968, p. 877.

[52] Taylor, 1969, p. 120.

[53] Bevans, 1968, p. 878; Spain ratified on 11 February 1921.

[54] Bevans, Charles I., compiler. Treaties and Other International Agreements of the United States of America 1776 – 1949, Volume II Multilateral 1918 – 1930. Washington, DC: Department of State, Division of Publishing and Reproduction, 1969 LG, Treaty of Peace with Germany (Treaty of Versailles), p. 175.

meant that practically all the countries on the planet would subscribe to an agreement originally signed by only a few.

On the other hand, the stipulations of the agreement were sensible. It was based on the principle of mutual respect: no nation would be able to export drugs as England, the United States and others had done to China in the nineteenth century. Such an agreement was acceptable to everyone.

Brent and Wright were the principal architects of an agreement that did not really satisfy their aspirations, though it contained the seed of possible future prohibitions. The fates of the two diverged. Brent continued to the end of his days a victorious crusader in the lands of the infidels. Wright was fired a little before the third and final conference in 1914 due to excessive drinking. America had become in those years singularly sensible of dipsomania. The Secretary of State William Jennings Bryan (1860 – 1925)

> increasingly uncertain about Wright's value and having occasionally detected liquor on Wright's breath, called him and demanded that he take the pledge of abstinence .... Humiliated, Wright refused and was thereupon dismissed from the State Department and from the Hague delegation.[55]

Two years later Wright died of bitterness and liver failure in equal parts.

If Wilbur F. Crafts (1850 – 1922), Brent and the other missionaries had advanced the ethical-theological argument, Wright must be credited with finding an effective path to give it legal force. He conceived the idea of presenting the American Congress with an international convention as a means of calling for urgent domestic measures, avoiding the long and difficult process of amending the

[55] Musto, 1999, Chapter Three The Harrison Act, p. 61.

Constitution. Wright's "own understanding was that when once a treaty was ratified it became the law of the land. If it were ratified by the Senate and approved by the President it would become law."[56] His legal instincts were the key to making the prohibitionist enterprise viable, and although his basic motivation was political ambition, he undoubtedly contributed decisively to the crusade.

Indeed, one byproduct of the Convention was the passing of national repressive legislation, except in the United States:

> [A] reflex effect of the initiation by the United States ... took the form of improved domestic legislation in nearly all the countries concerned .... The one nation which has not been vitally affected by the international movement initiated by the United States is the United States itself, except in the Philippines.[57]

Wright published these remarks less than two years before the passage of the *Harrison Act.*

---

[56] Unknown contributor. "The Proceedings," *BMJ*, 14 September 1912, p. 637.

[57] Wright, AJIL, Volume 7, 1913, p. 134.

B. The *Harrison Act*

From the international scene we have to return to the United States at the beginning of 1912. After the failures with the bills introduced by James Robert Mann (Rep. IL, 1856 – 1922) and David Johnson Foster (Rep. VT, 1857 – 1912), Wright sought a new sponsor to push through new federal bills, one Francis Burton Harrison (Dem. NY, 1873 – 1957). For manufacturers and pharmacists the new proposed bills had the same problems as the previous ones, in that they did not exempt specifics with small quantities of opiates and cocaine. This was even more unacceptable than the Hague agreement which did not submit such medicines to governmental control.

In this era public agitation for prohibitionist legislation grew steadily. Alcohol would soon be outlawed. Smoking tobacco in public was already illegal in twelve states and soon would be in twenty-eight. Charles Barnes Towns (1862 – 1947), known for his New York clinic that treated patients with *Atropa belladonna* (deadly nightshade) and *Hyoscyamus niger* (henbane),[58] also (as noted earlier) attacked cigarettes with apocalyptic fervor: "I consider that cigarette-smoking is the greatest vice devastating humanity to-day, because it is doing more than any other vice to deteriorate the race."[59] The country was ripe for prohibitionist measures.

---

[58] See GHDV4P1, Chapter 22, C. The Debate Over the Foster Bills, p. 1256, ftnt. 98.

[59] Towns, Charles B. Habits that Handicap: the Menace of Opium, Alcohol, Tobacco, and the Remedy. New York: The Century Co., 1916 AO, Chapter VIII The Injuriousness of Tobacco, p. 157; see also GHDV3P2, p. 1419.

Figure 311. "Francis Burton Harrison." Photograph, negative, glass, 1910. Bain News. Library of Congress, Prints and Photographs Division, Washington, DC LG.

Although the druggists, pharmacists and manufacturers had emerged victorious twice, they considered it inevitable that they would have to accept some kind of restrictive regulation. In the nineteenth and early twentieth centuries, they had formed organizations to set standards and affect legislation. "It was pressure from outside which forced the druggists in the United States to form their first associations. This pressure came from the medical profession."[60] Membership in the American Medical Association [AMA, established 1847], for example, had "increased from 8,500 in 1900 to 36,000 in 1913."[61]

It should be noted that alarm over these new proposed laws had not really spread throughout the pharmaceutical establishment because in this era two things appeared to be clear and indisputable that later would not turn out to be so: a) that both the opiates and cocaine were therapeutic agents of extraordinary value, and b) that chemists, pharmacists and physicians were the only ones competent to define the scientific and medical use of controlled drugs. Instead, they disagreed only on the details of who should dispense and who should prescribe.

---

60 Kremers, Edward and George Urdang. History of Pharmacy: *A Guide and a Survey*. Philadelphia, PA: J. B. Lippincott Company, 1940 AO, Part III, Chapter 12 The Growth of Associations, p. 173.

61 Musto, 1999, Chapter 3 The Harrison Act, "The AMA and Narcotic Legislation," p. 56.

1. The Controversy Over Dispensing

From 1912 to 1914 an interesting conflict arose in the pharmaceutical industry, exemplified in three consecutive editorials in the house organ of the National Association of Retail Druggists [NARD]. First, the retail druggists felt that the doctors were using lobbying and public relations to increase their sphere of influence within the Wilson Administration at the expense of the druggists, as well as other stakeholders and interested parties. In 1913, after an editorial in a "leading medical journal" decried the "not so organized" physicians, while praising the "most carefully organized" retail druggists, a reply editorial in the *Journal of the N.A.R.D.* provocatively compared the legislative influence of the doctors with that of the druggists:

> Possibly our editorial friend desires to 'return the compliment' THE JOURNAL [of the NARD] has been for years handing to the organized doctors. It has been pointing to the splendid, compact and efficient organization of medical men and the results they have accomplished, not only in legislation beneficial to the public, but in monopolistic legislation beneficial only to the physicians, as an example of what can be done and what should be done by our own people in so far as the results might be in harmony with N. A. R. D. principles and democratic rule in our organization and among the people. But lo and behold, the tables are turned on us, and our organization is now pointed out to the medical profession as the model organization of legislative forces for them to pattern after!
>
> All of which is to laugh, and laugh most heartily [quotation marks, capitalization and exclamation mark original].[62]

---

[62] Carr, Charles Mylert, editor and director. "Legislative Organization: Have a Laugh with Us," The Journal of the National Association of Retail Druggists (Formerly N. A. R. D. Notes), Volume XVII, October 9, 1913 to April 2, 1914. Chicago, IL: Published by the National Association of Retail Druggists, 1914 [hathitrust.org, hereinafter HTO], October 9, Issue No. 1, "With the Editor," p. 74.

A previous editorial in the same issue declared a new regulation regarding the retailing of cocaine to be not only "impracticable" but a gross intrusion of government bureaucracy into their business:

> The most important consideration, however, and the one that strikes terror to the hearts of the drug interests everywhere, is the fact that **under the provisions of the Food and Drugs Act the Department officials of the Government seemingly have power to issue and make binding such a decision or declaration** .... Are we a Government of Representatives chosen by the people, or are we a Bureaucracy? Has a Bureau or Department of the government the right to ... issue an edict which disposes of the matter, relieving the upper chamber of our Congress of the necessity of further action? There is food for thought in the present status of our anti-narcotic legislation and the exercise of bureaucratic power in connection therewith [bold emphasis original].[63]

The editor called cocaine "the most destructive of all drugs," adding that "the most strenuous regulations should be applied to the traffic therein,"[64] but objected to a rule-making bureaucracy. A third editorial illustrated the "dangers of medical dispensing, as well as the harm likely to arise from the promiscuous use of secret nostrums in cases that may develop into serious illness."[65]

Distrust stemming from the competition between the druggists and physicians continued to increase. In the face of the so-called betrayal by the AMA, the American Pharmaceutical Association [APhA] called a National Drug Trade Conference [NDTC] which met 15 January 1913 to consider "the subject of legislation, both state and national, in its relation to pharmacy."[66] Besides those from the APhA

---

63 Mylert, 1914, "That Federal Cocaine Declaration," pp. 70-71.

64 Mylert, 1914, p. 70

65 Mylert, 1914, "A Dispensing Doctor in Trouble," p. 73.

66 Beal, James H., editor. "Of General Interest, Proceedings Relating to the Organization of the National Drug Trade Conference, First Session," The Journal of

[established 1852], delegates with credentials included representatives from the National Wholesale Druggists Association [NWDA, 1876], NARD [1898], the American Association of Pharmaceutical Chemists [AAPC, 1908], and the National Association of Manufacturers of Medicinal Products [NAMMP, 1912].[67] Like the AMA which wholeheartedly supported the entry of the federal government in this arena, the APhA also adopted a position clearly supporting repressive legislation, although it was critical (as were the druggists, chemists and manufacturers) of the complexity of methods, multiplicity of records, inconsistencies and burdens involved in registering each and every sale in detail.[68]

Though each group protected its own interests, by the third session there was unanimous agreement

> heartily in favor of Federal Legislation of such a nature as to bring under control the importation and the interstate traffic in so-called habit-forming drugs in such a manner as to prevent their illegitimate use, without placing unnecessary burdens upon the manufacturer, jobber, retailer, physician, or veterinarian.[69]

The original project then suffered modifications by the Senate Committee on Finance that considerably softened its language. In particular, the prescription registry requirements became much less stringent, in that "physicians, dentists and veterinary surgeons" could dispense freely to patients even when not physically present during

---

the American Pharmaceutical Association, Volume II. Columbus, OH: Published by the Association, 1913 AO, No. 2, February, p. 234.

[67] Kremers, Edward and George Urdang. History of Pharmacy: *A Guide and a Survey*. Philadelphia, PA: J. B. Lippincott Company, 1940 AO, Part III, Chapter 12 The Gtowth of Associations, pp. 192-193; Beal, 1913, p. 235.

[68] Beal, 1913, p. 236.

[69] Beal, 1913, p. 241.

appointments (at the time it was possible to fill narcotic prescriptions by mail) when "specially employed to prescribe" for the patient:

> [I]t is unfortunate that the Senate Committee found it necessary to open the door so widely to possible abuse. Any physician who is disposed to supply habituees with the drugs will be able to claim, and to prove by his own testimony and the testimony of the alleged patient, that he was specially employed in the case although he may never have seen the person. The original reading that the physician should 'personally attend such patient,' would have required at least one bona fide consultation and examination [quotation marks original].[70]

Remedies with small quantities of opium, morphine and cocaine would continue to be sold in drug stores or through the mail and "the drugs can be sent direct from the manufacturer in one state to a consumer in another."[71] No bond was required, drugs were not taxed by weight, chloral hydrate (with effects similar to barbiturates), cannabis and heroin remained outside the proposed federal statute. The Harrison Subcommittee of the House Ways and Means Committee "assured the full committee that the bill now had approval

---

[70] Beal, James H. "The Senate Amendments to the Harrison Bill," The Journal of the American Pharmaceutical Association, Volume III, No. 4, April. Columbus, OH: Published by the Association, 1914 AO, p. 480; Biel mentioned this was due to the "efforts of a manufacturer of a proprietary asthma cure which is said to contain a small proportion of cocaine, and to be widely used throughout the United States. It is advertised only through the mails, and is not sold in drug stores" (p. 480); for example, Dr. Nathan Tucker's Asthma Specific "was an aerosolised preparation containing 1-3.5% cocaine" (Hamilton, Niall and Lutz Beckert. "Dr Nathan Tucker's Asthma Specific: a treatment for asthma preceding inhaled steroids and beta-agonists," *The New Zealand Medical Journal*, Volume 123, No. 1323, 24 September 2010 [nzma.org, hereinafter NZM], p. 49).

[71] Beal, April 1914, JAPhA, p. 481.

of both the medical and trade interests."[72] In the end the law was approved on 14 December 1914, after a few minutes of deliberation.

Figure 312. "Dean Roscoe Pound." Shaw, Albert, ed. The American Review of Reviews, Vol. 53, Jan – June. NY: The Review of Review Co., 1916 AO, p. 734.

[72] Musto, 1999, p. 60.

Only a week later, on 22 December 1914, at the Third Session of the Sixty-Third Congress it was noted that the legislators had received six million signatures calling for a Dry Law. Oscar Wilder Underwood (Dem. AL, 1862 – 1929), the Speaker of the House of Representatives who had been instrumental in passing the *Harrison Act*, did not hesitate to qualify this condemnation of wine and liquor in the harshest terms. In his opinion he did not care if the petition had been signed by fifty million, and he read into the record an editorial from the Louisville *Courier-Journal* condemning prohibition generally:

> The prohibition movement – a tyrannous scheme to establish virtue and morality by law, to regulate personal appetite and individual habit by the will of the majority ... is quite as mischievous a delusion as any of those that have gone before it. ... If prohibition prohibited, if law reached morals, the argument in favor of drastic legislation would be cogent, indeed. But the actual experience had everywhere shows exactly the contrary. The scheme is the offspring of emotional insanity. It would in nowise accomplish the ends it aims at. It would simply ruin whole classes and regions ... leaving the drink evil untouched ... as it has done everywhere that prohibition has laid its blight.[73]

The Dry Law claimed in principle to illegalize any traffic in alcohol. The *Harrison Act* only tried, in principle, to regulate the registration and taxation of substances that could continue to be manufactured and used, without other limitations than those envisaged by the medical establishment. In other words, the Dry Law attempted to prohibit something at the federal level, and for this reason required amending a Constitution that had sought in part at least to enshrine

[73] Underwood, O. W. Congressional Record: Containing the Proceedings and Debates of the Sixty-Third Congress, Third Session, Volume LII, Part I. Washington, DC: Government Printing Office, 1915 AO, Congressional Record - House, 22 December 1914, p. 520, column 1.

into law the right of every white male citizen of property to certain freedoms based upon the principles in the Declaration of Independence including the pursuit of personal happiness. On the surface the *Harrison Act* only claimed to regulate something, like the *Pure Food and Drug Act* for example. If Underwood had understood its true purpose, perhaps he would have included it also in the list of machinations confusing morality and law.

Who perceived foresightedly the difficulties in enforcement that both laws would engender was Nathan Roscoe Pound (1870 – 1964) then Dean of Harvard Law School, one of the fathers of American sociology:

> For when men demand little of law, and enforcement of law is but enforcement of the ethical minimum necessary for the orderly conduct of society, enforcement of law involves few difficulties. All but the inevitable anti-social residuum can understand the simple program and obvious purposes of such a legal system, and enforcement requires nothing more than a strong and reasonably stable political organization. On the other hand, when men demand much of law, when they seek to devolve upon it the whole burden of social control, when they seek to make it do the work of the home and of the church, enforcement of law comes to involve many difficulties.[74]

---

[74] Pound, Nathan Roscoe. "The Limits of Effective Legal Action," The American Bar Association Journal, Volume III. Baltimore, MD: Published by the American Bar Association, 1917 AO, No. 1, January, pp. 55-56.

2. The Legal Nature of the Precept

The originality of the *Harrison Act* was to present itself as merely regulating the administrative registration of manufacturers and dispensers of opium, morphine and cocaine with penalties for non-compliance with such requirements. None of its clauses prohibited the possession, consumption or sale of those products. To do otherwise would of course have required an amendment to the Constitution, and in 1914 it was extremely doubtful, not to say impossible, to get the therapeutic estate or the bar associations to lend their support; more impossible still would have been to get six million signatures on a petition, much less the overwhelming majorities in both chambers needed to modify the right to useful medicine. In 1914 there was not a single competent physician or pharmacist anywhere in the world who considered opium or its derivatives useless. Daring to ban them like alcohol, a drug widely used recreationally, would have produced howls of protest.

Indeed, in the beginning there were vehement denials of its true nature. In reply to a letter alleging that the bill "would aim at police regulation without showing any connection with the taxing or inter-state commerce power of the Federal Government,"[75] the editor of the *Journal of the American Pharmaceutical Association* (and one of the chief negotiators at the National Drug Trade Conference) wrote:

[75] Freericks, Frank H. "More About the Harrison Bill," The Journal of the American Pharmaceutical Association, Volume III. Columbus, OH: Published by the Association, 1914 AO, No. 1, January, p. 1.

The Harrison Bill does not propose to interfere in the police regulations of a state any further than is necessary to insure the collection of the tax levied. ... The Harrison Bill does not go even so far as this. It requires the tax from every dealer alike, whether sold for the purpose of a medicine or for ministering to a previous habit.[76]

This criterion was shared by any jurist with minimal notions of American constitutional law, and even by the federal Public Health Service:

[T]o a woman who had taken morphine for many years and now complained that her supply would be cut off because of the Harrison Act, the Surgeon General replied in March 1915 that the Act was intended to gather information, and she could continue to receive morphine from her physician.[77]

The law's legitimacy was theoretically based on the United States remaining faithful to the international treaties signed by its representatives. But the US federal Constitution (as with the immense majority in existence) foresaw that no convention with another country could derogate fundamental civil rights. The greatest irony is that the Treaty of Versailles (within which in fine print had been added adherence to the Hague Convention) was never ratified by the American Congress. Moreover, these international conventions did not establish a prohibitionist law, as we will see.

However, the *Harrison Act* in actuality constituted a substantive criminal statute which was intended (albeit indirectly) to outlaw certain painkillers and one of the major known stimulants. But because of the

---

[76] Beal, J. H. "The Editor's Reply to Mr. Freericks," The Journal of the American Pharmaceutical Association, Volume III. Columbus, OH: Published by the Association, 1914 AO, No. 1, January, pp. 5, 7.

[77] Musto, 1999, p. 64; see also note 33, p. 275.

way it had been written as a tax measure, in the early years of its enforcement it encountered serious difficulties in the judicial sphere each time its regulatory provisions were manifested in their true nature as substantive criminal precepts. The *Harrison Act* was instead an anomalous precept, in reality a law without a legislator.

On the one hand it was supported by the necessity of saving face before other countries at the Hague Conference. On the other by it could be argued that Congress had authorized something different from what had actually been authorized by the treaty. At no time had any assembly of legislators ever considered (within the requisite requirements for legislating on similar matters) to erase from the pharmacopoeia such products, or even to restrict their availability to the medical profession.

Curiously, both the *Harrison Act* and the *Volstead Act* (referring to the prohibition of alcohol) ultimately were only possible because of the newly instituted federal income tax. Recommended by President Taft in 1900, passed by Congress in 1909 and ratified in 1913, the Sixteenth Amendment established direct federal taxation, requiring the Treasury Department (an administrative authority) to ensure its collection through its Bureau of Internal Revenue. Only then did the basic conditions begin to exist for the ratification six years later of the Eighteenth Amendment [the *Volstead Act* or Dry Law].

The *Harrison Act* sidestepped these highly complex formalities, but it was also enforced by the Treasury, as in the case of the *Volstead Act*. Hence, both agents of the Bureau of Prohibition and of the Narcotic Division were Treasury officials within the Bureau of Internal Revenue. In 1930, enforcement "was transferred to the Department of Justice while a standalone federal agency, the Federal Bureau of Narcotics (FBN), was established within the Treasury to handle narcotic enforcement."[78] In 1973, the DEA was created to replace the FBN.

Figure 313. "Dr. Lawrence Kolb." Photograph by Kay Harris, Medical Press, Inc., 1957 [profiles.nlm.nih.gov, hereinafter PN].

[78] Sacco, Lisa N. "Drug Enforcement in the United States: History, Policy, and Trends," Congressional Research Service Report, October 2, 2014 [crs.org, hereinafter CRS], p. 3.

a. The Medical and the Nonmedical

In essence, the *Harrison Act* was based on Brent's principle that any nonmedical use of a drug is immoral. But this immediately raised the problem of what was understood by the terms medical and nonmedical. To begin with, the vast majority of American addictions were iatrogenic or of medical origin, meaning they had been acquired using drugs prescribed by a physician. Secondly, no one dared to discuss the fact that physicians and their therapeutic staff were the most prone by far to acquiring a habit. Adding one thing to the other, it seemed obvious that cases of addiction were medical problems.

At the same time, until the law came into force, it was generally accepted that a certain proportion of the population could not exist without some sort of lenitive, just as a certain proportion was born color blind, mongoloid or otherwise handicapped. Whether by the influence of unfavorable social conditions or due to congenital defects, a patient's ailments could be mitigated by a physician using the pharmacopoeia to reduce a basic quantum of anxiety or apathy, it being preferable of course to have a drug-dependent patient rather than a desperate or useless subject. This orientation had been accepted practice in Western medicine since the 17th century and in pagan medicine for millennia. In serious cases, both somatic and psychic, the physician might prefer the establishment of a habit as the lesser of two evils, and it was up to his professional ethics to inform the patient of the foreseeable consequences. It was a totally different thing to deceive him in one way or another, promising him impossible cures, giving him up to an unanticipated dependence, or taking advantage of him by similar means, but such cases were a matter for the civil or criminal courts as negligence, fraud and poisoning.[79]

Now, however, this picture of motives and circumstances was substantially altered. Although not explicitly stated, the use of certain drugs would no longer depend on the physician nor the user, but on third parties linked to the police and delinquency. In order to prepare the ground for such a transformation, it was necessary to establish something so novel from the pharmacological point of view as that opium and morphine *per se* promoted criminal appetites, genetic defects and dementia, while other drugs such as barbiturates, ether, chloral hydrate or bromides were innocuous medicines. Onto medical use was superimposed a morality that ultimately ended in nonuse. Behind the appearance of a technical or statutory question were an alternative of political ethics and a redefinition of the State's functions in relation to the citizen.

This was seen clearly within the first decade of enforcement of the new law. Dr. Lawrence Kolb (1881 – 1972), a career medical officer, psychiatrist and administrator of the United States Public Health Service (1909 – 1945), appeared in a 1924 congressional hearing. When he was asked about the nexus between narcotics and crime, he replied that the main narcotics were ether, chloroform and dentist's nitrous oxide, and that while they had caused some disorderly conduct in Europe, in the United States he was not aware of any abuse. When asked about the connection between the use of opium and crime, he replied:

---

[79] Thus, for example, Section 22 of the English Offences Against the Person Act of 1861 (24 & 25 Vict., Chapter 100) punished with "Penal Servitude for Life" those who used "Chloroform, Laudanum or other stupefying or overpowering Drug, Matter, or Thing" to facilitate "any indictable Offence" (Offences Against the Person Act 1861 [legislation.gov.uk, hereinafter LGU], pp. 5-6).

I was quoted by Captain Hobson as saying that 1 gallon of alcohol would produce more crime than a ton of opium. That was not my statement. I said a single gallon of alcohol has more potentialities for violent forms of crime than a ton of opium. I repeat that, and my psychiatric studies prove it. ... No form of opium impels a man to commit violent crime. It does exactly the opposite.[80]

In fact, Kolb had just finished a thorough investigation of the lives of a hundred or so addicts, without finding anything to justify Brent and Wright's claims. But the *Harrison Act* was beginning to create a black market and, by the same token, crime. Dr. Kolb had seen the process unfold as previously legal users now were imprisoned for the same conduct that had now been made illegal:

In 1923 there were more than 4,000 convictions for violations of the narcotics laws resulting in over 4,000 years of penitentiary sentences. These people did not go to jail because they committed rape or robbery or some other crime. They went because they had some narcotic in their pockets or sold some in violation of law, and such cases account largely for the increased population of the jails and penitentiaries. That explains the cause of the large increase in crime – a new crime has been created by law. ... The explanation is that we put them in jail now, and we did not do it before.[81]

The so-called Father of American Prohibition, the former Democratic representative from Alabama Richmond Pearson Hobson (1870 – 1937) also testified at the same hearing and was outraged enough by Kolb's remarks that he referenced them in his own preemptive testimony, stating that in his opinion "it is against public

---

[80] Moses, George H., Chairman. Hearing Before the Committee on Printing United States Senate, Sixty-Eighth Congress, First Session on S. Con. Res. 10. Washington, DC: Government Printing Office, 1924 AO, 3 June, "Statement of Dr. Lawrence Kolb, Surgeon, United States Public Health Service," p. 27.

[81] Moses, 1924, "Statement of Dr. Lawrence Kolb," p. 26.

Figure 314. "Richmond Pearson Hobson." Photograph, negative, glass. Bain News Service, 1916. Library of Congress, Prints and Photographs Division, Washington, DC LG.

policy to minimize this terror."[82] Hobson never shied away from the florid. In a Senate hearing four years later he compared heroin addicts to lepers:

> Suppose it were announced that there were more than a million lepers among our people. Think what a shock the announcement would produce. Yet drug addiction is far more incurable than leprosy, far more tragic to its victims, and is spreading like a moral and physical scourge.[83]

A decade or so earlier, the most respected manuals, encyclopedias and textbooks considered opium and morphine to be the best remedy in all of the scientific pharmacopoeia, while now methods for suppressing the habit overnight were all the rage.

By far the most famous of these methods (which made its inventor a millionaire) was a concoction based on *Atropa belladonna* (deadly nightshade), *Hyoscyamus niger* (henbane) and *Zanthoxylum americanum* (prickly ash).[84] Congressman and later Senator Charles B. Towns, the originator of the potion, had no medical degree and clearly represented the so-called quack sector; one detractor later called it

---

82 Moses, 1924, "Statement of Hon. Richmond Pearson Hobson ...," p. 4.

83 Unknown compiler. Congressional Record Proceedings and Debates of the First Session of the Seventieth Congress, Volume LXIX – Part 2, January 9 to January 31, 1928. Washington, DC: Government Printing Office, 1928 [govinfo.gov, hereinafter GIG], Wednesday 18 January, Richmond P. Hobson on The Peril of Narcotic Drugs, Sociology, p. 1647, column 2.

84 "The treatment ... was given to me by Mr. Charles B. Towns .... Briefly stated, it consists in the hourly dosage of a mixture of belladonna, hyosyamus and xanthoxylum. This mixture is given every hour, day and night, for about fifty hours" (Lambert, Alexander. "Care and Control of the Alcoholic," *The Boston Medical and Surgical Journal*, Volume CLXVI, January – June. Boston, MA: W. M. Leonard, 1912 AO, 25 April, p. 618); see GHDV4P1, Chapter 22, The Debate Over the Foster Bills, p. 1256.

"diarrhea, delirium and damnation."[85] Towns charged from two to three hundred and fifty dollars for administering his extravagant remedy for five days,[86] and prided himself on "never having had a negative result," a proven fact (in his opinion) because "less than 10 percent returned to us for a second treatment."[87] But a former presidential physician treated 131 patients at Bellevue Hospital using the novel cure. Eighteen months later, of "the 85 in whom we could judge accurately of the results, 67 had reverted and 18 had remained abstinent. That is, 78.8% had reverted and 21.2% had remained abstinent."[88] In spite of that the Commissioner of Narcotic Control "declared that institutional treatment should be preferred" to a gradual withdrawal or maintenance dose.[89]

b. Possession and Dispensation

When the *Harrison Act* was passed, the main legal question was whether violations of the law could be anything other than failure to register in a special registry[90] or negligence in the keeping of statutory books. If it was an administrative rule, this was the reasonable thing to

---

85 Musto, 1999, p. 82.

86 Pittman, Bill. AA The Way it Began. Seattle, WA: Glen Abbey Books, 1988 AO, Chapter Five The "Prohibition Cure," p. 86.

87 Pittman, 1988, p. 86.

88 Lambert, 1912, pp. 618-619.

89 Musto, 1999, p. 119.

90 By June 30, 1915 roughly 124,000 physicians, 36,000 dentists, 10,000 veterinarians, 47,000 retail dealers and 1,100 wholesale dealers were "registered during the first three months, for the fiscal year ending June 30, 1916" (Osborn, W. H., Commissioner of Internal Revenue. Annual Report of the Commissioner of Internal Revenue for the Fiscal Year Ended June 30 1915. Washington, DC: Government Printing Office, 1915 AO, p. 147).

do; but if it was not merely an administrative rule but a substantive criminal precept, its relationship to the Constitution was highly problematic. For four years the subject matter remained in suspense, although leaning towards a restrictive interpretation. However, the spirit of the statute militated in favor of prohibitionism pure and simple.

The changeover was not abrupt, however. In the beginning, addiction was seen as a disease and early emphasis was put upon helping the "unfortunate ... regain his self-respect and take his place in the community as a self-respecting, self-supporting citizen."[91] For example, New York State set up its own Department of Narcotic Drug Control [DNDC] which began operations in February of 1919.[92] When the DNDC was first created, its new director proposed the establishment of narcotics clinics

> in every city and community in the State where the unfortunates suffering from the disease of drug addiction can receive treatment. ... [T]hey are of necessity driven to peddlers or to physicians and druggists who take unfair advantage of these unfortunates. ... [U]ntil provision is made by the establishment of Narcotic Clinics where the patients can be treated, the Department does not feel justified in revoking the authority of the physician and druggist to treat and dispense narcotic drugs to those addicted. ... In addition to the Narcotic Clinics there is urgent need of hospital accommodations where addicted patients can be committed and receive scientific treatment.[93]

---

[91] Richardson, Frank, Commissioner. First Annual Report of the Narcotic Drug Control Commission. Albany, NY: J. B. Lyon Company, 1919 AO, p. 4.

[92] Herrick, Walter R., Commissioner. Second Annual Report of the Narcotic Drug Control Commission. Albany, NY: J. B. Lyon Company, 1920 AO [filed under First Annual Report], p. 3.

[93] Richardson, 1919, pp. 4-5.

Treatment however often meant a relatively rapid withdrawal.[94]

Was possession of a substance listed by the *Harrison Act* a crime? Section 8 read, in part:

> That it shall be unlawful for any person not registered under the provisions of this Act, and who has not paid the special tax provided for by this Act, to have in his possession or under his control any of the aforesaid drugs; and such possession or control shall be presumptive evidence of a violation of this section, and also of a violation of the provisions of section one of this Act.[95]

Thus, possession became presumptive evidence of violating the statute. Exempt were physicians, dentists, veterinarians, their employees, those with prescriptions, law enforcement, wholesalers and transporters. The last sentences of Section 8 removed the burden of proof from a prosecutor and placed it squarely on the shoulders of the defendant:

> *Provided further*, That it shall not be necessary to negative any of the aforesaid exemptions in any complaint, information, indictment, or other writ or proceeding laid or brought under this Act; and the burden of proof of any such exemption shall be upon the defendant [italics original]. [96]

---

[94] For example, an unscientific survey of ten "American and European physicians in China" as to the treatment time needed for an opium addict to taper off ran from "no treatment at all" to "four weeks" though two reported the deaths of older, confirmed smokers who suddenly stopped (Crafts, Wilbur F. Opium Cures, Third Abridged Edition. Washington, DC: International Reform Bureau, 1908 AO, pp. 7, 10, 11, 16).

[95] Secretary of State, Director. The Statutes at Large of the United States of America from March, 1913, to March, 1915, Volume XXXVIII. Washington, DC: Government Printing Office, 1915 AO, Public Acts of the Sixty-Third Congress, Session III, Chapter 1, Section 8, p. 789.

[96] Secretary of State, 1915, p. 789.

Essentially it was up to the defendant to demonstrate that he or she possessed a listed drug under one of the exemptions. This type of proof was normally not admissible in law; in medieval law it was termed *probatio diabolica* [a legal requirement to achieve an impossible proof], because proving a negative involves extraordinary difficulties and perverts the rational course of the judicial process to the point where the burden of proof is now on the accused, not the accuser. No longer was a defendant innocent until proven guilty.

Moreover, some tended toward a more pharisaical class-dependent distinction. If the defendant had obtained the listed substance after a quick, cheap consultation with a physician who served the poor, such possession only indulged the hidden urges of dope fiends. On the other hand, if the physician dispensed a small amount at a time to a small number of addicts, with a small fee appropriate to a distinguished clientele, his conduct could be accepted as treatment. In other words, conceptions of medical ethics were being derived from a tax and registration rule, creating a situation of legal uncertainty for ordinary citizens. Some judges pushed back.

3. Judicial Reservations

Almost as soon as the *Harrison Act* went into effect, judges around the country objected, refusing to read more into the law than what had been written. A federal district judge in Tennessee quashed the indictment against a physician for "giving a prescription for said drugs *in quantities more than was necessary, and not in good faith and as a medicine* [italics original]."[97] Although this interpretation was exactly

[97] *United States v. Friedman*, 224 Federal Reporter 276, 278 (1915) [digital.library.unt.edu, hereinafter UNT].

what was intended by its prohibitionist backers, the *Harrison Act* contained no actual language making such actions illegal.

A case before a federal district judge in Montana was similarly dismissed against six defendants for possession of smoking opium because a) "there is nothing in the act imposing the duty of registration and payment of taxes upon mere consumers of the drugs," and b) "the indictments do not show that defendants are of any of the classes by the act required to register and pay the tax."[98] Though decided narrowly, the same judge included *dicta* excoriating the poorly drafted legislation because its draconian punishment certainly did not fit the supposed crime:

> Any person convicted of its most trivial violation – the most law-abiding druggist or physician or like person in legitimate possession of the drugs, who inadvertently allows the annual tax to become delinquent for a day – though fined but $1, is made a felon and infamous! And this for a mere legal infraction, and not a true crime, is a consequence shockingly disproportionate to the offense, is antagonistic to sound criminal economics, and is abhorent to justice [exclamation point original].[99]

A federal district judge in Pennsylvania also quashed an indictment against a physician for conspiring with a patient by issuing a prescription for "one dram[100] of morphine sulphate" not in "good faith" and "not given for medicinal purposes, but for the purpose of supplying one addicted to opium and the compounds, salts, and derivatives and preparations thereof."[101] But the district court found that the patient was not required to register and pay the tax because he

---

[98] *United States v. Woods (and five like cases)*, 224 Federal Reporter 278, 280 (1915), UNT.

[99] *US v. Woods*, 224 Fed. Rep. 278, 279 (1915).

[100] 1.771845 grains or 0.0625 ounces.

[101] *United States v. Jin Fuey Moy*, 225 Federal Reporter 1003, 1005 (1915), UNT.

did not "import, produce, manufacture, deal in, dispense, sell, or distribute"[102] said morphine sulphate. The judges reasoned:

> And there is no allegation in the indictment that [the patient] had in his possession these drugs for any of these purposes. The indictment, therefore, could not be sustained, unless the mere fact of having the drug in his possession is a violation of the law. If so, any person would be presumptively guilty ... if he had any small amount of the prescribed drug in his possession, without any reference to the purpose for which it was to be used, whether legitimate or otherwise.[103]

In the midst of a serious uproar and pressure from all sides, the latter case of *Jin Fuey Moy* was elevated to the United States Supreme Court, which by a seven-to-two majority upheld the previous rulings. The highest judicial authority in the country rejected outright the government's arguments soliciting police powers to enforce the *Harrison Act*. In fact, by adding penalties in Section Nine of "a fine of not more than $2,000 or imprisonment for not more than five years, or both," wrote Mr. Justice Holmes who delivered the opinion of the high court,

> Congress meant to strain its powers almost if not quite to the breaking point in order to make the probably very large proportion of citizens who have some preparation of opium in their possession criminal or at least *prima facie* criminal and subject to the serious punishment made possible by § 9 [section mark and italics original].[104]

However, the case was decided more narrowly, observing that Section 1 did not apply to any person but, taken in the context of the law itself, only any person required to register:

---

102 *US v. Moy*, 225 Fed. Rep. 1003, 1005 (1915).

103 *US v. Moy*, 225 Fed. Rep. 1003, 1005 (1915).

104 *United States v. Jin Fuey Moy*, 241 U.S. 394, 401-402 (1916) LG, Opinion of the Court.

Approaching the issue from this point of view we conclude that 'any person not registered' in § 8 cannot be taken to mean any person in the United States but must be taken to refer to the class with which the statute undertakes to deal – the persons who are required to register by § 1 [section and quotation marks original].[105]

Two curiosities were noted but not ruled upon by the court. One, though the government argued the law was in fulfillment of a treaty (and treaties under Article Six of the US Constitution were the supreme law of the land), Holmes noted:

But the question arises under a statute not under a treaty. The statute does not purport to be in execution of a treaty but calls itself a registration and taxing act. The provision before us was not required by the Opium Convention, and whether this section is entitled to the supremacy claimed by the Government for treaties is, to say the least, another grave question ....[106]

The second oddity was that the physician was not charged with writing a prescription outside of the good faith exemption but only with conspiring to place the drugs in possession of the patient:

It is true that the exemption of possession of drugs prescribed in good faith by a physician is a powerful argument taken by itself for a broader meaning. But every question of construction is unique, and an argument that would prevail in one case may be inadequate in another.[107]

The good faith prescription was not tested in *Moy*.

It's important to remember that all of these were exclusively judicial rulings. Judges were not intrinsically opposed to interpreting a law prohibiting the consumption of opium, morphine and cocaine; but

---

[105] *US v. Jin Fuey Moy*, 241 U.S. 394, 402 (1916).

[106] *US v. Jin Fuey Moy*, 241 U.S. 394, 401 (1916).

[107] *US v. Jin Fuey Moy*, 241 U.S. 394, 402 (1916).

they demanded that the particular law be applied in accord with its nature, a revenue act that only demanded registration and a small tax, not a police measure assuming the right to explain to physicians and druggists their duties. As we will see, what one Supreme Court may give, another may taketh away.

Figure 315. "Oliver Wendell Holmes, Jr." Harris & Ewing, 1930. Library of Congress, Prints and Photographs Division, Washington, DC LG.

In this initial era the prevailing mood in the medical establishment was one of satisfaction that the poorly constructed statute would have to be changed. In the opinion of an editor of the *New York Medical Journal*, the law was so full of holes it needed to be recast:

> In June, Justice Holmes of the United States Supreme Court handed down a decision in the Jin Fuey Moy case which interpreted the Harrison Narcotic Act as a revenue measure, controlling dealers and physicians, but in no way holding the mere possessor or user of narcotics liable to the law. This resulted in making it impossible for United States attorneys to continue prosecutions, as formerly under the act, against mere possessors of the drug .... It has all along been evident that the law has been so soldered over by departmental rulings as to make a clear view of the statute impossible. The courts are slowly melting this away, until the act now seems so leaky that it will hold nothing unless Congress soon does some recasting.[108]

But this reworking of the law could only occur either through a recognition of the right of prosecutors and police to distinguish the medical from the nonmedical (the opposite of the *status quo* in the rest of the world), or else through a constitutional amendment banning the substances altogether. If, so far, the first was repulsive to the judiciary (though long sought by prohibitionists), the second appeared to be unfeasible.

The Treasury Department quickly declared that it was the lack of collaboration from the magistrates (not the inconsistencies in the law) that threatened to sink this most humanitarian of initiatives. The Commissioner of Internal Revenue's opinion of the *Jin Fuey Moy*

---

[108] Sajous, Charles E. de M., et al, editors. New York Medical Journal, Volume CIV, July to December, Inclusive New York: A. R. Elliott Publishing Co., 1916 AO, No. 19, Whole Number 1979, Saturday, November 4, Contemporary Comment, "Holes in the Harrison Law," pp. 905-906.

decision might well have been written by Craft's International Reform Bureau:

> This decision makes it practically impossible to control the illicit traffic in narcotic drugs by unregistered persons, as the mere possession of any quantity of the drugs is not evidence of violation, and therefore the Government is forced to prove in every case, even where the circumstances indicate sale and dispensing, actual sales by this class of offenders, which it had been found difficult to do.[109]

In other words, both prohibition agents and prosecutors considered adherence to the general principles of law (with their substantive and procedural safeguards in force for defendants indicted for any other crime), as abusive when applied to narcotics. The possession of a machine gun, a stick of dynamite, a strain of smallpox, a flask of arsenic or the plans to the underground utilities of a bank would not be considered automatic proof of a crime, but possession of two grains of morphine should be. This example was expressed by the consulting physician to the New York Prison Commission Dr. Ernest S. Bishop (1876 – 1926), of whom we will speak more of in the next chapter.

For three years, while the *Volstead Act* is clearing away all the obstacles in its path, the *Harrison Act* is only applied as an administrative precept, and its sanctions fall only on unlicensed importers or dispensaries which are negligent in keeping their books or recording prescriptions. Physicians could not be cited for making lawful prescriptions for addicts and addicts did not need to register.

Behind the scenes, however, a nucleus of militant prohibitionists in the Congress disputed the admissible options with

---

[109] Osborn, W. H., Commissioner of Internal Revenue. Annual Report of the Commissioner of Internal Revenue for the Fiscal Year Ended June 30 1916. Washington, DC: Government Printing Office, 1916 AO, Narcotic Law, p. 24.

federal magistrates. The judiciary would not compromise on a lax interpretation of the law. Nor was it clear that a prohibition on widely used medicines would have the unconditional support of the therapeutic establishment.

Then, in 1919 a new president of the AMA took office, accusing members of his own profession of aiding and abetting the illicit drug trade: "A few crooked doctors, at present, can undo all the honest endeavors of the rest of the profession in stopping this evil business."[110] He also offered the following resolution to be adopted by the House of Delegates of the AMA calling on closer cooperation between the government and the therapeutic estate:

> *Resolved*, That the American Medical Association respectfully requests the Internal Revenue Department of the federal government to call together a conference composed of representatives of the medical profession, the wholesale and retail drug interests, and representatives of each state [italics original].[111]

Of the nearly three columns devoted to his inaugural address, almost two and half were devoted to narcotic addiction.

That same year the Supreme Court issued two rulings on Section 2 of the *Harrison Act*. The first decision of *United States v. Doremus* concerned a doctor who had prescribed

---

[110] Lambert, Alexander. "Address of the President Elect, Dr. Alexander Lambert," The Journal of the American Medical Association, Volume 72. Chicago, IL: American Medical Association, 1919 AO, Number 24, June 14, Atlantic City Session, p. 1767, column 2; see also GHDV3P2, Chapter 22, 2. The Compromise of Autonomy, p. 1213.

[111] Lambert, 1919, p. 1768, column 1.

> five hundred one-sixth grain tablets of heroin ... the sale not being in pursuance of a written order on a form issued on the blank furnished for that purpose by the Commissioner of Internal Revenue ... [and] not for the treatment of any disease ... [but] for the purpose of gratifying his appetite for the drug as an habitual user thereof.[112]

The district court had held that Section 2 of the act was beyond "the constitutional power of Congress to enact because ... the statute was a mere attempt by Congress to exert a power not delegated, that is, the reserved police power of the States."[113] The Supreme Court, however, reversed because an act "may not be declared unconstitutional because its effect may be to accomplish another purpose as well as the raising of revenue."[114] Section 2 was held to be constitutional because at least some of its provisions were related to raising revenue, something well within the purview of Congress.

The second case of *Webb et al. v. United States* was more significant. Section 2 (b) of the *Harrison Act* exempted "the sale, dispensing, or distribution of any of the aforesaid drugs by a dealer to a consumer under and in pursuance of a written prescription issued by a physician, dentist, or veterinary surgeon registered under this Act."[115] The notion of a prescription was only qualified as needing to be signed and dated and kept for two years for inspection.

The question now being asked was, what exactly constituted a prescription? For example, was prescribing a maintenance dose to an addict allowed?

---

112 *United States v. Doremus*, 249 United States Reports 86, 90 (1919) LG.

113 *US v. Doremus*, 249 US Rep. 86, 95 (1919), Dissent by Chief Justice and three others concurring.

114 *US v. Doremus*, 249 US Rep. 86, 94 (1919).

115 Secretary of State, Statutes at Large, Vol. XXXVIII, 1915, Session III, Chapter 1, Section 2 (b).

> If a practicing and registered physician issues an order for morphine to an habitual user thereof, the order not being issued by him in the course of professional treatment in the attempted cure of the habit, but being issued for the purpose of providing the user with morphine sufficient to keep him comfortable by maintaining his customary use, is such an order a physician's prescription under exemption (b) of § 2 [parentheses, section and question mark original]?[116]

This was exactly the issue so avoided by the prosecutors in their indictment in *Jin Fuey Moy*, and thus not ruled upon by Justice Holmes.

Bad facts make bad law. The facts of *Webb* may have helped sway five members of the court. The druggist fulfilling the prescriptions written by the physician had purchased "thirty times as much morphine as was bought by the average retail druggist doing a larger general business," that the physician had written in less than a year "over 4,000 such prescriptions" for fifty cents apiece, and that the druggist had filled some ten of the physician's prescriptions for an out of state client "although each was made out in a separate and fictitious name."[117]

The high court declared the doctor's prescription a semantic perversion unworthy of a physician, writing that "to call such an order for the use of morphine a physician's prescription would be so plain a perversion of meaning that no discussion of the subject is required."[118] As in *Doremus*, the court split five to four on the issue.

In 1919 it could be said that the crusade on narcotics was given the green light in the United States. The first trimester of that year saw not only Lambert's speech and the two devastating Supreme Court rulings, but also an article about the retiring New York Commissioner of Health declaring that addicts were everywhere, that all violent crime

---

[116] *Webb et al. v. United States*, 249 United States Reports 96, 99 (1919) LG.

[117] *Webb v. US*, 249 US Rep. 96, 98-99 (1919).

[118] *Webb v. US*, 249 US Rep. 96, 99 (1919).

was committed by addicts, and that doctors writing too many cheap prescriptions should be boiled in oil:

'You will find them,' he said, 'among lawyers, judges, doctors. In fact, in every layer of society. In the underworld of New York you will find 10,000 drug addicts, and every crime of violence committed you may know has been perpetrated by one of them. It is safe to say that in all New York one person in thirty is a victim.' ... 'And worse han [sic] all is the fact that there are physicians, members of my own profession, writing from 100 to 200 prescriptions a day for 25 cents a prescription. They should be boiled in oil, and if there is a hell they should go there and sizzle for all eternity [quotation marks original].'[119]

Clearly the political climate had changed.

To complete the picture, at a 1924 hearing before the Committee on Printing of the US Senate the number of addicts in the country was absurdly exaggerated. Captain Hobson's International Narcotics Education Association requested the government foot the bill for printing some fifty million copies of a pamphlet entitled "The Perils of Narcotics – a warning to the people of America."[120] The article estimated the number of addicts in the entire country at 1,750,000 while a survey made by the Federal Narcotics Control Board put the number "well within the half-million mark,"[121] deprecating the sources relied on in the pamphlet:

---

119 Unknown writer. "Copeland to Resign Soon, He Intimates," *The New York Times*, Volume LXVIII, No. 22,346, Monday 31 Mar 1919 AO [indexed as Mar 16-31, 1919], p. 8. column 3.

120 Moses, 1924, p. 1; see also this chapter, section a. The Medical and the Nonmedical.

121 Moses, 1924, p. 2.

> With regard to the organization known as the International Narcotic Education Association, you are informed that this office has no information other than that gained through newspaper articles which have been published, purporting to be from that organization, and the article now presented to you for publication.[122]

Dr. Lawrence Kolb of the Public Health Service testified at the same hearing that the real number was much smaller: "Now, as to the number of drug addicts, those of us who have studied it carefully, have concluded that the maximum limit for the United States is 150,000, and that the probable number is about 110,000."[123]

On the other hand, the American people would have accepted with the same horror any number. The triumph of the Soviet revolution, the military victory of their country in Europe, the internal trade union conflicts and the imminent Dry Law exacerbated both the messianic and nationalistic elements always present in the nation. Attacks against leaders and institutions attributed to Bolsheviks, anarchist plots, large scale strikes and the Red Raids unleashed that year are concomitant political phenomena of a post-war purification ritual, from which neither could some users of a few common medicines escape being included, a complex *cliché* of Germanophobia, barbarism and crime.

C. The *Volstead Act*

As stated above, the American Congress had received petitions by 1917 with six million signatures demanding a wartime prohibition on alcohol:

---

[122] Moses, 1924, p. 3.

[123] Moses, 1924, p. 22.

Figure 316. "Andrew John Volstead." Harris & Ewing, ca. 1915. Library of Congress, Prints and Photographs Division, Washington, DC LG.

It was estimated that six million separate petitioners asked Congress to enact a war prohibition law. This was without a parallel in the history of the country. The heads of great business corporations and manufacturing plants, leading economists and publicists, presidents and student bodies of colleges and universities, great mass meetings of citizens and conferences and assemblies of all kinds joined in strong and earnest petitions for total war-time prohibition.[124]

This helped set in motion a bill known as the *Volstead Act*, named after Andrew John Volstead (Rep. MN, 1860 – 1947) but substantially drafted[125] by the general counsel of the Anti-Saloon League Wayne Bidwell Wheeler (1869 – 1927). Its purpose was to give enabling legislation to the Constitutional amendment which Congress voted on and submitted to the states where it was quickly ratified:

It passed the Senate on August 1, 1917, by a vote of 65 to 20 and passed the House on December 17 by a vote of 282 to 128. Having been amended in the House, it repassed the Senate on December 18, 1917. Including both houses, the percentage of each major party voting for submission was the same, 70 per cent of the Republicans and 70 per cent of the Democrats, the Prohibition party voting 100 per cent for it. Submitted to the states on December 22, 1917, it was ratified on January 16, 1919, and went into effect one year later.[126]

---

124 Colvin, D. Leigh. Prohibition in the United States: A History of the Prohibition Party and of the Prohibition Movement. NY: George H. Doran Company 1926 AO, Chapter XXIII The Progress of State and National Prohibition, 1914-1919, p. 443.

125 "Mr. Wheeler made the draft of the National Prohibition Law, defended it in the courts and before the Judiciary Committee in Congress," (Editor's comment. Wheeler, Wayne B. "The Meaning of the Supreme Court Decision on National Prohibition," *The Christian Advocate*, Volume XCV, No. 22, 1 July 1920 HTO, p. 886); see also Okrent, Daniel. "The Man Who Turned Off the Taps," *Smithsonian Magazine*, May 2010 [smithsonianmag.com, hereinafter SM].

126 Colvin, 1926, p. 448.

While the National Prohibition Party (established in 1869 "for the legal prohibition of the liquor traffic")[127] was electorally insignificant, it (and especially the Anti-Saloon League) pragmatically built coalitions with countless groups and sects on the local and state level to achieve their goal. Party leaders "generally did not envision replacing one of the major parties. Their chief aim became one of pressure politics. They joined in coalitions with other organizations ...,"[128] a strategy that was clearly successful:

> The total vote in the Senates of the forty-six states was 1,309 to 240 – 84 per cent for prohibition. The total House vote was 3,775 to 1,025 – 79 percent for prohibition. Combining both houses of forty-six states the total vote on ratification was 5,084 to 1,265. More than 80 per cent of the representatives of the people, more than four to one, voted for the adoption of the Eighteenth Amendment.[129]

To an even larger degree than with opium, morphine and cocaine, those who would ban alcoholic beverages embraced social and political *clichés*. Mr. Hobson of Alabama, who had previously campaigned for government largess to print misinformation regarding opiates, also campaigned against alcohol with the same racist fervor when he introduced his own prohibitionist amendment in 1914. His observations regarding liquor causing the degeneration of the Indian, the brutalization of the Negro and the devolution of the White Man were noted earlier.[130]

---

127 Colvin, 1926, Chapter IV The First National Prohibition Convention, p. 73.

128 Storms, 1972, Foreword, unpaged.

129 Colvin, 1926, p. 449.

130 Unknown compiler. Congressional Record: Proceedings and Debates of the Sixty-Third Congress, Third Session, Volume 52, Part I – Bound Edition. Washington, DC: Government Printing Office, 1915 LG, Speech of Mr. Hobson, December 22, 1914, p. 605, column 2, p. 606, column 1; see GHDV3P2, Chapter 18,

His commitment to the prohibitionist cause, the "greatest question of history," was also very nearly apocalyptic:

This question, Mr. Speaker, antedates human slavery. This question has baffled every civilization that has passed through the panorama of history. It is the greatest question in the life history of the human species, actually determining more than all other questions combined the perpetuity of any civilization.[131]

Of course, those who felt prohibition should be left to the states were equally apocalyptic and racist:

I tell you all that the very civilization of my State and of every Southern State depends upon the survival of the principle for which we of the South who oppose this [Hobson] amendment are fighting. We have disfranchised [sic] the ignorant negro vote; we were forced to do it to preserve our civilization and our institutions and to have peace. We did what was best for the white man and what was best for the colored man. We did not deprive him of the right to vote in anger or with malice. We took away the ballot as the adult takes the pistol from the hand of a child. And I want to tell you that the negro himself is better satisfied under the new order of things.[132]

Though prohibition of alcohol would be enforced more fiercely against minorities than whites, many black leaders embraced the policy, at least initially. Writing in 1908, for example, the educator, orator, and first leader of the Tuskegee Normal and Industrial Institute Booker Taliaferro Washington (1856 – 1915) approved of the policy

---

pp. 1290-1291.

[131] Unknown, Congressional Record, Volume 52, 1915, December 22, 1914, Speech of Mr. Hobson, p. 603, column 2.

[132] Unknown, Congressional Record, Volume 52, 1915, December 22, 1914, Speech of Mr. Pou (Dem. NC), p. 507, column 1.

after viewing the effects of "two months of prohibition" in two major Southern cities:

> The prohibition movement is based upon a deep-seated desire to get rid of whiskey in the interest of both races .... The prohibition sentiment is as strong in counties where there are practically no colored people as in the Black Belt counties. ... In Birmingham the negroes ... cast nearly all of the registered colored vote for prohibition .... It is at the same time, if I may say so, an intellectual awakening and a moral revolution.[133]

Indeed, one modern historian argues that the country's

> most vocal prohibitionists weren't privileged white evangelicals, but its most marginalized and disenfranchised communities: women, Native Americans and African Americans. Indeed, temperance and prohibitionism worked hand-in-glove with other freedom movements – abolitionism and suffragism – that fought against the entrenched system of domination and subordination. Consequently, nearly every major Black abolitionist and civil rights leader before World War I – from Frederick Douglass, Martin Delany and Sojourner Truth to F. E. W. Harper, Ida B. Wells, W. E. B. Du Bois, and Booker T. Washington – endorsed temperance and prohibition.[134]

---

[133] Washington, Booker. "Prohibition and the Negro," *The Outlook*, Volume 88, No. 11, Saturday, 14 March 1908 AO, pp. 587, 589.

[134] Schrad, Mark Lawrence. "The Forgotten History of Black Prohibitionism," *Politico Magazine*, 02/06/2021 [politico.com, hereinafter POL], unpaged, filed under Black History Month, History Department.

Figure 317. "Booker Taliaferro Washington." Harris & Ewing, 1905. Library of Congress, Prints and Photographs Division, Washington, DC LG.

Hobson would go on to win the Medal of Honor for scuttling the *Merrimac* in the channel to the harbor at Santiago, Cuba in 1898 where "Admiral Cervera's fleet had taken refuge"[135] during the Spanish American War. On a subsequent cross-country heroes tour he became "the champion kisser in the universe," defending himself saying: "Now, what on earth am I to do – run away? Shall a man dodge, when pretty women crowd around him? It may be silly, but any man with any gallantry or decency in him would do just as I have done – kiss 'em all."[136]

Nor should we ignore international political factors. Even prior to the entrance of the United States into the First World War, the Anti-Saloon League noted approvingly that during "the period of mobilization in Germany the sale of alcoholic liquors was absolutely forbidden in all German towns"[137] while in Austria-Hungary the government took "the attitude that the prohibition was necessary in order to conserve the food supply, especially the supply of barley."[138] Once in the war, war-time prohibition in the United States became an anti-German patriotic duty:

---

135 Hobson, Richmond Pearson. The Sinking of the Merrimac: A Personal Narrative. NY: The Century Co., 1899 AO, p. 7.

136 Unknown writer. "Cross-Country Kissing Record," *St. Louis Post-Dispatch*, Volume 50, No. 127, Wednesday, 21 December 1898, p. 3, column 2.

137 Cherrington, Ernest Hurst, editor. The Anti-Saloon League Year Book 1917. Westerville, OH: Published by the Anti-Saloon League of America, 1917 AO, p. 322.

138 Cherringon, 1917, p. 324.

> The German saloon, the wrecking place of our industrial efficiency, and the foul spawning nest of spies, incendiaries and traitors; the German brewery gulping into its insatiable maw precious man-power, transportation facilities which would clear the yards and terminals of American fuel so necessary to maintain the war machine at its highest speed, and food sufficient to feed twice our army – these must go.[139]

Domestically, the Governor of North Dakota (a dry state) felt sure that with saloons would come "all the other vices and criminals that it fosters and propagates."[140] The Scientific Temperance Federation of Boston published leaflets with self-explanatory titles like:

> <u>Hand in Hand, Feeblemindedness, Alcoholism</u>; <u>How Drink Leads to Immorality</u>; <u>More White Plague in Children of Drinkers</u>; <u>More Drinkers Died Early</u>; <u>Do You Know? One Insane Person in Every Four Owes His Insanity to Drink</u>; and <u>Drink's Cost to the Taxpayer in Poverty, Crime, Pauperism, Etc</u> [capitalization, underlining original].[141]

Dry zones were mandated around military bases:

> HOBOKEN, N. J. – A War Department order establishing a dry zone of one-half mile about the embarkation piers in Hoboken, N. J., went into effect November 3, 1917, closing nearly 300 saloons. ... These saloons, mostly operated by Germans, were of the most vicious character, and ... conditions became so bad that the federal authorities were forced to act. ... NEW ROCHELLE, N. Y. – In the vicinity of this city are some of the most important military posts in the United States, including Fort Slocum, Fort Totten, Fort Schuyler, and the Naval Training Station at Pelham Bay Park, yet ... the local authorities of New Rochelle allowed saloons and resorts to

---

[139] Cherrington, Ernest Hurst, editor. <u>The Anti-Saloon League Year Book 1918</u>. Westerville, OH: Published by the Anti-Saloon League of America, 1918 AO, p. 61.

[140] Cherrington, 1918, p. 106.

[141] Cherrington, Ernest Hurst, editor. <u>The Anti-Saloon League Year Book 1916</u>. Westerville, OH: Published by the Anti-Saloon League of America, 1916 AO, unpaged advertisements, 318/322, 319/322.

run wide open night and day seven days in the week. Twenty-seven deputy marshals swooped down upon the place and secured evidence which resulted in the closing of all the saloons. In one of the places raided, run by an unnaturalized German, the deputies found 100 soldiers and between 30 and 40 Blue Jackets on the floor dancing. Most of the soldiers and sailors were under the influence of liquor. Some of the girls were masqueraded in the uniform of the army and navy [capitalization original].[142]

But the reformers made little progress in places where drinking openly was an accepted tradition like Coney Island, near New York City, which remained a refuge for thirsty off-duty military personnel:

A Captain Pfeiffer of the U. S. Army made a personal survey of Coney Island and confirmed his worst suspicions. "When a soldier or a sailor from the far-off places gets his pay and a little liberty," the captain complained, "he makes directly for Coney Island. Day and night you'll see men in uniform on the beach and taking in the varied amusements of the place, for you know Coney Island's fame is not only country-wide but international. "We have been shocked to find that many of the young men succumb to the alcoholic opportunities of the place in a way that we did not at first understand. But we know now: they go to some bathhouse, get into a bathing suit and then can drink all they wish, undistinguished from any other citizen."[143]

Economically, Prohibition caused big changes in the sources of revenue for the government. According to Szasz, "[b]etween 1870 and 1915, the tax on liquor provides from one-half to two-thirds of the whole of the internal revenue of the United States, amounting, after

---

142 Cherrington, 1918, "Liquor and Vice Regulations around Army cantonments in the United States and France," pp. 65-66.

143 Pilat, Oliver and Jo Ranson. Sodom by the Sea: An Affectionate History of Coney Island. NY: Garden City Publishing Co., Inc., 1943 [annas-archive.org, hereinafter AA], Chapter IV Trident of Entertainment, 2. Beer, p. 115.

the turn of the century, to about $200 million annually."[144] The shortfall in the budget would be partially offset by the newly passed income tax and the shift to a wartime economy.

Socially, while the *WASPS* led a moral crusade, the therapeutic establishment and important sectors of industry advocated a ban in order to reduce absenteeism and accidents at work. State governors agreed. A Dry State like Arizona had seen a "marked decrease of commitments to penal and pathological institutions. Crime and insanity, seemingly, have been greatly reduced under prohibitory legislation relative to intoxicants."[145] Florida lauded the benefits:

> Wherever Prohibition has been enforced in Florida the ... churches are better attended, preachers better paid, schools better attended, roads better kept up, less debts on the counties than formerly, and in fact a general air of peace and prosperity exists all over the districts where Prohibition is enforced.[146]

Kansas noted increased worker efficiency and home ownership:

> Its strongest advocates in the state are the large employers of labor, the managers of the big railroad corporations, and the labor organizations. ... The general manager of the Santa Fe Railway says the books of the company show these shopmen turn out more work, consistently and promptly the year round, than the men of any other railroad shops. Seventy-two per cent of the married men in these shops own their own homes – a showing not equaled by any other railway town in America.[147]

---

[144] Szasz, Thomas. Ceremonial Chemistry: The Ritual Persecution of Drugs, Addicts, and Pushers. Garden City, NY: Anchor Press/Doubleday, 1974 AA, Appendix, p. 196.

[145] Cherrington, 1918, "The Progress of Prohibition According to the Testimony of the Chief Executives of the Several States, Arizona, George W. P. Hunt, Governor," p. 99.

[146] Cherrington, 1918, p. 101.

[147] Cherrington, 1918, p. 103.

Even discounting its strictly pharmacological benefits, no one denies that alcohol is by far the single most important contributing factor in crimes against property and persons, and of many accidents. Neither does anyone deny that alcoholism is a more deleterious condition, physically and psychologically, than a mania for morphine or opium.

In January 1919, the acting Secretary of State certified that "the Amendment aforesaid has become valid to all intents and purposes as a part of the Constitution of the United States."[148] In January 1920, the XVIIIth Amendment (also called the *Volstead Act* or *Dry Act*) would come into force. Section 1 prohibited "the manufacture, sale, or transportation of intoxicating liquors within, the importation thereof into, or the exportation thereof from the United States and all territory subject to the jurisdiction thereof for beverage purposes ...."[149] Section 2 declared that the "Congress and the several States shall have concurrent power to enforce this article by appropriate legislation."[150]

That legislation was the *National Prohibition Act* passed 28 October 1919.[151] Exempt under Title II, Section 1 were any "beverage or liquid produced by the process by which beer, ale, porter or wine is produced, if it contains less than one-half of 1 per centum of alcohol by volume."[152] Section 4 of the same title exempted denatured alcohol,

---

148 Secretary, 1919, p. 1942.

149 Secretary of State, Director. The Statutes at Large of the United States of America from April 1917, to March, 1919, Volume XL. Washington, DC: Government Printing Office, 1919 AO, Session II, Proposed Amendment to the Constitution, Joint Resolution, S. J. Resolution 17, p. 1050.

150 Secretary, 1919, p. 1050.

151 Secretary of State, director. The Statutes at Large of the United States of America from May, 1919, to March, 1921, Volume XLI, Part 1. Washington, DC: Government Printing Office, 1921 LG, Sixty-Sixth Congress, Session I, Chapter 85, An Act to Prohibit Intoxicating Beverages, p. 305.

152 Secretary, 1921, p. 308.

medicinal preparations, patented and proprietary medicines, antiseptic solutions, flavoring extracts, as well as "[v]inegar and preserved sweet cider."[153] Section 6 exempted "wine for sacramental purposes" while Section 7 prohibited anyone but "a physician holding a permit" to "issue any prescription for liquor."[154] Under Section 21 any establishment in violation could be declared a "common nuisance" and its operator could be "fined not more than $1,000 or be imprisoned for not more than one year, or both."[155] Section 29 declared:

> Any person who manufactures or sells liquor in violation of this title shall for a first offense be fined not more than $1,000, or imprisoned not exceeding six months, and for a second or subsequent offense shall be fined not less than $200 nor more than $2,000 and be imprisoned not less than one month nor more than five years.[156]

On Friday, January 16, 1920, one day before the new law would take effect, the radio and the newspapers recorded a revivalist speech by former baseball player turned evangelist preacher William Ashley "Billy" Sunday (1862 – 1935) at his tabernacle in Norfolk, Virginia where he held a mock funeral service for John Barleycorn:

> Twenty pall bearers placed the coffin on a carriage and marched it through the streets to Sunday's tabernacle, while His Satanic Majesty trailed behind in deep mourning and anguish. At the tabernacle door Sunday met the cortege with a delighted grin. The Devil, wearing a mask and simulating a state of deep dejection, sat with the mourners. "Good-bye, John," said the evangelist at the end of his sermon. "You were God's worst enemy; you were Hell's best friend. I hate you with a perfect hatred; I love to hate you [quotation marks original]."[157]

---

153 Secretary, 1921, p. 309.

154 Secretary, 1921, p. 311.

155 Secretary, 1921, p. 314.

156 Secretary, 1921, p. 316.

157 Unknown writer. "Billy Sunday Speeds Barleycorn to Grave," *The New York*

Figure 318. "William Ashley Sunday." Widesmuth & Stearns, c. 1913. Library of Congress, Prints and Photographs Division, Washington, DC LG.

Times, Volume LXIX, No. 22638, Saturday, 17 January 1920 AO, p. 3, column 8.

1. Alcohol and Heredity

When the United States was taking these measures, knowledge about the effect of alcohol on successive generations was extensive but inconclusive. In addition to the physical and intellectual limitations[158] of habitual drunkards, the damage to their offspring needed to be taken into account. Alcohol, according to a widely respected investigator of the era, was one of a group of substances that,

> like chloroform, ether, benzene, carbon sulphide, etc., are capable of dissolving the fatty matter (lecithin, etc.) contained in the organic complex. The possibility of such action is also present in the case of the sperma and the ovum. Both of them may be deteriorated in their functions. ... This can be proved experimentally in fertilized eggs (parentheses original).[159]

In one such experiment this researcher injected some twenty-four eggs with ethyl alcohol, which allowed 62.5% of the eggs to hatch normally while 16.66% were undeveloped and 20.83% were described as abnormal.[160] In another experiment sixty-three eggs were injected with ethyl alcohol leaving only 53.96% normal, 11.11% undeveloped,

---

[158] Organically, these include serious vascular, hepatic, cardiac and renal illnesses. Mentally, there are profound disturbances in affectivity and will. Socially they include the incapacity to work and a tendency toward violence.

[159] Lewin, Louis. Phantastica: Narcotic and Stimulating Drugs, Their Use and Abuse, tr. P. H. A. Wirth. NY: E. P. Dutton & Company, Inc., 1964 AO, Inebrantia, Alcohol, 2. Chronic Alcoholism, a) Alcoholism and Heredity, p. 152; *die gleich Chloroform ... nachweisen* (Lewin, L. *Phantastica: Die Betäubenden und Erregenden Genusmittel, Für Ärzte und Nichärzte*. Berlin, DE: Verlag von Georg Stilke, 1924 AO, p. 155).

[160] Lewin, 1964, p. 175; *Beeinflussung der Entwicklung von Eiern ... Äthylalkohol ... Mißbildungen* (Lewin, 1924, p. 179).

while 34.93% were labeled monsters.[161] In contrast, an injection of water left 75% percent normal, 16.66% not developed, and 8.34% monsters.[162]

In humans the most common inherited defects were children born addicted to alcohol, with mental disorders that include idiocy, epilepsy, and various other psychopathies, as well as simple malformations of the body. Of 600 chronic alcoholics examined in one study, 40 percent of "the parents and nearest relations were alcoholic or affected with mental diseases."[163] Of 1000 "abnormal" children investigated at the Bicêtre Hospital in Paris, sixty-two percent reported alcoholism in the father, the mother, or both.[164]

A famous nineteenth century study of a single family was used to purportedly show the "influence of parental alcoholism on the criminal propensities of the offspring."[165] A member of the Prison Association of New York in 1874 "was appointed a committee of one to inspect thirteen of the county jails of the State of New York."[166] In particular, he studied the descendants of one family, the Jukes. The first Juke to settle in the territory, Max, "was born somewhere between 1720 and 1740. He is described as 'a hunter and fisher, a hard drinker, jolly and companionable, and averse to steady toil [quotation marks original].'"[167] One of his descendants, Ada, "better known both in Z

161 Lewin, 1964, p. 152; *Aethylalkokhol ... Monstra* (Lewin, 1924, p. 155).

162 Lewin, 1964, p. 152; *Wasser ... Monstra* (Lewin, 1924, p. 155).

163 Lewin, 1964, p. 153; *Von 600 Trinkern waren ... 40,4 Proz.* (Lewin, 1924, p. 156).

164 Lewin, 1964, pp. 153-154; *anormalen Kinder ... 62 Proz.* (Lewin, 1924, p. 157).

165 Lewin, 1964, p. 154; *Daß die Trunksucht in der Aszendenz ...* (Lewin, 1924, p. 157).

166 Estabrook, Arthur H. The Jukes in 1915. Washington, DC: Published by the Carnegie Institute of Washington, 1916 AO, Historical Note, p. v.

167 Estabrook, 1916, IV. The First Two Generations of Jukes, p. 2.

County and to the general public as 'Margaret, the mother of criminals,' was born about 1755 [quotation marks original]."[168]

In all, this researcher looked at some

> 709 persons, 540 being of Juke blood and 169 of "X" blood who had married into the Juke family. He estimated that the Juke family would consist of 1,200 persons were it possible to have traced all the lines of descent from the original 6 sisters. Of the 709 whom he studied, 180 had either been in the poorhouse or received outdoor relief to the extent of 800 years. There had been 140 criminals and offenders, 60 habitual thieves, 7 lives sacrificed by murder, 50 common prostitutes, 40 women venereally diseased contaminating 440 persons, and 30 prosecutions in bastardy. The total cost to the State of New York of this one group of mental and social degenerates was estimated, for a period of 75 years beginning in 1800, at $1,308,000 [quotation marks original].[169]

Few of the nearly eight hundred persons in his study had avoided prison, the poorhouse, or the asylum. A follow up study concluded that half of the Jukes "were and are feeble-minded, mentally incapable of responding normally to the expectations of society ...."[170]

These statistics were certainly more impressive in the 1920s than they are today, partly because we tend to attribute a more decided influence to factors of social marginalization and less to genetic determinism. For this reason, the conclusions established between alcoholism and heredity can only be admitted with great reservations. Our present understanding does not allow us to speak, as the Italian eugenicist, criminologist and phrenologist Ezechia Marco Lombroso ("Cesare," 1835 – 1909) did, of the born criminal.[171]

---

[168] Estabrook, 1916, p. 2.

[169] Estabrook, 1916, II. Summary of Jukes, 1. Jukes of Dugdale, pp. 1-2.

[170] Estabrook, 1916, XXV. General Summary, p. 85.

[171] See for example Ferrero, Gina Lombroso. Criminal Man, According to the Classification of Cesare Lombroso. NY: G. P. Putnam's Sons, 1911 AO, Chapter I

At first glance, it seems clear that there is a marked, even very marked, convergence between harm to offspring and alcoholism, judging only by the case of Ada Juke. The German physician who investigated the connections between alcohol and crime described Ada Juke so: "She was a drunkard ...."[172]

But the original study of 1874 described her in two different charts as "temperate."[173] Instead, the most common description of Ada Juke is "Ada, a harlot."[174] Certainly, the original data from New York in 1874 does not support the conclusions written in Berlin in 1924, fifty years later. Besides, rare is the human who does not have several dipsomaniacs in his or her genealogy, affecting the genetic endowment and threatening to disrupt their offspring in an unpredictable way.

From a strictly pharmacological point of view, alcohol admits of some disturbing depths. But early prohibitionists rarely plumbed them. What was really harmful in their view was the unnatural euphoria and, ultimately, the sin of getting drunk, combined with the slavery to a habit.

The Born Criminal, p. 3; see also Lombroso, Cesare. *L'uomo Delinquente*. Milano, IT: Ulrico Hoepli, Libraio-Editore, 1876 AO, Capitolo I, p. 3.

172 Lewin, 1964, p. 154; *Sie war Trinkerin* ... (Lewin, 1924, p. 157).

173 Dugdale, Richard L. "The Jukes" A Study in Crime, Pauperism, Disease and Heredity, Third Edition, Revised. NY: G. P. Putnam's Sons 1877 AO, Chart I – The Illegitimate Posterity of Ada Juke, with the Persons They Married, as recorded in 1874, unpaged, between pages 14 and 15, Chart II – The Posterity of the Legitimate Children of Ada Juke, with the Persons They Married, as recorded in 1874, unpaged, between the pages of 16 and 17.

174 Dugdale, 1877, pp. 19, 20, 22, 23, for example.

2. The Therapeutic Estate

Although the *Volstead Act* did not come into force until the beginning of 1920, the imminence of prohibition was clearly manifested in 1916 when the pharmacopoeia of the United States erased whiskey and brandy from its list of medicinal drugs.[175] Shortly thereafter, the president of the American Medical Association endorsed a policy of complete abstinence, nationwide. The AMA's House of Delegates passed a motion stating the following:

> Whereas, We believe that the use of alcohol as a beverage is detrimental to the human economy, and
> Whereas, Its use in therapeutics, as a tonic or a stimulant or as a food has no scientific basis, therefore be it
> *Resolved*, That the American Medical Association opposes the use of alcohol as a beverage, and be it further
> *Resolved*, That the use of alcohol as a therapeutic agent should be discouraged [italics original].[176]

To what extent American medicine of the period inherits clerical functions is expressed by a second resolution, on sexual continence, from a different committee reading in part:

---

[175] See GHDV3P2, Chapter 18, 1. Spiritual Values and Union Interests, p. 1262, fn 110.

[176] Graves, M. L., Chairman of the Reference Committee. Journal of the American Medical Association, Volume LXVIII, Number 24, Saturday, 16 June 1917, Minutes of House of Delegates, New York Session, Report of Reference Committee on Legislation and Political Action, p. 1837.

1. That sexual continence is compatible with health and is the best prevention of venereal infections.
2. That steps be taken toward the prevention of venereal infections through the prevention of prostitution, and by the provision of suitable recreational facilities, the control of alcoholic drinks, and other effective constructive measures.[177]

The Hippocratic Oath, of course, enjoins physicians from sexual intercourse with patients, their families or slaves: "Into whatsoever houses I enter, I will enter to help the sick, and I will abstain from all intentional wrong-doing and harm, especially from abusing the bodies of man or woman, bond or free."[178] Forgotten was the Hippocratic advice that sex was healthy: "Here is another trait in women. If they have relations with men, their health is better; worse, if they do not have them. ... In fact, in the case of a man too, if he indulges much in intercourse, the veins become free-flowing and attract the semen more."[179]

But concern for the moral side of things would not be incompatible with ultimate developments. As soon as the *Volstead Act* was enacted, the American Medical Association decided that it could no longer continue to maintain what had been agreed to in 1917. It continued to advise against the recreational use of alcoholic beverages, but considered the therapeutic efficacy of certain wines and spirits as sedatives and in the cure of neurasthenia to be undeniable: "Hospital pharmacies stocked large amounts of wine, and it was prescribed as an

---

[177] McCormack, Arthur T., Chairman. "Report of Reference Committee on Hygiene and Public Health," JAMA, 16 June 1917, p. 1837.

[178] Jones, W. H. S., tr. Hippocrates, Volume I. Cambridge, MA: Harvard University Press, 1984 AO, The Oath, p. 301; *ἐς οἰκίας ... δούλων* (p. 300, lines 24-28).

[179] Ellinger, Tage U. H., translator. Hippocrates On Intercourse and Pregnancy. NY: Henry Schuman, Inc., 1952 AO, On Intercourse, Chapter 4, p. 29; On Pregnancy, Chapter 21 (10), p. 75.

appetite stimulant, diuretic, and sedative, as well as a treatment for psychosomatic illnesses like neurasthenia."[180]

As for the APhA, if in 1917 they had withdrawn all beverages from the US Pharmacopoeia, six months after Prohibition was approved they returned nine classes of alcohol to it, several of which were the most popular among drinkers. Doctors and druggists were quick to take advantage of the exception for medicinal alcohol:

> More than 57,000 druggists, retail and wholesale, and manufacturers of proprietary medicines, flavoring extracts, syrups, &c., have been licensed in the United States and its consular possessions to date under the National Prohibition act .... The records of the Internal Revenue Bureau also show that nearly 16,000 physicians in the United States, Hawaii and Porto Rico have received permits to write prescriptions calling for the dispensation of intoxicating liquors for medicinal purposes and that additional permits at the rate of 1,000 a month are being issued to physicians.[181]

Distillers also took advantage of the same loophole:

> Since only bottled-in-bond whisky and brandy can be sold for medicinal purposes, the Large and Barett companies are putting their product into warehouses for the four years' aging required before it can be bonded, and count on the blended whisky finding a market for medicinal purposes six, eight or ten years hence, when the present supply is gone.[182]

The result was more illegal liquor than ever before:

---

[180] Grinspoon, Lester and James B. Bakalar. Cocaine: A Drug and its Social Evolution, revised edition. NY: Basic Books, 1985 AO, p. 252.

[181] Unknown writer. "'Dry Act' Licenses Now Exceed 57,000," *The New York Times*, Volume LXVIIII, Issue 22,807, Sunday, 4 July 1920 AO, Section 2, Editorial Section, p. 1, column 3; Sinclair, Andrew. Prohibition: the Era of Excess. Boston, MA: Little, Brown and Company, 1962 AA, Chapter 22. The Blighted Roots, p. 410.

[182] Unknown, NYT, 4 July 1920, p. 1, col. 3.

The clauses dealing with medicinal and sacramental alcohol in the act provided more illicit liquor in America. In the House debate, Congressmen had voiced their fears of scalawag and jackleg physicians, although no one foresaw the possibility of bootlegging ministers. The testimony of Dr. Bevan that doctors made roughly $40,000,000 in 1928 by writing medical prescriptions for whisky, the opposition of the National Association of Retail Druggists to the vast profits of the speakeasy drugstores, and proof that even sacramental wine often reached the dinner table rather than the communion cup provided damning evidence against these loopholes in the Volstead Act.[183]

This implies twenty percent of the annual total tax revenues of the United States obtained before the illegalization of these products was now going to doctors, not saloon keepers. By 1931, as Prohibition was being increasingly challenged, evaded and ignored, there were huge numbers of therapists in the special registry, earning by some estimates every bit of what previously had been received in tax revenue by the Treasury.

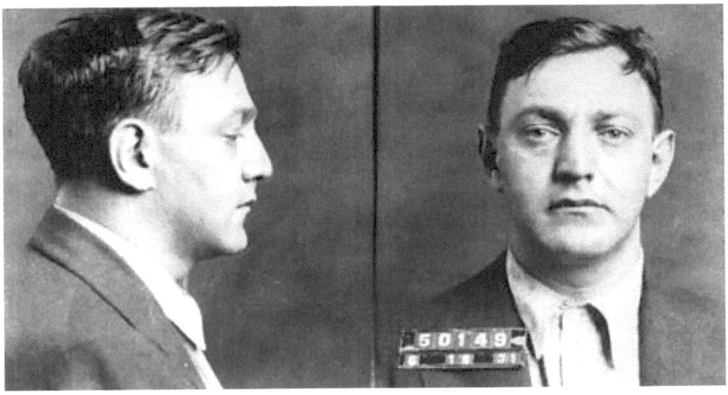

Figure 319. "Dutch Schultz." NYPD Mugshot, 1931. Burton B. Turkus Papers, Lloyd Sealy Library, John Jay College of Criminal Justice/ CUNY [dc.lin.jay.cuny.edu, hereinafter, CU].

---

183 Sinclair, 1962, p. 191.

3. Crime

Prohibition opened up new opportunities for graft and corruption in the bureaucracy created to enforce it. In all, according to Szasz:

> [d]uring the first eleven years of the Volstead Act, 17,972 persons are appointed to the Prohibition Bureau, 11,982 are terminated "without prejudice," and 1,604 are dismissed for bribery, extortion, theft, falsification of records, conspiracy, forgery, and perjury [quotation marks original].[184]

Most of these offenses appear to have happened in the latter years of the prohibition.

At higher levels the moral situation is similar. Warren Gamaliel Harding (1865 – 1923) came into office at the head of a campaign guided by a catchy slogan equating business and government. A providential heart attack, during the summer of 1923, spared him the fallout from one of the biggest bribery cases then known in the history of the country. His Secretary of the Interior, Albert Bacon Fall (1861 – 1944) became the first cabinet minister to go to prison, convicted for leasing oil reserves without competitive bidding in the Teapot Dome scandal. His Attorney General, Harry Micajah Daugherty (1860 – 1941), part of the so-called Ohio Gang, was investigated also but never convicted.

Nor among the citizens was there much ethical progress. "Only a small number of liquor sellers were arrested and prosecuted, but even this number overwhelmed the courts. In some cases, juries refused to convict liquor sellers out of principle."[185] Szasz computes:

---

[184] Szasz, 1974, Appendix, p. 198.

[185] Andersen, Lisa M. F. <u>The Politics of Prohibition: American Governance and the Prohibition Party, 1869 – 1933</u>. NY: Cambridge University Press, 2013 AO,

"In 1932 alone, approximately 45,000 persons receive jail sentences for alcohol offences."[186] More than three times as many were sentenced to fines and preventive detention. Another estimate figures the overall effect of a decade of prohibition:

> From 1920 to 1930 federal prohibition agents arrested, in round numbers, 577,000 suspected offenders, of whom slightly less than two-thirds were convicted. The agents seized 1,600,000 distilleries, stills, worms and fermenters, 9,000,000 gallons of spirits, 1 billion gallons of malt liquor, 1 billion gallons of wine, hard cider and mash, 45,000 automobiles and 1,300 boats presumed to have transported liquor. The appraised value of confiscated property totaled $49,000,000. The figures on state and municipal enforcement were never computed but during the early years probably surpassed the federal total.[187]

Alcohol was quickly adulterated: "About one gallon of denatured industrial alcohol in ten is diverted into bootleg liquor. About 40 Americans per million die each year from drinking illegal alcohol, mainly as a result of methyl (wood) alcohol poisoning."[188] How much responsibility devolved upon the government's denaturing became the subject of some debate. One medical examiner, commenting on some sixteen recent deaths, opined: "The government knows it is not stopping drinking by putting poison in alcohol. It knows what bootleggers are doing with it, and yet it continues its poisoning processes. Knowing this to be true, the government must be charged with the deaths that poisoned liquor causes."[189] A federal

---

Epilogue, pp. 279-280.

186 Szasz, 1974, Appendix, p. 198.

187 Kobler, John. Ardent Spirits: The Rise and Fall of Prohibition. NY: G. P. Putnam's Sons, 1973 AO, p. 269.

188 Szasz, 1974, Appendix, p. 200.

189 A. P. writer. "U. S. Liquor Poison Blamed in 25 Deaths from Rum," *The Washington Post*, No. 18,457, Tuesday, December 28, 1926 AO, p. 3, column 3.

prohibition administrator defended the practice, saying the denaturing was "done in order that users of alcohol for non-beverage purposes might avoid payment of the high tax on grain alcohol and there was no intent on the part of the government to risk the lives of citizens. The denaturing has been going on since 1906 ...."[190]

Another adulterant, tri-ortho-cresyl phosphate (added to Fluid Extract of Jamaica Ginger) was responsible for so-called Jake paralysis:

> The usual story is that the patient drank one or more two-ounce bottles of "Jake" which produced the desired alcoholic effect in a short while. Then, after a variable period (usually about two weeks), he first noticed a sensation of numbness, tingling, fatigue, or cramp-like pain in his calf muscles. This was not a marked sensation and usually caused no alarm. This peculiar cramp-like sensation in the calf muscles persisted one or two days, after which the patient noticed weakness of the legs which rapidly progressed into paralysis with "foot-drop" or inability to walk or to stand still [quotation marks original].[191]

The phenomenon became the subject of a number of blues songs with lyrics like: "Jake leg, jake leg, what in the world you trying to do? Seems like everybody in the city's messed up on account of drinking you."[192] The concoction "paralyzed tens of thousands of people" resulting in a group, the "United Victims of Jamaica Ginger Paralysis, which claimed to speak for thirty-five thousand stricken people across the country."[193]

---

190 A. P., "U. S. Liquor," *Washington Post*, 1926, p. 3

191 Kidd, John G. and Orthello R. Langworthy. "Jake Paralysis: Paralysis Following the Ingestion of Jamaica Ginger Extract Adulterated with Tri-Ortho-Cresyl Phosphate," *Bulletin of the Johns Hopkins Hospital*, Volume LII, Number 1, January 1933 AO, IV. Clinical, *a. History*, p. 44.

192 Baum, Dan. "Annals of Epidemiology, "Jake Leg: *How the blues diagnosed a medical mystery*," *The New Yorker*, September 15, 2003 AO, 2003, p. 50.

193 Baum, 2003, p. 57.

Figure 320. "Jamaica Ginger." Munsey, Cecil. "Paralysis in a Bottle (The 'Jake Walk' Story)," *Bottles and Extras*, Volume 17, No. 1, Winter 2006, Federation of Historical Bottle Collectors [fohbc.org, hereinafter FO], p. 7.

Gangsterism caused unprecedented turbulence. Responding to the demand, trafficking surged throughout the country. The profession of bootlegger (seller of contraband alcohol) became the most lucrative of all, often thanks to the complicity of the police.[194] A

194 *Pour répondre ... la police* (Schoell, Frank A. Histoire des États-Unis. Paris, FR: Payot, 1985 AO, p. 233).

few years of Prohibition were enough to create local syndicates, which fundamentally work for the benefit of a financial oligarchy, smoothing out small difficulties while taking over the sector of public vice.

In Chicago, Johnny Torrio ("The Fox," 1882 – 1957) "looked far beyond the confines of the First Ward to the latent opportunities throughout metropolitan Chicago. He saw a vice-monopoly of an entire county – and acted promptly."[195] Considered

> one of the smartest criminals in American history, Torrio saw the benefit of eschewing violence in favor of cooperation and sharing profits with rivals, politicians, law enforcement officers, and members of the bench. He quickly moved to unite the various gangs of Chicago, offering them protection and shared profits in exchange for his leadership. Though it rankled some, particularly Irish gang leaders whose hatred toward Italians was common in those days, Torrio enjoyed much success in the early 1920s. Chicago was a relatively peaceful community. Cooperation was achieved not only on the alcohol front, but in gambling as well.[196]

Torrio would then bring in Alphonse Gabriel Capone ("Scarface," 1899 – 1947) as a bodyguard and successor.

Others who took advantage of Prohibition were the legendary New York mobster Dutch Schultz (Arthur Simon Flegenheimer, 1901 – 1935), Jack "Legs" Diamond (John Thomas, 1897 – 1931) of Philadelphia and New York, New York kingpin Arnold Rothstein ("The Brain," 1882 – 1928), Meyer Lansky (Maier Suchowljansky, "The Accountant," 1902 – 1983) and Charles "Lucky" Luciano (Salvatore Lucania, 1897 – 1962).

---

[195] Paisley, Fred D. Al Capone: *The Biography of a Self-Made Man*. Garden City, NY: Garden City Publishing Company, 1930 AO, p. 15.

[196] Iorizzo, Luciano. Al Capone: A Biography. Westport, CT: Greenwood Press, 2003, p. 14.

CH. 23 JUNKIES AND JUICERS

Over time, the Italians came to control much of the alcohol business, only after violent battles with other families. By 1928, there was a meeting of the heads of various families from all over the country, where a policy of coexistence was finally agreed upon, with a scrupulous distribution of zones and a supreme council to handle disputes.

> The first known conference was held in Cleveland, Ohio, in December 1928. The conferees were all Italian, many of whom were the upcoming leaders of organized crime. Fearful of losing some of his power if he attended, Capone stayed away. He sent a representative instead. ... Virtually every profession and industry in America had its annual conferences. Though not meeting yearly, organized crime was no exception. ... When gangland leaders met again the next year in Atlantic City, Capone was there. He must have figured it was better to keep an eye on what was going on than have racketeers possibly conspiring behind his back. Criminals were taking a big step forward in allocating turf and rackets to major bosses and putting an end to chaos and bitterness. ... The conferees agreed on establishing an organization of equals that would have jurisdiction throughout the nation. There would be no boss of bosses. Murder would be outlawed. Rule would be by a commission that would recognize the sovereignty of leaders on their turf as long as they abided by the rules for the syndicate on which all had agreed. There was plenty of money to be made in providing consumers with liquor, women, and gambling. Everyone stood to profit by agreeing to assigned territories and sticking to their promises.[197]

Billy Sunday purportedly promised that the jails and correctional facilities would be emptied, closing the gates of hell forever. A decade later, the attempt to outlaw an individual vice with indiscriminate general restrictions had produced a system to satisfy that vice. Deeply infiltrated into the public machinery, prohibition enhanced both the demoralization and corruption of the federal repression and a tendency to disregard the law in much of the country.

---

[197] Iorizzo, 2003, pp. 51-52, 53.

Figure 321. "Meyer Lansky." Photograph, 1958, Al Ravenna. *The New York World-Tribune* and *Sun* Collection, Library of Congress, Prints and Photographs Division, Washington, DC LG.

Figure 322. "Lucky Luciano." Photograph, B&W film copy negative, 1936. *New York World-Tribune* and *Sun* Collection, Library of Congress, Prints and Photographs Division, Washington DC LG.

In his own mind, Capone felt

> he was a benefactor of Chicago, much better than the white-collar criminals who stole the people and the city blind and never gave back as he did to the poor, the homeless, and the countless victims of the Depression. ... Capone did honestly believe that he did nothing wrong in violating Prohibition laws. In an age where the establishment tried to eliminate drinking and minimize gambling and prostitution, he became a hero of sorts, making it possible for the common individual to partake of fruit that, though forbidden in his day and age, had been legally available throughout the nation's history. Capone knew that and capitalized on it. ... He could rationalize his gangster life because he understood that corruption was part and parcel of life in urban America.[198]

[198] Iorizzo, 2003, pp. 90, 108.

Capone himself would say seriously, "I'm just a businessman who supplies people with what they want to buy, in the good old American way."[199]

Figure 323. "Al Capone Leaving a Federal Courthouse." Wide World Photos, 1931. Everett Collection. Encyclopedia Britannica [britannica.com, hereinafter BR].

[199] Iorizzo, 2003, p. 12.

BIG SCENIC SENSATION
KING OF THE OPIUM RING
BY
CHAS. E. BLANEY
& CHAS. A. TAYLOR
- POLICE RAIDING AN OPIUM JOINT -

Figure 324. "*King of the Opium Ring.*" Charles E. Blaney (1866 – 1944), writer and producer. H. C. Miner Lithograph Company, 1899. Library of Congress, Prints and Photographs Division, Washington, DC [loc.gov, hereinafter LG].

24

The Crusade Begins (I)

We laugh when we hear that among the ancients even the arts were subject to the civil code. But we are not always right when we do so. Unquestionably, laws must not exercise any constraint on the sciences, for the ultimate goal of knowledge is truth. ... But the ultimate goal of the arts is pleasure, and this pleasure is not indispensable. Hence it may be for the lawmaker to determine what kind of pleasure and how much of each kind he will permit.[1]
Lessing, Ephraim Gotthold (1729 – 1781)

You abuse snuff! Perhaps it is the final cause of the human nose.[2]
Coleridge, Samuel Taylor (1772 – 1834)

A. The Initial Dissidents
- **1. The American System**
- **2. The British System**

B. Closing the Clinics
- **1. Numbering the Addicts**
- **2. Changing Demographics**

C. Opening the Farms

D. Medical, Legislative and Judicial Dissent

E. Militant Prohibitionists React

---

1 Laocoön: An Essay on the Limits of Painting and Poetry, tr. Edward Allen McCormick. Indianapolis, IN: The Bobbs-Merrill Company, Inc., 1962 [annas-archive.org, hereinafter AA], Chapter Two, p. 14.

2 Table Talk of Samuel Taylor Coleridge. London: George Routledge and Sons, 1884 [archive.org, hereinafter AO], *January* 4, 1823, p. 36.

For the traditional State it was enough that its subjects paid their taxes, bowed before the emblems of its reigning majesties, and conceded males of military age for its wars. Except in those centuries marked by crusades against witches, the political authorities were not concerned with what a subject used privately to modify her state of mind. Once the security offered to the citizen began to include norms on her pharmacological diet, the interest in various drugs undergoes an enormous expansion.

It is as if a river were approaching its estuary, not only gaining depth and width but also bifurcating into channels while receiving tributaries, fast-moving and slow. If in 1900 only the therapeutic professions seemed interested in ending self-medication, by 1920 this principle has become part of class progress and a pillar of the social order. Following the vigorous Northamerican initiatives, other nations are going to assume that the duty to protect the public health consists not so much in protecting the citizen from danger that threatens from without as it is in protecting him from certain internal temptations, especially those which cause him to alter by chemical means his way of feeling about the world. This happens precisely in those countries whose population enjoys an economic comfort never before seen, where there are political liberties, and where atheism is spreading with great velocity, or at least a deism refractory to any dogma. There, the place once occupied by theological dissidents begins to be occupied by pharmacological dissidents, as the authorities are as liberal in matters of faith as they are severely orthodox in matters of drugs.

This change betrays strategic displacement in the physics of social power, obedient to considerations of political control. However, this new activity is born out of a religious crusade, grows stronger because of it, and is sustained (nominally at least) by its arguments; its justification is that there is at least as much difference between this or that psychotropic drug as there is between the miracle and black magic, good and evil, holy water and the potion of the sorceress. Amplified by a nascent mass media, this Manichean dichotomy sets in motion a confused crusade whose ultimate enemy is the experiment in libertarian individualism being tried since the end of the 1700s. Without the imprint of fundamentalism, it is doubtful that the path chosen would have been prohibition.

Human history does not know of a single drug that has ceased to be consumed or has disappeared because it was prohibited. But it does show that drug use is much more likely to become delirious when banned. The phenomena attached to illegalization (adulterations, contact with a criminal environment, usurious prices, insecurities in the supply, myths) erode the critical sense, causing it to be consumed with abandon. A drug is not only a particular chemical compound, but a thing whose effects depend on the prevailing conditions for its access. Tobacco was prohibited in Russia, with penalties of torture and mutilation, and its risk-taking adepts tended to smoke it avidly; the Tsarist attributed the increase in use to the intoxicating nature of the substance, and augmented the repression accordingly, though in good measure this irrational use was a consequence of the repression. An identical expansion of use happened in Paraguay with its prohibition of *maté*, in China with the prohibition of opium and in the United States with the prohibition of alcohol. Was there any reason to hope for something different with the so-called narcotics?

It would be an error to think that this line of reasoning was not present from the beginning of the crusade. True, there were those who strove to create a moral conscience about the subject. But there were also others (pharmacologists mostly) who dated the appearance of problems from the moment of the imposition of the prohibition itself.

Figure 325. "Dr. Ernest Simons Bishop (1876 – 1926)." Photograph, c. 1914. Stafford, Hartwell. Empire State Notables 1914. NY: Hartwell Stafford Publisher, Inc., 1914 AO, Physicians and Surgeons, p. 333.

CH. 24 THE CRUSADE BEGINS (I)

A. The Initial Dissidents

The *Harrison Act* passed practically unperceived in non-therapeutic circles. Its very nature was that of a tax, regulating the registration of certain products and their distribution. However, it did not fail to arouse opposition from certain physicians.

The most outspoken among them in the beginning was a doctor working in the Alcohol, Narcotic and Prison Service of Bellevue Hospital, Dr. Ernest S. Bishop (1876 – 1926),[3] an undisputed authority on opiate dependence,[4] who in various articles[5] had attempted to combat what he called "the stigma of mental and moral taint"[6] imposed upon narcotic addicts. In his opinion, gradually reducing the dose was impractical, and forcible reduction cruel and useless: "The method of gradual reduction of dose to the point of

---

[3] See GHDV4P1, Chapter 23, p. 1613.

[4] Speaking of himself in the third person, Bishop modestly demurs: "He is not a 'specialist' in the treatment of narcotic drug addiction. He is a practitioner of diagnostic and clinical medicine, in whose professional work the care of the narcotic addict has constituted much the smaller part of his activities and studies ... [quotation marks original]" (Bishop, Ernest S. The Narcotic Drug Problem. NY: The MacMillan Company, 1920 AO, Preface, first page).

[5] "Morphinism and its Treatment," *Journal of the American Medical Association*, Volume LVIII, No. 20, 18 May 1912 [jama.jamanetwork.com, hereinafter JJN], pp. 1499-1504; "An Analysis of Narcotic Drug Addiction," New York Medical Journal, Volume CI, *January to June ... Inclusive*, NY: A. R. Elliott Publishing Company, 1915 AO, 27 February, pp. 399-403; "Some Fundamental Considerations of the Problem of Narcotic Drug Addiction," American Medicine, Volume XXI, Complete Series, Volume X, New Series, January – December 1915 AO, November, pp. 807-816; "The Narcotic Addict, the Physician and the Law," The Medical Economist, Volume IV. Brooklyn, NY: The Physicians' Economist Publishing Company, Inc., 1916 AO, No. 6, June, pp. 121-128.

[6] Bishop, 1920, Chapter I Introduction, p. 3.

ultimate discontinuance is practical and feasible ... to but very few addicts. The forcible reduction of dose ... is barbarous, harmful and futile."[7]

On the contrary, a legal and cheap supply of drugs should be given to addicts, at least until there existed some better remedy:

> Until the addict can be offered rational treatment, the profession should do what it can in making the lives of addicts less unbearable by removing from the public mind some of the gross misconceptions concerning addiction, seeing to it, especially, that these unfortunates are not stigmatized as 'morphine fiends' and that they are given the means of obtaining, without risk and hardship and almost prohibitive cost, the supply of their drug which, until they are cured, is to them as necessary as the air they breathe [quotation marks original].[8]

No one becomes dependent upon opiates without serious pre-existing conditions, either mental or physical, and attempting to cure dependence by calling it a crime is an infallible way to convert it into a crime. According to Bishop, addiction should be treated as simply another disease:

> One of the essentials for the practical solution and management of the narcotic drug problem is the realization by the medical profession, legislators, administrators and laity that opiate drug addiction is a definite disease entity, to be treated as such, and calling for extensive clinical and laboratory investigation and study such as have been accorded other diseases over which we have gained the mastery.[9]

---

[7] Bishop, 1920, Chapter VI The Rational Handling of Narcotic Drug Addiction-Disease, p. 69.

[8] Bishop, 1920, Appendix Human Documents – Personal Statements, Drug Addiction from the Viewpoint of an Afflicted Physician, By a Prominent Medical Man, Formerly a Health Official of an American City, p. 155.

[9] Bishop, 1920, Chapter VI, p. 61.

If a physician pretended to ignore these factors he was betraying the most elemental principles of his profession: "It seems a crime that we of the profession have gone so long without any attempt to study or understand the disease which we in our daily rounds are constantly creating."[10] Doctors were not missionaries, but only, as Claudius Galenus (Galen, 129AD – c. 210AD) said, servants of the individual nature of the patient.[11] Bishop certainly would have agreed: "Studying them – not as drug addicts, but as individual human beings – I found them in their personal, mental, moral and other characteristics, as various as people suffering from any other disease condition."[12]

With The Narcotic Drug Problem, a book which collected together collaborations from scientific journals and unpublished essays, Bishop was out front of his colleagues in declaring the drug problem an invention of drug prohibition. When he began treating addicts, there

> were no narcotic laws at that time and opiates were easily and cheaply obtainable. Very many, perhaps most of those who came to my wards were not forced in either by fear of the law or by scarcity of opiate supply. They did not have to come for treatment, but voluntarily presented themselves in the hope of cure.[13]

---

[10] Bishop, 1920, Appendix A Plea for a Broader Consideration of Narcotic Drug Addiction by the Medical Profession, By a Practicing Physician Who has Met the Problem in his own Family, p. 158.

[11] See for example, Galenus, Claudius. How to be Healthy: An Ancient Guide to Wellness, tr. Katherine D. Van Schaik. Princeton, NJ: Princeton University Press, 2024 AA, On Hygiene, pp. 158-159: "So, if we then function in different ways, the good balance of each individual's elements is also different – and this is the very thing we said health was (*εἴπερ οὖν διαφόρως ... ἡ ὑγεία*)."

[12] Bishop, 1920, Chapter II Fundamental Considerations, p. 12.

[13] Bishop, 1920, p. 12.

Superstition and cruelty, disguised as benevolence and science, treated some people's pain by outlawing their remedies. But what was truly harmful at the physical level for an opiate addict was to undergo repeated periods of abstinence and overdose:

> Less than the definite amount required for nervous and glandular and circulatory support and organic balance deprives the patient of reaction, places his vitality and energy far below par and for a long time hinders his betterment. More than this amount displays the inhibitory effects of opiates, locks up or slows secretions and body functions, and causes malnutrition, autotoxemia, autotoxicosis, and the consequent mental and physical deterioration commonly and erroneously attributed to the direct action of opiate drug.[14]

But this was going too far. In the same month that his book appeared Bishop was indicted for violation of the *Harrison Act* reputedly for prescribing morphine tablets to an agent of the Narcotic Division of the Prohibition Unit of the Treasury Department which had decided to "close all clinics and prevent almost all maintenance."[15] Although it received wide publicity (and caused the professional ruin of Bishop), the case was eventually dismissed.

According to an editorial in *American Medicine*, the dismissal was influenced by the fact that the Department of the Treasury was accused of trying to silence a strong position contrary to its prevailing interpretation of the *Harrison Act*:

---

[14] Bishop, 1920, Chapter IV The Mechanism of Narcotic Drug Addiction-Disease, p. 38.

[15] See Musto, David F. The American Disease: Origins of Narcotic Control, Third Edition. NY: Oxford University Press, 1999 AA, Notes, pp. 329-331, fn 23.

Therefore Be It Resolved, that we, the American Medical Editors' Association, confident of the absolute innocence of Dr. Ernest S. Bishop and believing that the situation today in regard to narcotic drug addiction calls for scientific study and investigation as never before ... respectfully requests and urge that the Secretary of the Treasury, the Hon. A. W. Mellon, undertake an inquiry looking to an investigation into all the facts and conditions surrounding the indictment of Dr. Ernest S. Bishop ... thereby making it possible not only for Dr. Bishop to take up the scientific study and teaching of a problem, to the solution of which he has already contributed so much, but also, the resumption of research and investigation of this serious disease by honest, conscientious and law-abiding physicians all over the country ....[16]

Along the same lines, a virulent editorial appeared a year later in the *Medical Record*, decrying the scapegoating of physicians by fanatical legislatures resulting in the increasing "enslavement" of the medical profession by the less than qualified:

The antivivisectionists and the antivaccinationists we have always with us. Nearly every year some new group of 'healers,' with little education or no education ... are made by law the equals of medical practitioners who have given years of study to qualify themselves to treat the sick.

Who is to blame for this ever-increasing interference with the liberty of medical practitioners? If the medical societies of the land ... were in general more alive to their responsibilities, possibly a halt might be called to this meddling by politicians and cranks with the practice of medicine [question mark and quotation marks original].[17]

---

16 Lewis, H. Edwin, ed. American Medicine, Volume XXVIII, Complete Series, Volume XVII, New Series, January – December. Burlington, VT: American Medical Publishing Company, 1922 AO, December, No. 12, News, Notes and Announcements, *Resolution in behalf of Dr. Ernest S. Bishop*, p. 721.

17 Stedman, Thomas L., ed. "The Growing Enslavement of the Medical Profession," Medical Record, Volume 99, January 1, 1921 – June 25, 1921. NY: William Wood and Company, 1921 BGU, No. 1, Whole No. 2617, 1 Jan 1921, p. 18.

Figure 326. "Dr. Willis Pollard Butler (1888 – 1991)." Handbook of North Louisiana Online. LSU – Shreveport [nwla-archives.org, hereinafter NWLA].

Another physician in agreement with the general position of Bishop was the chemist, pathologist and coroner Dr. Willis Pollard Butler (1888 – 1991) who operated a maintenance clinic for narcotic addicts in Shreveport, Louisiana in the early 1920s:

> The treatment for morphinism should be as humane and as free from pain and suffering on the part of the patient as possible if we are to expect good or permanent results. ... I take it that it goes without saying that the incurable case should be supplied with his medicine. ... For old, infirm, incurable, or any other class of cases that are not treatable, I believe that a well-regulated dispensary, having a treatment institution to care for the curable cases, both run on honest, humane but practical and business like principles with the cooperation of the whole community is necessary. It is our duty to show these patients the some [sic] consideration that we have for those suffering from other kinds of sickness.[18]

Unsurprisingly, a narcotic agent called him "the most subtle opponent of the Harrison Narcotic Act in that part of the country."[19] One of his patients was driven out of town by a so-called Public Committee, the Ku Klux Klan.[20] After a cursory investigation based on biased interviews accompanied by inconsistent and false accusations of opiate trafficking to street hustlers, Butler's clinic was closed in 1923.[21] Needless to say, the narcotics police viewed Bishop and Butler as degenerate drug dealers making profits from prostitutes and dope fiends.

---

[18] Butler, Willis P. "How One American City is Meeting the Public Health Problems of Narcotic Drug Addiction," American Medicine, Volume XXVIII, Complete Series, Volume XVII, New Series, January-December. Burlington, VT: American Medical Publishing Company, 1922 AO, No. 3, March, pp. 161-162.

[19] Musto, 1999, p. 172.

[20] Musto, 1999, p. 171.

[21] Musto, 1999, p. 172.

For their part, the yellow press served up sensationalism, pure and simple. Favorite themes included Negroes coked up out of their minds, sinister Chinese plotting in opium dens, Mexican marijuana orgies, German morphine addicts bent on revenge, and drunken Irish and Italians. An exception to this peddling of fear and hysteria was an article by the physician in charge of the Philadelphia House of Corrections Robert A. Schless (1894 – 1972) adopting an unusually radical perspective on the issue, denying the menace of drug addicts and blaming drug addiction squarely on the legislation that created it:

> The menace of the drug addict to society exists, I believe, mainly in the minds of the uninformed .... I believe that most drug addiction today is due directly to the Harrison Anti-Narcotic Act, which forbids the sale of narcotics without a physician's prescription. Prior to the passage of this act, there was a limited number of drug addicts who went to the corner druggist for their day's or week's supply. They paid a moderate price for the then legitimate article of sale .... Addicts who are broke act as *agents provocateurs* for the peddlers, being rewarded by gifts of heroin or credit for supplies. The Harrison Act made the drug peddler, and the drug peddler makes drug addicts [italics original].[22]

Another physician and ex-president of the Society for the Study of Inebriety observed the same from the other side of the Atlantic:

> It appears that not only has the Harrison Law failed to diminish the number of drug takers – some contend, indeed, that it has increased their numbers – but, far from bettering the lot of the opiate addict, it has actually worsened it; for without curtailing the supply of the drug it has sent up the price tenfold, and this has had the effect of impoverishing the poorer class of addicts and reducing them to a condition of such abject misery as to render them incapable of gaining an honest livelihood.[23]

---

[22] Schless, Robert A. "The Drug Addict," The American Mercury, Volume IV, No. 4, February 1925 AO, Arts and Sciences, Sociology, pp. 196, 198.

[23] Campbell, Harry. "The Pathology and Treatment of Morphia Addiction," The

Nor were they alone as the uneasiness which the official interpretation of the *Harrison Act* produced in certain members of the American Medical Association (AMA) prompted a number of interesting field studies underwritten by the United States Public Health Service which also would contradict official Narcotics Division dogma.

Figure 327. "Dr. and Mrs. Willis P. Butler." Photograph, 1978. Courtwright, David et al. Addicts Who Survived: An Oral History of Narcotic Use in America before 1965. Knoxville, TN: University of Tennessee Press, 2012 AA, p. 276.

British Journal of Inebriety, Volume XX [found together with Volume XIX], 1922-23. London: Baillière, Tindall and Cox, 1923 AO, No. 4, April 1923, p. 151.

1. The American System

On the other hand, some physicians joined the anti-narcotic bandwagon. One member of the AMA's Committee on Narcotic Drugs wrote an editorial in 1921 denying both that addiction was a treatable disease as well as that maintenance doses prescribed by a physician was anything other than exploitation:

> Conspiracy
>
> From the beginning ... evidence has accumulated of a widespread and well organized conspiracy .... Those who find it profitable to exploit the victims of drug addiction by supplying them with narcotic drugs ... over prolonged periods or quite indefinitely ... desire to ... continue their exceedingly profitable traffic ... carried on under the pretense of medical treatment for an assumed 'disease.'
>
> Propaganda
>
> Public opinion regarding the vice of drug addiction has been deliberately and consistently corrupted through propaganda in both the medical and the lay press. Cleverly designed appeals ... plausible reiteration of certain pseudoscientific fallacies designed to confuse the unscientific mind ... are brought to bear on an unsuspecting public ....
>
> The shallow pretense that drug addiction is 'a disease' ... has been asserted and urged in volumes of 'literature' by the self-styled 'specialists.' ... [A] physician who supplies narcotic drugs to an addict ... is either grossly ignorant, or ... would exploit the miserable creatures of the addict world for sordid gain. ... For such there can be only one verdict. Suspend or revoke his license to practice medicine, by all means. Let him suffer the penalty of the law, and may God have mercy on his soul [quotation marks and exclamation mark original]![24]

[24] Prentice, Alfred C. "The Problem of the Narcotic Drug Addict," *The Journal of the Amercian Medical Association*, Volume 76, Number 23, 4 June 1921 AO, pp. 1552-1553, 1556.

Instead, the same physician argued for the use of various treatments along the lines of those advocated by Charles Barnes Towns (1862 – 1947),[25] including the use of "scopolamin hydrobromate ... sulphonal, choral [sic], paraldehyd," vomiting, and the "method of immediate and complete withdrawal of the drug ... in all cases not complicated with organic disease."[26]

Thirty years after the fact, in 1953 the US Bureau of Narcotics issued a pamphlet justifying their closing of the narcotic clinics in the early 1920s:

> During and after the year 1919, forty-four or more narcotic clinics or dispensaries were opened by municipal or State health officials in large cities throughout the United States .... In some clinics addicts were given diminishing amounts of narcotics until reaching a minimum dosage which would prevent withdrawal symptoms; in others cures of addiction were attempted in hospitals operated in conjunction with the clinics .... In still others the customary dosage was maintained, or often increased upon the demands of addicts. ... By the end of 1925 all of these clinics had been closed ....[27]

Most of the information in the self-congratulatory pamphlet was sourced from those with little or no medical training, newspaper articles, and cherry-picked opinion pieces. For example, the acting director of the Bureau of Public Health Education for the city of New York advocated in the 1920s for sudden forced withdrawal: "A plan called by the addicts 'cold turkey' ... is not only possible but practical. It does occasion some suffering [quotation marks original] ...."[28] Citing

---

25 See GHDV4P1, Chapter 22, C. The Debate over the Foster Bills, p. 1560 and GHDV4P1, Chapter 23, B. The *Harrison Act*, p. 1586.

26 Prentice, 1921, pp. 1553-1554.

27 Bureau of Narcotics. Narcotic Clinics in the United States. Washington, DC: Government Printing Office, 1953 BGU, pp. 1-2.

28 Bureau, 1953, p. 4.

"[e]xcerpts from press reports," the same source supposedly advised "*against the clinic plan and recommending institutional treatment solely. ... [T]here is no need for prolonging addiction by a continued supply of narcotics* [italics original].[29] Something similar to the Towns cure was used: "The drug was withdrawn within the first five days and hyoscin was administered for 3 days thereafter."[30] Official optimism about the therapeutic virtues of rapid institutional withdrawal dominated throughout the pamphlet. In Syracuse, New York the "doctor in charge expressed the opinion that at least 90 percent of the 92 clinic addicts could be cured of drug addiction if institutional treatment could be provided."[31]

Such optimism would prove to be unfounded. Andrew Grover DuMez (1885 – 1948), a physician on the Treasury's Special Committee tasked with reviewing the treatment of narcotic drug addiction for the Surgeon General found that in state institutions "only about 10 percent of cures have been reported. ... Our present methods of treating drug addiction must be considered failures."[32] Only private for profit centers reported any progress in rehabilitation, a success that quickly evaporated when evaluated under controlled conditions. For example, in 1919 the same committee reported that of "the total number of addicts treated in these [private] institutions, 74 per cent are stated to have been benefited to some degree, and 61 per cent are said to have been permanently cured of their addiction."[33]

---

29 Bureau, 1953, p. 5.

30 Bureau, 1953, p. 5.

31 Bureau, 1953, p. 7.

32 Musto, 1999, p. 145, citing "A. G. DuMez, 'Treatment of Drug Addiction,' memorandum to the Surgeon General, 28 Feb. 1919 (PHSR)" [fn 67, p. 355].

33 Rainey, Henry T., Chair, et al. <u>Traffic in Narcotic Drugs: Report of the Special Committee of Investigation Appointed March 25, 1918 by the Secretary of the Treasury</u>. Washington, DC: Government Printing Office, 1919 AO, p. 19.

However, as reported in Chapter 23, although Towns claimed a ninety percent success rate, when his collaborator tried the same cure at a state hospital, within eighteen months nearly eighty percent had reverted.[34]

In fact, even these numbers were too flattering. Of those discharged from the Public Health Service Hospital in Lexington, Kentucky in the early 1950s, few remained voluntarily abstinent (even loosely defined) over the course of a five year follow up study:

> It is estimated that only about 9 percent of the study population were voluntarily abstinent at 6 months after discharge from Lexington. ... Two years after discharge the estimated voluntarily abstinent rate increased to 17 percent. ... Only 12 of the patients in the sample group were voluntarily abstinent for the full 5 years [roughly three percent of the study cohort still living]. In this study, a patient is considered voluntarily abstinent at some time only if he refrains from the use of drugs willingly for at least one period of at least 3 consecutive months.[35]

A twelve year follow up study found similarly dismal results:

> In spite of ... relatively favorable conditions, within two years all but ten of the 100 patients again became addicted – at least temporarily .... Of the ten who did not, three died less than four years after discharge, two turned to alcohol, three had never used narcotics more than once a day and one used drugs intermittently after discharge. In other words, virtually all patients who had been physically addicted and did not die, relapsed. After leaving, 79 percent of the discharged patients used several shots of narcotics a day for at least 12 months. Although prior to coming to Lexington, only 46 percent of the patients had been imprisoned, after leaving Lexington 92 percent of the patients were imprisoned. ... Almost as many patients

---

[34] See GHDV4P1, Chapter 23, a. The Medical and the Nonmedical, pp. 1603-1604.

[35] Duvall, Henrietta J., et al. "Followup Study of Narcotic Drug Addicts Five Years After Hospitalization," *Public Health Reports*, Volume 78, No. 3, March 1963 [ncbi.nlm.nih.gov, hereinafter NIH], pp. 186, 188.

gave up drugs on their own ('cold turkey') without any formal treatment. Three of the patients who did not relapse after voluntary hospitalization had never been physically addicted [quotation marks, parentheses original].[36]

A twenty year follow up study of the same cohort of 100 narcotic addicts reported that "35 men had achieved *stable abstinence* [italics original]."[37] Confidence in this number should be tempered as "data derived from institutional records are inferior to using repeated urine testing and interviews."[38] Indeed,

more than *half* of the actively addicted men in this study were able to go for five years or more without being reported to the Federal Bureau of Narcotics and Dangerous Drugs. Over 25% of active addicts went for five years without being reported to the New York Narcotics Register [italics original].[39]

One quarter were still addicted after twenty years of long stays in hospitals and prisons: "[O]nly 25 of the original sample were thought to be still addicted. ... Since 1952, each of these 25 men had averaged seven voluntary hospitalizations, eight imprisonments, and had spent an average of four years in institutions."[40] However, of the seventeen classified as "uncertain," one had a record of active addiction in the past five years, four were on methadone, one had

---

[36] Vaillant, George E. "A Twelve-Year Follow-Up of New York Narcotic Addicts: I. The Relation of Treatment to Outcome," *American Journal of Psychiatry*, Volume 122, Issue 7, January 1966 AA, pp. 730-731.

[37] Vaillant, George E. "A 20-Year Follow-Up of New York Narcotic Addicts," Archives of General Psychiatry, Volume 29, Number 2, August 1973 AA, p. 238.

[38] Vaillant, 1973, p. 240.

[39] Vaillant, 1973, p. 240.

[40] Vaillant, 1973, p. 238.

relapsed to heroin, two were chipping, and six were actively addicted.[41] Twenty three were dead, only two from natural causes.[42]

Abstinence rates were three percent or less after voluntary hospitalization or less than nine months of imprisonment, while prison for more than nine months followed by parole of more than a year was more effective. So was supervised methadone maintenance, though the "average previous treatment record for *each* methadone success was one long imprisonment, five short imprisonments, and nine voluntary hospitalizations – all followed by relapse within a year [italics and exclamation mark original]!"[43] On average only three percent of addicts became stably abstinent each year.[44]

Figure 328. "Lexington, Kentucky PHS Hospital."
Aerial photograph. Courtwright (2012), p. 275.

---

41 Vaillant, 1973, pp. 238-239.

42 Vaillant, 1973, Table 2, p. 238.

43 Vaillant, 1973, Table 6, pp. 239, 241.

44 Vaillant, 1973, Table 3, pp. 238-239.

Figure 329. "Sir Humphry Davy Rolleston (1862 – 1944), seated holding a mace." George Henry (1858 – 1943). Oil on canvas, 1925. St. George's Hospital, London [artuk.org, hereinafter AR].

2. The British System

The British model could not be more different from the one in the United States. The obvious failure of the regime in the US led to the first serious medical and sociological investigations of those dependent on opiates in the United Kingdom. In 1924 Sir Humphry David Rolleston (1862 – 1944) was appointed chairman of a committee to "consider and advise as to the circumstances ... in which the supply of morphine and heroin ... to persons suffering from addiction to those drugs may be regarded as medically advisable."[45] His report two years later recommended a system which, from the middle 1920s to the middle 1960s [when it was disbanded], produced a "very small" number of addicts and a "negligible" number of illicit suppliers:

> 24. After careful examination of all the data put before us we are of the opinion that in Great Britain the incidence of addiction ... is still very small. ...
> 25. According to the Home Office and the police ... the purveyors of illicit supplies ... for addicts in this country is so small as to be almost negligible.[46]

The amount of bureaucracy devoted to the addicts was also small:

---

[45] Rolleston, Humphry, chair. Report of the Departmental Committee on Morphine and Heroin Addiction. London: His Majesty's Stationery Office, 1926 AO, 1/22.

[46] Brain, Russell, chair. The Report of the Second Interdepartmental Committee on Drug Addiction. London: Her Majesty's Stationery Office, 1961 [University of Stirling, onlinelibraryaddictions.stir.ac.uk, hereinafter UST], Extent of the Problem in Great Britain, 5/14.

26. We would emphasize that there is, in Great Britain, no system of registration of addicts, nor any scheme by which the authorities allocate to them regular supplies of the drugs they are taking. ... [H]owever, ... nearly all addicts are known to the Home Office, to the Ministry of Health and the Department of Health of Scotland.[47]

The recipe for achieving such excellent results from the Rolleston Committee was simple:

Section III. Circumstances in which it may be medically advisable to administer morphine or heroin to persons known to be suffering from addiction to these drugs.
45. ... [T]he use of morphine or heroin for the relief of pain, etc., due to organic disease ... such as inoperable cancer. In such cases, the administration of the drug for prolonged periods may, no doubt, produce a craving which might persist and develop into an addiction if the disease were cured. But there can be no question of the propriety of continuing to administer the drug in quantities necessary for relief of the disease, so long as it persists, ignoring for the time being the question, of possible production of addiction. ...
46. It is, of course, also necessary for a time to administer morphine or heroin to persons suffering from addiction to these drugs who are under treatment by the gradual reduction method. ...
47. [A]ny recommendations for dealing with the problem of addiction at the present time must take account of and make provision for the continued existence of two classes of persons, to whom the indefinitely prolonged administration of morphine or heroin may be necessary:
(a) Those in whom a complete withdrawal of morphine or heroin produces serious symptoms which cannot be treated satisfactorily under the ordinary conditions of private practice; and,
(b) Those who are capable of leading a fairly normal and useful life so long as they take a certain quantity, usually small, of their drug of addiction, but not otherwise [parentheses original].[48]

---

[47] Brain, 1961, 5/14.

[48] Rolleston, 1926, 10/22.

These recommendations were adopted and an official review commissioned by the British government forty years later found no reason to change the policy that had worked so well:

> Good results are more likely to be obtained with co-operative rather than coerced patients. At a time when the compulsory treatment of the mentally sick is being steadily diminished we see no ground for seeking new powers of compulsion for the treatment of drug addicts.[49]

This perspective, long since advocated by Bishop and Butler, had begun to be debated in the 1920s. Physicians opposed to the government's interpretation of the *Harrison Act* conducted several carefully detailed studies in that decade. These unequivocally described what was happening with US addicts, affected and not yet affected by the new restrictions on the dispensing of opiates.

One of the first was led by a surgeon with the Hygienic Laboratory of the Public Health Service, Lawrence Kolb (1881 – 1972),[50] who examined 119 cases of medical addiction, caused either iatrogenically (prescribed by physicians) or by self-medication for a disease, rheumatism being the most prevalent. Altogether, ninety individuals were steadily employed while twenty-nine were employed only part-time or not at all. In contrast with any cohort of chronic alcoholics, the general state of health of the opiate addicts and their ability to perform work, maintain social and domestic relations and so forth were incomparably better. According to Kolb:

---

[49] Brain, 1961, p. 5/14.

[50] See also GHDV4P1, Chapter 23, a. The Medical and the Nonmedical, pp. 1600 et seq.

Judged by the output of labor and their own statements, none of the normal persons had their efficiency reduced by opium. Twenty-two of them worked regularly while taking morphine for twenty-five years or more; one of them, a woman, aged 81, and still alert mentally, had taken 3 grains (0.19 Gm.) of morphine daily for sixty-five years. She gave birth to and raised six children and managed her household affairs with more than average efficiency. A widow, aged 66, had taken 17 grains (1.1 Gm.) of morphine daily for most of thirty-seven years. She is alert mentally but is bent with age and rheumatism. However, she does physical labor every day and makes her own living [parentheses original].[51]

Kolb's conclusions with regard to the physical health of addicts were confirmed a year later in a second careful study centered on the physical health of addicts:

We have been unable to detect any marked physical deterioration or impairment of physical fitness aside from the addiction per se in the series of cases of opium addiction studied during the administration of morphine. ...
A careful study of the data presented in this paper does not reveal any obvious deviation from the normal of the heart and circulation in human opium addicts during the administration of morphine sulphate to prevent withdrawal symptoms. ...
Studies of the stomach, kidney, liver, basal metabolism, thymus temperature, dextrose response to epinephrine and dextrose response to morphine revealed no fundamental differences from normal in addicts to whom morphine was administered to supply their needs ....[52]

---

[51] Kolb, Lawrence. "Drug Addiction: A Study of Some Medical Cases," Archives of Neurology and Psychiatry, Volume 20. Chicago, IL: American Medical Association, 1928 AA, No. 1, July, p. 178.

[52] Light, Arthur B. and Edward G. Torrance. "Opium Addiction," Archives of Internal Medicine, Volume 43. Chicago, IL: American Medical Association, 1929 AA, "II. Physical Characteristics and Physical Fitness of Addicts During Administration of Morphine," No. 3, March, p. 334; "III. The Circulation and Respiration of Human Addicts During the Administration of Morphine," No. 4, April, p. 563; "V. Miscellaneous Observations of Human Addicts During the Administration of Morphine," No. 6, July, pp. 888-889.

CH. 24 THE CRUSADE BEGINS (I)

The cases investigated by Kolb and others corresponded mainly to the type of addict in the United States before the prohibitionist machinery was fully operational. One must take into account that in 1920 there were only 170 narcotics agents in the entire country,[53] a number insufficient to effectively harass a large part of those long habituated to opiates. The typical addict then was sometimes referred to as a white southerner, part of a middle class made up of landlords, professionals and older women. Until prohibition marks them with its stigma, the vast majority were never even detected as assiduous drug users. Many were doctors using formidable quantities of morphine daily, working steadily and regarded eminently in their communities:

> Some addicts ... live to an advanced age. For example, the grandfather of an Indian graduate student in Indiana University has been using opiates since he was about twenty and is now more than ninety years old. There are many examples of drug addicts who have continued to engage in productive work and who have even had positions of eminence while they were using drugs.[54]

A century later, there will be a hundred times more agents dedicated to the repression and a hundred times more users of prohibited drugs. The DEA alone will employ "approximately 10,000 personnel throughout the world – Special Agents, Diversion Investigators, Intelligence Analysts, Chemists, and professional staff – across 24 domestic offices in 23 Divisions and 93 foreign offices

---

[53] Musto, 1999, p. 147, citing L. F. Schmeckebier's The Bureau of Prohibition: Its History, Activities, and Organization. Washington, DC: Lord Baltimore Press, 1929, pp. 309-310.

[54] Lindesmith, Alfred R. The Addict and the Law. Bloomington, IN: Indiana University Press, 1965 AA, Introduction, pp. x-xi.

across the globe."[55] Today the typical user is an adolescent who has committed a property crime to buy adulterated poison at an astronomical price, and whose death is euphemistically termed an overdose.

The evidence of those earlier long-lived and socially integrated stabilized addicts contrasts with the short lives and self-destructiveness of contemporary addicts who consume substitutes in a vampirish ritual, buying irresponsibility because the circumstances imposed upon them by law for the satisfaction of their vice demand it. By the same definition, those middle-aged and elderly habitués at the beginning of the twentieth century were also dope fiends, though they scrupulously obeyed all other laws. Today, he who commits parricide to purchase cornstarch and strychnine is a victim not of the vague trace of an opiate but of a specific system that foments such deception and poisoning.

Few facts so nakedly illustrate the circular and self-referential reasoning of those early moral entrepreneurs. In reality, what they deemed inadmissible was the fact that the majority of users of opiates led satisfactory lives without harassment or stigma. From the United States, this demonization will spread to the rest of the world.

---

[55] "About the DEA," Dea.gov, first page, retrieved February 2024.

B. Closing the Clinics

From its founding, the agents of the Narcotics Division of the Prohibition Unit of the Treasury Department[56] tried to intimidate or incarcerate doctors who prescribed opium, morphine and cocaine outside of the operating room or for cases of great temporary pain. But this very enforcement then led previously unrecognized addicts to come to the attention of the political authorities who recognized the need for the creation of narcotic dispensaries:

> In the spring of 1919 a situation arose that had to be met. There were a large number of people ... who were using morphine – some because of suffering from incurable diseases, some from untreated or unsuccessfully treated physical conditions ... and some because they had a morphine habit .... All of these people were in some manner obtaining the drug previously, but now the supply was almost suddenly stopped, and there was great suffering. ... Due to a fear or natural disinclination on the part of doctors and druggists to have anything to do with an addict ... many sick people were caused to suffer terribly, or to seek the peddler. These people began coming to the officers of the law and to the board of health officials begging for relief. ... To meet the situation our dispensary was started.[57]

As a result, the agents of the Narcotics Division now needed to close these new institutions dedicated to maintenance therapy or gradual reduction. Of course, when this policy begins to be enforced, relations between the therapeutic and political estates are already strained.

---

[56] "Shortly after the passage of the Harrison Act, the Narcotic Division was organized in the Bureau of Internal Revenue. When the Prohibition Unit was established in the Bureau of Internal Revenue in 1920, the Narcotic Division became one of its branches; it continued in this status until the Prohibition Bureau was created in 1927, when it was transferred to that organization" (Schemeckebier, 1929, Chapter I History, p. 3).

[57] Butler, 1922, pp. 154-155.

While they were fighting a losing battle against government intrusion, the medical profession was also trying to enforce its own rigorous monopoly on the most effective psychotropic medicines in the pharmacopoeia, in the process feeding the public every kind of popular superstition about the magical and sinister power of certain drugs. The APhA had been supporting prohibitionist principles since the beginning of the century, officially affirming that assassins were angels compared to dispensers without a diploma, as well as suggesting expelling minorities for their pharmacological preferences: "If the Chinaman cannot get along without his 'dope,' we can get along without him [quotation marks original]."[58] The AMA had collaborated even more with the strict prohibitionists, and in the 1920s its compromises with the apparatus of the State bore fruit in the form of substantial increases in political and economic power.

These professional guilds could hardly lament that lay society had made the stereotype of the dope fiend its own, the very existence of such an infernal creature betraying the avidity of diabolic doctors, dedicated to their own pocketbooks. Neither of the major medical associations understood that their monopoly on drugs really meant putting themselves at the mercy of prohibitionists, and that practicing professionals will from now on suffer massively from accusations provoked by police disguised as patients. As with any crime of pure risk (and inquisitional inquiries), the *Harrison Act* implied that its enforcers could preempt the commission of a crime, inducing it through various strategems.[59] They did not fail to do so, since a good

---

[58] Hynson, Henry B. "Report of the Committee on Acquirement of the Drug Habit," Proceedings of the American Pharmaceutical Association at the Fiftieth Annual Meeting held at Philadelphia, PA, September, 1902. Baltimore, MD: Published by the APhA, 1902 AO, Minutes of the Section on Education and Legislation, p. 572.

[59] In 1928 Congress "authorized the advance of money to narcotic agents to

service record could be constructed by incriminating traitorous doctors as much as by arresting Capone's henchmen. Few physicians opted for heroism.

Clinic doctors generally did not feel that addicts should be deprived of their supply unless there was some real chance of a cure, and we have already seen that the leading scholars of addiction did not consider deprivation to be a cure. In marked contrast, the Treasury considered the policy of the doctors perverse. But it understood its position was especially dangerous in the realm of public opinion, because its agents had observed that judges and juries also demanded some kind of alternative to maintenance or gradual disintoxication in order to convict.

Finally, it is worth noting that this tense relationship between the administration and a sector of the medical estate happens at a moment when the stereotype of the dope fiend is experiencing both a significant expansion as well as an important retraction. The expansion occurs as the crusade begins to inflame the population, the passive belief in the prohibitionist becoming an active belief in individuals who consider themselves dope fiends. The retraction comes from the practitioners of psychoanalytic thought just then taking shape in the US, with new professions integrating themselves into traditional therapy like psychoanalysts, social workers and counselors who consider addiction a complex psychic dynamic, capable of appearing not only in malignant beings but in anyone at all.

---

purchase drugs in order to obtain evidence of sale. Prior to the passage of the act an agent was required to make purchases with his own funds, reimbursement afterward being made to him by the Treasury (Schemeckebier, 1929, p. 35).

Figure 330. "Stephen Geyer Porter (1869 – 1930)." Harris & Ewing. Glass negative, c. 1915. Bain News Service. Library of Congress, Prints and Photographs Division, Washington, DC LG.

1. Numbering the Addicts

Coincident to the dismantling of the clinic system, the Chairman of the House Foreign Affairs Committee, Stephen Geyer Porter (Rep. PA, 1869 – 1930) quoted from a 1919 Treasury committee report which, after noting the "difficulties in obtaining information," reported that the "committee is of the opinion that the total number of addicts in this country probably exceeds 1,000,000 at the present time."[60] Although demonstrably false, what is most interesting about these statements repeated in 1923 is that they will become true some forty years later when the laws will be as strict as the ones he was asking for.

He did not quote from another section of the 1919 report which exaggerated the numbers even more while admitting they were all mere guesses:

> *Extent of drug addiction.* – The number of individuals addicted to the use of opium, its preparations or alkaloids, and coca leaves, their preparations and alkaloids, in the United States has, at various times, been estimated to be from 200,000 to 4,000,000. These estimates must, however, be looked upon as mere guesses in most cases because of the fact that there have been no means available for reaching an accurate estimate in the past [italics original].[61]

Nor did he quote from the first sentence in the Foreword, absolving the report's creators of any responsibility for the inaccuracy of the numbers:

---

[60] Porter, Stephen G. Remarks of Hon. Stephen G. Porter, Chairman, Committee on Foreign Affairs in the House of Representatives February 26, 1923. Washington, DC: Government Printing Office, 1923 HT, p. 3.

[61] Rainey, 1919, p. 20.

In publishing the report of the Special Narcotic Committee the department does not vouch for the accuracy of the figures given nor assume finality for the conclusions arrived at. A careful reading of the report will make clear the reasons for this statement. Complete and accurate statistics of the extent of drug addiction have never been compiled and are not now available.[62]

Even more fatuously, another report on the total number of addicts in the United States cited estimates ranging from 100,000 to 500,000 based on a very limited consensus of three colluding bureaucrats before concluding [honestly] that no one knows:

In April, 1924, Colonel Nutt, Chief of the Narcotic Division under the Treasury Department, in a survey made by himself, estimated there were 500,000 drug addicts in the United States ... [while in 1926 three other bureaucrats] made estimates of the number of drug addicts in the United States, on blank pieces of paper ... and curiously enough, each of the three estimates was 500,000. ... Unofficially, Mr. Ralph Oyler, Chief Narcotic Agent, New York City, estimates there are probably 330,000 or more drug addicts in the United States, while an official of the Public Health Service estimates that there are only 109,000. ... Colonel Arthur Woods, Former Police Commissioner of New York City, and United States representative at the International Opium Conference, estimated that there were approximately 200,000 drug addicts in the United States .... No one knows the actual amount of drug addiction in the United States, and it is doubtful whether it can ever be ascertained to any degree of accuracy ....[63]

Exaggerated numbers were still being quoted in 1927 at the first world conference on narcotic education:

---

[62] Rainey, 1919, p. 3.

[63] Brewster, Sidney W. "Actual Trend of Drug Addiction and its Relation to Crime," *Narcotic Education Bulletin of the World Conference on Narcotic Education and the International Narcotic Education Association*, Volume 1, No. 1, July, 1927 AA, Part I, p. 12.

> While it is probably impossible to estimate accurately the number of drug addicts in the United States, the special committee appointed by the Secretary of the Treasury, in their report dated April 15, 1919 ... stated that it is their opinion that the total number of addicts in this country probably exceeds 1,000,000. This was in the year 1919. ... I am, however, satisfied that the number of addicts has increased greatly since 1919 .... Some observers claim that the number of addicts is greatly overestimated, that there are not more than say 110,000 in the United States today, that it is on the decrease because of the less available supply of the drug ....[64]

The number of addicts in New York City was said to range from 39,000 to 75,000, numbers never before questioned:

> Several years ago, Dr. Carleton Simon, Special Deputy Commissioner, New York City Police Department, in charge of the Narcotic Squad, stated that the Police Department of New York City had records of 75,000 narcotic violators. ... The Drug Control Commission of New York State recorded 39,000 addicts in the State of New York .... The figures, however, are authentic, and have never been questioned.[65]

They should have been. The lower figure came via the Commissioner of the New York Narcotic Drug Control Commission who based it upon his own personal recollection of only a few of the actual registered addicts [13,000] with whom he had had conversations:

---

[64] Owens, Clarence J., Jr., Secretary. Report of the First Annual Conference of Committees of the World Conference on Narcotic Education and International Narcotic Education Association. Washington, DC: World Conference on Narcotic Education, 1927 AA, First Session, Thursday, November 3, Address by Dr. Amos Osborne Squire, pp. 14-15.

[65] Brewster, 1927, p. 12.

One of the first questions that is asked by those who are interested in the subject of drug addiction is, How many drug addicts are there in the State? ... I think a safe and conservative approximation would be 39,000. The records of the Department show in round numbers 13,000 registered addicts. This number is composed of those who obtain habit-forming drugs through legitimate sources, that is directly from a doctor or on prescriptions issued by a doctor, filled by a druggist, or from the different clinics established throughout the State. To these figures should be added twice the number, which is an approximation of the users who obtain drugs from peddlers, or other illicit sources. Of course, this latter figure, as I have stated, is only an approximation. I base it on the percentage of addicts among the great number with whom I have personally conferred, who have admitted that they obtained their drugs from peddlers and other illicit sources [question mark original].[66]

The director of a large city hospital expressed his disgust with such apocalyptic estimations attempting to provoke panic and unrest in the masses, when in reality these exaggerations arrived only via bureaucratic functionaries trying to obtain more funding for their own departments. According to the hospital director, the figures from the moral entrepreneurs were as mythical as the belief in gradual reduction:

Of 7,464 cases observed from April 10, 1919, to Jan. 15, 1920, in the Department of Health clinic .... In the clinic, 7,464 cases were cared for; and while gradual reduction (one-half grain every other day) was the custom, yet it was extremely difficult to hold our patients to schedule. A number openly opposed reduction; and when the amount was cut down about half, they left the clinic, not to return, or to return under a different name to commence again at the maximum dosage (15 grains) and pursue another course of reduction. Many were detected doubling in this manner [parentheses original].[67]

---

[66] Herrick, Walter R., Commissioner. Second Annual Report of the Narcotic Drug Control Commission. Albany, NY: J. B. Lyon Company, 1920 AO, Bulletin No. 1, Work of the State Department, p. 5 [included together with the First Annual Report].
[67] Hubbard, S. Dana. "Some Fallacies Regarding Narcotic Drug Addiction," *The Journal of the American Medical Association*, Volume 74, No. 21, 22 May 1920 AO, pp.

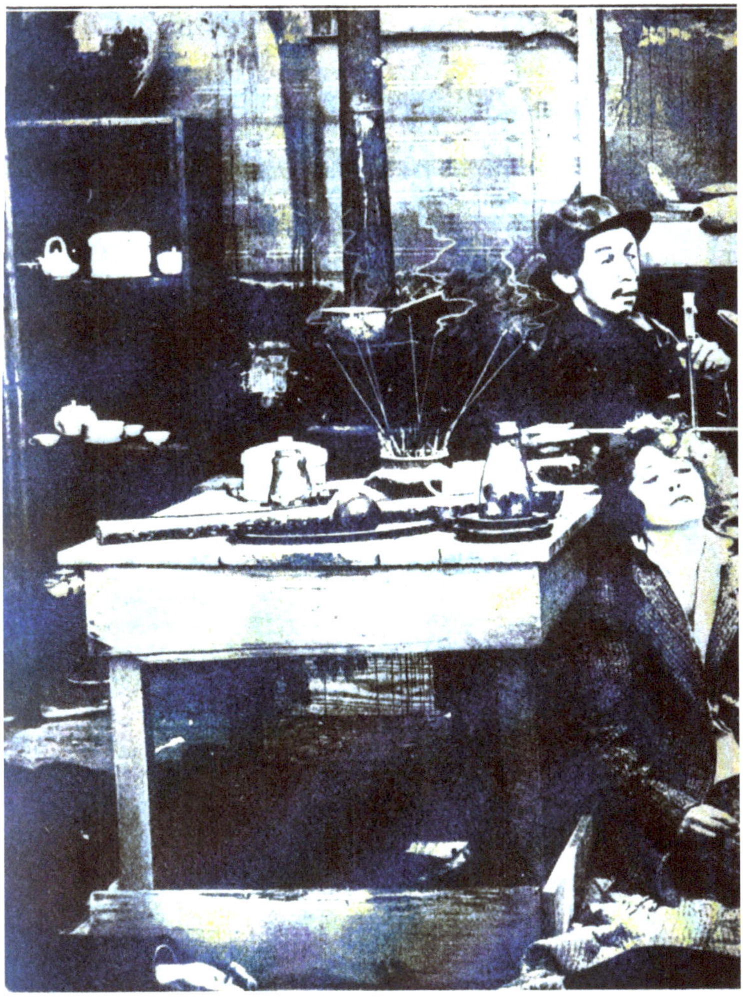

Figure 331. "While the morphine, heroin, and cocaine addict desires above all else to be alone, the opium smoker goes to a 'joint' that other smokers frequent [quotation marks original]." Rowell, Earl Albert. Battling the Wolves of Society: the Narcotic Evil. Mountain View, CA: Pacific Press Publishing Association, 1929 [hathitrust.org, hereinafter HT], p. 26.

1439, 1440.

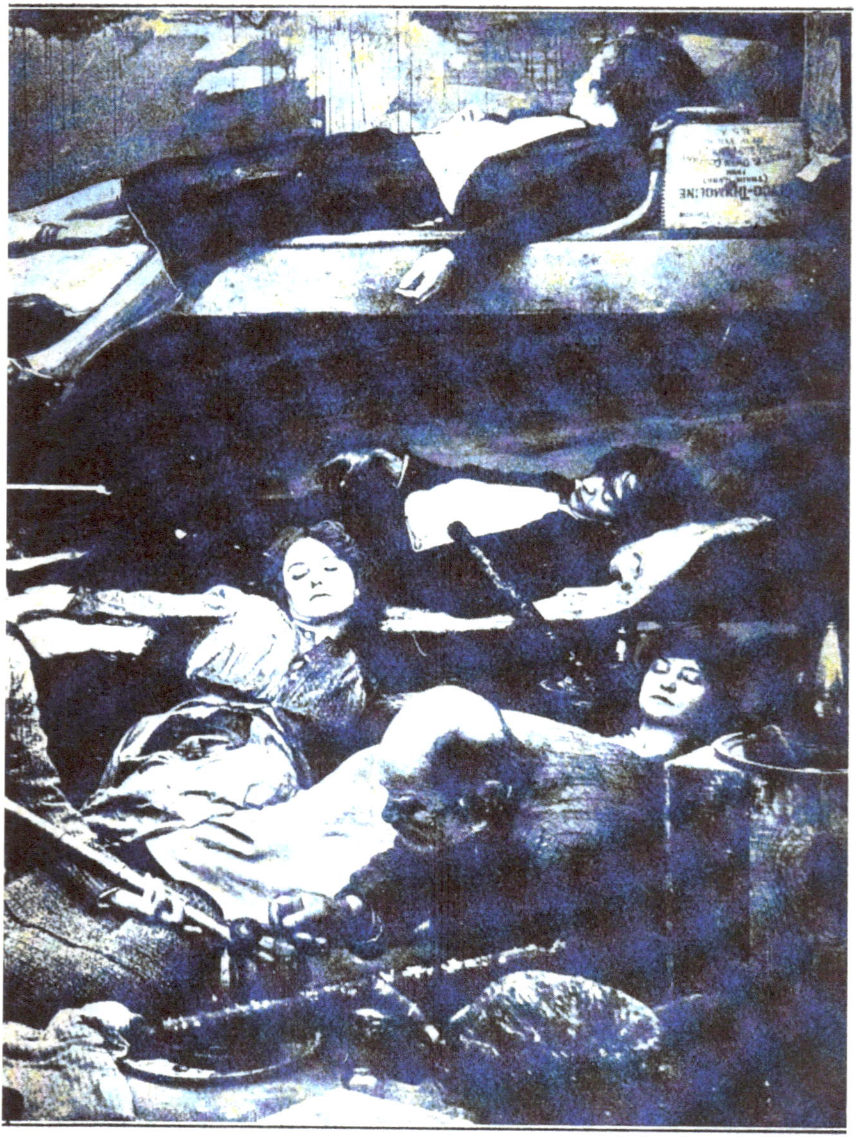

Figure 332. "Here, reclining on a dirty bench, he cooks his 'pill,' and inhales the pungent vapors of burning opium, and immediately is at peace with every one [quotation marks original]." Rowell, 1929, p. 27.

2. Changing Demographics

Throughout the 1920s the age, sex, wealth, ethnicity and choice of drug began to change as the clinics were forced to close. In 1922 the median age of an addict at Butler's Shreveport clinic was forty one, males outnumbering females.[68] The median ages at other clinics were similar. Within a few years succumbed the narcotic clinics in Albany, Houston, New Haven, Atlanta, New Orleans and Shreveport.

At Shreveport, the aforementioned Dr. Butler (who continued to treat 129 registered patients in the face of federal attacks) had received the

> cooperation, assistance, hearty approval and commendation of every branch of our government locally, including the City Judge, Police Department, City Commission Council, State Board Inspector, City and Parish Boards of Health, Sheriff and his department, City and Parish Medical Society, the U. S. Marshal, U. S. District Attorney and U. S. Judge.[69]

Butler was soon denounced by an undercover agent who he described "as vile and vulgar a man as I ever had to converse with."[70] The agent claimed Dr. Butler was freely distributing drugs to street peddlers and prostitutes. Lacking any evidence for his accusations, the agent interviewed "40 percent of the registrants" hoping to find the proof needed to close the clinic. The recorded interviews betrayed more about the agent and his purposes and prejudices than about the interviewees:

---

[68] Butler, 1922, p. 158.

[69] Butler, 1922, p. 155.

[70] Musto, 1999, p. 170.

E. W. – 39 years old, occupation sign worker, not working. ... [R]eceiving 11 grains daily from Dr. Butler .... '[A] drug addict, pure and simple.'
Mrs. M. – 'Looks good and healthy but claims she feels bad if she doesn't get her daily allowance of morphine ... a typical drug addict ... no visible means of support.'
Mrs. S. – 37 years old, 8 years an addict, received 10 grains daily, had no visible means of support. Appeared to the agents as 'a good healthy plain everyday drug addict.'
J. R. – 54 years old, morphinist for 20 years, 'a physical wreck' receiving 10 grains daily. Although 'appearing in very poor condition' the agents were 'naturally unable to tell if he was affected with any ailment' but warned against his use as a witness in any prosecution due to his 'physical appearance.'
B. J. – Prostitute, 32 years old, addict for 12 years .... '[T]he picture of health; strongly built, and to our minds is a simple vicious addict.'
W. M. – 'a well-known bootlegger in liquor and narcotics' who had been driven out of Oil City by 'a Public Committee' (the Ku Klux Klan).
M. P. – 52 years old, storekeeper, 'a respectable man' .... He would like to stop taking the drug and could do so 'providing it is hard to get same.' ...
S. W. H. – 39 years old, claimed to have been off morphine several times for as long as 2 weeks at a time 'when he was unable to obtain it [italics, quotation marks, parentheses original].'[71]

It's significant that the ages of the patients at the Shreveport clinic (in Musto's excerpt from the agent's report) range from thirty-two to fifty-four and include not a single adolescent. Butler (as noticed) records the average age of his patients as being forty-one: "Since our beginning we have had a total of over 740 patients on roll. We now have about 120. The ages run from 21 to 81 years, averaging about 41 years of age."[72] This appears to contradict Congressman Porter's claim that most of the heroin addicts in the country were

[71] Musto, 1999, pp. 170-172.

[72] Butler, 1922, p. 158.

young, many under the age of twenty,[73] quoting from the 1919 Treasury report.[74]

But Butler was generally not seeing heroin addicts: "Morphine is the drug of addiction almost exclusively, and we seldom see a heroin addict."[75] Further, his clinic only dispensed to incurable cases:

> Only incurable cases and those in which after examination and investigation we think treatment not at present indicated are dispensed to. Curable cases are put into the institution for a cure as soon as practical. Each incurable case is examined and classified as such by from two to seven reputable physicians.[76]

For these older morphine addicts, the "average length of time of addiction is about 13 years."[77] Within months of the closing of Butler's clinic, the "Shreveport *Journal* investigated the city's drug traffic and claimed that morphine and cocaine were being freely sold, whereas before the closing of the clinic the traffic was practically unknown [italics original]."[78]

Practically the same thing happened with the Atlanta clinic which "provided narcotic prescriptions for about 200 addicts."[79] After a Treasury agent's investigation, "the Atlanta clinic dropped half its registrants and retained ninety-five who were described, at least by the city physicians, as incurable for medical reasons or of such long-

---

[73] Porter, 1923, p. 3; see previous section.

[74] Rainey, 1919, p. 24.

[75] Butler, 1922, p. 155.

[76] Butler, 1922, p. 155.

[77] Butler, 1922, p. 158.

[78] Musto, 1999, p. 174.

[79] Musto, 1999, p. 176.

standing addiction that they must be continued on the rolls."[80] A second investigation led to its closing, recommending that

> city physicians be informed ... that prescriptions from then on would be scrutinized with great care. In cases of narcotic law violation, prosecution would be recommended. ... By 1925 the Atlanta clinic had faded away. It had succumbed to repeated investigations and threats to the physicians, although no indictments are known to have been sought or obtained.[81]

The agent responsible for the initial investigation (along with an accomplice) were later "arrested and dropped from the service" because they "would visit a town, blackmail addicts, *shake down* druggists and doctors and vanish [italics original]."[82]

It is unnecessary to clarify that none of the agents charged with discerning the difference between incurable and curable patients held diplomas from a medical school or even qualified as health care assistants, while Butler's clinic (as previously noted) relied upon the services of from "two to seven reputable physicians"[83] to make such a determination. By 1925 there was not a single institution ministering to inveterate addicts. Only a few doctors continued to prescribe opiates to patients on an individual basis because of the obvious risk. Cocaine and opiates began to flow into the country from elsewhere, as yet without high levels of adulteration, but with prices that invited those less favored by fortune to crime.

Compare the economics of the Shreveport clinic:

---

[80] Musto, 1999, p. 176.

[81] Musto, 1999, p. 176.

[82] Howard, Sidney. "The Inside Story of Dope in this Country," *Hearst's International*, Volume XLIII, No. 2, February 1923 AO, p. 142.

[83] Butler, 1922, p. 155.

The morphine which we dispense is bought wholesale for about 3c. a grain, and sold at 6c. a grain. This is less than the retail price of about 10c. a grain and the peddler's price of about $1.00 a grain. No profit is allowed to anyone, and the difference between the cost and the selling price pays the actual operating expenses of the dispensary and the treatment department. There is no appropriation for this work, but it is entirely self-supporting.[84]

The age, wealth, sex, ethnicity and choice of drug of the typical addict changed as a result of the repression. An older group composed mainly of white, suburban, middle-class, over 40-year-old men and women consuming prescribed pharmaceuticals like morphine was giving way to a younger group of poor, urban, black and brown adolescent males concentrated in the ghettoes of New York, Chicago, Washington and Puerto Rico, as well as scattered along the Mexican frontier with Arizona, New Mexico and Texas. These younger consumers were harassed by the persecution and high prices, stealing and dealing to subsist, with high instances of common criminality and absenteeism. They belonged to more or less segregated ethnic minorities, using illicit drugs to better suffer their daily misery, internalizing the cliché of the dope fiend.

Two sociologists later found they could connect the characteristics of an addict with that country's so-called control policies toward that addict's choice of drug:

The general nature of the addicted population of any nation can be most easily predicted from a knowledge of the type of control policy in use. Control by prohibition and police suppression seems to be regularly associated with a concentration of addiction among young, urban males of the lower or criminal classes who also have the easiest access to illicit sources of supply. [Where] ... opiates are available primarily by medical prescription ... the addicts are older, the sex ratio is

[84] Butler, 1922, p. 157.

about even, there is a disproportionate number of addicts from the medical profession, and there is little connection between addiction and delinquency or crime.

The analysis of *availability* inevitably leads one into the midst of a public debate on policy questions. If the structure of access to the drugs defines the terms and conditions of drug addiction, and the techniques of public policy and legislative enactment are latently supportive of the illegal traffic, then it is inescapable that the risk population in addiction could be changed by instituting new policy. ... A theory which attributes addiction rates to strains inherent in our culture and social structure, without considering the impact of present policies, makes our drug problem appear more like an act of God than a consequence of the way it is handled [italics original] ....[85]

Figure 333. "*Narcotic* (1933)." Directed by Dwain Esper and Vidal Sodar't, written by A. J. Karnopp and Hildegarde Stadie, starring Harry Cording, Joan Dix and Patricia Farley [imdb.com, hereinafter IMDB].

[85] Lindesmith, Alfred R. and John H. Gagnon. "Anomie and Drug Addiction," Anomie and Deviant Behavior: A Discussion and Critique, ed. Marshall B. Clinard. NY: The Free Press, 1964 AA, The Effects of Control Policies, pp. 167-168.

Figure 334. "Andrew W. Mellon (1855 – 1937)." Harris & Ewing, photographers. Glass negative, c. 1905 – 1945. Library of Congress, Prints and Photographs Division, Washington, DC LG.

C. Opening the Farms

Prohibitionist logic was based on the premise that without maintenance clinics (and with doctors and druggists maintained in a state of permanent intimidation) the problem of addiction would be resolved. In other words, it would be enough to cut the supply to some 10,000 registered addicts and block the supply to (by at least one estimate) some 100,000 others in order to achieve the desired decontamination of society. But what happened afterwards was a different story that led to creation of the so-called narcotic farms.

Converted into a business by any risk-taking gang, mythologized by both the aspirational poor and the most powerful (especially in the world of fashion and spectacle), aided and abetted by the corruption of the repressors, the opiates and cocaine flourished even more than before 1914, all of which will scandalously occur with alcohol after that drug is prohibited. What Narcotics Division propaganda overlooked was the very relevant growth and consolidation of a black market their actions had created.

While the hunt for diabolic doctors and infernal pharmacists was at its peak, at the highest levels what stands out is the lack of any hope of ending rapidly or even slowly the growing imports of narcotic drugs. In a 1921 letter to the Chairman of the House Ways and Means Committee, the Secretary of the Treasury Andrew William Mellon (1855 – 1937) warned:

> Another result of the limitation of imports of narcotic drugs is the stimulus which this is likely to give to smuggling. Reports made to the office of the chief of the customs division show conclusively that smuggling of narcotics in the United States is on the increase to such an extent that the customs officers seem to be unable to suppress the traffic to any appreciable extent.[86]

---

[86] Hadley, Lindley H., Chairman Committee on Ways and Means. Sixty-Seventh

In spite of this, the agents at the lower levels of his Narcotics Division maintained a posture of complete intransigence toward maintenance therapies. They promised to free the country from an infectious plague once it had closed all the clinics dedicated to treating addicts by these and similar methods. But it seems Mr. Mellon did not take into account that doing away with the supply of cheap, pure and legal opiates meant turning the market over to the very smugglers his customs officers were so far unable to suppress.

The impotence of the customs services mentioned by Secretary Mellon meant that massive duty-free imports would now supply clandestine traffickers in the newly prohibited drugs. Though this would affect the work of domestic narcotics agents, importation was the purview of the Bureau of Customs:

> The Bureau of Prohibition is a branch of the Treasury Department having charge of the enforcement of all laws prohibiting or authorizing the manufacture, sale, and use of intoxicating liquors and narcotic drugs. It is not directly concerned with the prevention of smuggling of these articles, which is part of the work of the Bureau of Customs and the Coast Guard.[87]

Estimates of the amount of narcotics smuggled into the country was difficult because they were "smuggled in small packages usually concealed on the person"[88] but some idea of the amount of liquor smuggled [up 75%] across the Canadian border was possible

---

Congress, Second Session, December 5, 1921 – September 22, 1922, House Reports (Public), Volume 2. Washington, DC: Government Printing Office, 1922 HT, Importation and Exportation of Narcotic Drugs, 27 March 1922, Report No. 852, Report to Accompany H. R. 2193, p. 19.

[87] Schmeckebier, The Brookings Institution, 1929 AO, Service Monographs of the United States Government No. 57, Chapter I, History, p. 1.

[88] Schemeckebier, 1929, p. 16.

because a substantial amount of the liquor passes through Canadian customs and official record is made thereof. In practice, the liquor runner clears his cargo regularly through the Canadian customs before proceeding to evade the United States customs in making delivery. No one would contend that all of the liquor which is smuggled across the northern boundary passes regularly through the Canadian customs. ... Based on the figures supplied by the Canadian Department of Trade and Commerce it will be noted that in the course of three years the volume of this traffic [in whisky only] has increased more than 75 per cent.[89]

Naturally, Congress threw money at the problem they themselves had created. In 1915 appropriations to the Bureau of Prohibition for restricting the sale of opium were $150,000, not all of which was spent; by 1930 appropriations were roughly $1,600,000 for narcotics control generally.[90] The budget tripled in the decade of the 1920s: "Annual appropriations for narcotic control gradually rose during the decade from almost half a million dollars in fiscal year 1920 to $1.6 million for fiscal year 1930."[91] In 1919 the political authority had enormously exaggerated the size of the problem, raising the number of addicts in the country to over a million. In 1930, when the bureaucrats in charge of the repression were required to show progress, the Chief of the Narcotics Division Levi G. Nutt (1866 – 1938) denied before Congress that there was any change in the number

---

89 Schemeckebier, 1929, pp. 16-17, citing Attorney General, Annual Report, 1928, pp. 36-37.

90 Schemeckebier, 1929, Appendix 5, Financial Statement, p. 309.

91 Musto, 1999, p. 189, citing on page 371, footnote 29, 'Hearings before House Appropriation Committee,' Treasury Dept. Appropriations Bill 1931, 29 Nov 1929, 71 Cong. 2nd Sess., p. 345.

Figure 335. "Levi G. Nutt (1866 – 1938)." National Photo Company. Glass negative, 1920-1921. Library of Congress, Prints and Photographs Division, Washington, DC LG.

of addicts: "At these [congressional] hearings Nutt estimated that there were fewer than 100,000 addicts in the U. S. and strongly disagreed that the addiction problem was increasing."[92]

Refusing to abide by this stereotype, the United Kingdom had in 1930 scarcely a thousand addicts, all under the control of physicians. With its moral crusade, the US incarcerated nearly 80,000 of its citizens for violations of the *Harrison Act* between 1916 and 1928, and faced hundreds of thousands more, born literally out of the prohibition, as much from simple passive resistance to a law considered

[92] Musto, 1999, p. 371, fn 29.

unconstitutional as from, more frequently, the secondary benefits derived from violating its precepts. Where Crafts, Brent and Wright had been opposed to a group of older, employed addicts, Nutt and his successors now confronted political protests and an army of the wretched (self-identifying with the oppressor) driven to a life of crime to satisfy a pharmacological preference.

By 1929 the Narcotics Division had grown from 170 to around 270 agents.[93] Those Treasury personnel devoted to alcohol prohibition had twenty times as many, and not arbitrarily so, as there were many more violations of the *Volstead Act* as there were of the *Harrison Act.* However, the penalties for the latter were much more severe than for the former:

The average number of federal liquor convictions with prison sentences during the years 1922-24 was about 31,000 annually, the average sentence between 20 and 30 days. For the same period the annual average number of federal narcotic convictions with prison sentences was about 4,000 with an average sentence that grew from 10 months in 1922 to 14 months in 1924.[94]

By 1928 nearly a third of all federal prisoners had been arrested for drug crimes:

On June 30, 1928, of the 7738 federal prisoners in the four federal penitentiaries for men and in the Federal Institution for Women, 2529, almost a third, were imprisoned for violation of the drug laws. The next largest distribution for crime groups was 1156 for violation of the National Prohibition Act [alcohol] and 1148 for transporting a stolen motor vehicle in interstate commerce.[95]

---

[93] Musto, 1999, p. 184.

[94] Musto, 1999, p. 368, fn 6.

[95] Schemeckebier, 1929, Chapter II Activities, p. 143, citing House Hearings on Department of Justice appropriation bill, 1930. Seventieth Congress, second session, pp. 134, 136.

This data is important because it shows that by the end of the 1920s so-called drug addiction accounted for the largest single category of inmates.

The figures for violations of the *Harrison Act* from 1916 to 1928 are as follows:

1916: 1,900	1921: 4,300	1924: 10,300
1917: 1,100	1922: 6,700	1925: 10,300
1918: 1,300	1923: 7,200	1926: 10,300
1919: 2,400		1927: 8,900
1920: 3,900		1928: 8,700.[96]

The first five years sum to 10,600 while the last five years sum to 48,500, an enormous increase in the number of arrests of over 400 percent. The increase was very nearly equal to the increase of the legal importation of opium and coca leaves which three decades earlier was said to justify the concerns of the US Congress; except that then the investigating committee did not want to admit the influence of a change in the tariff which had distorted the calculations.

The number of addicts in custody was so high it led to the creation of so-called narcotic farms in Lexington, Kentucky and Fort Worth, Texas "for the treatment of all federal prisoners addicted to narcotics, and not merely those convicted under the narcotic laws."[97] One consequence of these institutions being administered by the Public Health Service occurred when Dr. Kolb was appointed director

[96] Musto, 1999, p. 368, fn 6, citing 'Hearings before the House Appropriation Committee,' Treasury Dept. Appropriation Bill 1930, 23 Nov. 1928, 70th Cong., 1st Sess., p. 475.

[97] Schemeckebier, 1929, Chapter II Activities, p. 143, fn 17, citing the "act of January 19, 1929 (45 Stat. L., 1085)" and noting that: "An inmate of the farm is not entitled to parole unless he is certified as being no longer a narcotic addict."

of the Lexington farm in 1935 and began rigorously to study the issue. He realized quickly that the regimen of forced rehabilitation under prison conditions was radically opposed to both medicine and law. Thanks to him and to the volunteers at Lexington, the hysteria surrounding the opiates would begin to subside, and he remained until he retired as Assistant Surgeon General an implacable critic of this kind of legislatively mandated treatment. By the time he left, he had scientifically established that simply administering a maintenance dose of morphine was incomparably less harmful than repeatedly going through withdrawal symptoms from the various so-called treatments then in vogue:

> The belladonna group of drugs has been widely used in the treatment of opium addiction .... Treatment by these drugs is absolutely useless and even harmful to addicts in withdrawal .... [T]hose receiving sodium rhodanate suffered more than the controls. ... Two of these cases had been taking only four grains of morphine daily for two and six years, respectively, and both of them became wildly delirious and psychotic during withdrawal .... [T]he narcosan treatment was not only not beneficial, but it increased all the distressing symptoms of withdrawal and was positively dangerous to life. ... [I]nsulin had no effect on withdrawal symptoms. ... The only effect ... noticed from the blister treatment was that the blister caused considerable discomfort. ... While employing a five-day 'sleep method' in which the patients were kept in a semi-sleep condition through the administration of luminal and certain hypnotics, sedatives and analgesics, [investigators] lost two patients out of fifty treated by them. ... [R]ossium had no value in the treatment of drug addiction. ... Sudden or too rapid withdrawal may cause death but unwise treatments have contributed to most withdrawal deaths [quotation marks original].[98]

---

[98] Kolb, Lawrence and C. K. Himmelsbach. "Clinical Studies of Drug Addiction, III. A Critical Review of the Withdrawal Treatments with Method of Evaluating Abstinence Syndromes," Supplement 128 to *Public Health Reports*, January 1938 AA, Summary and Conclusions, pp. 762, 768, 772, 774, 776-777, 782, 783, 793.

His lack of influence, though he occupied one of the highest posts in the Health Department, indicates once again the extent to which the informed opinions of the foremost physicians and pharmacologists on the drug habit were ignored from the very beginning.

Figure 336. "Lester David Volk (1884 – 1962)." Harris & Ewing. Photograph, 1920. Library of Congress, Prints and Photographs Division, Washington, DC LG.

D. Medical, Legislative and Judicial Dissent

In the beginning the initial dissidents were members of the medical estate. But the obvious escalation of trafficking, when the so-called problem had seemed so containable years before with simple repressive measures, raised new doubts not only among doctors, but also among lawmakers and especially judges. To the highest tribunal of the latter was conferred the Damoclean sword of declaring the *Harrison Act* unconstitutional due to its irregular nature as a criminal precept masquerading under an administrative regulation.

Doctors came to abhor agents from the Narcotic Division. At the end of the 1930s statistics from the Health Department showed that the *Harrison Act* had motivated the detention of some 25,000 doctors, of whom 3000 were still completing their sentences eight years later:

> In the course of the past twenty years, upward of 25,000 registered physicians have been arraigned for criminal violation of one Federal law. ... About 20,000 of the physicians thus charged were allowed to cancel their 'liability,' by payment of what is facetiously termed a 'commensurate sum in compromise' or by merely acknowledging their guilt and, in effect, labeling themselves felons. ... About 2,000 of the physicians thus convicted were penalized only with fines .... The remaining 3,000 physicians were sentenced to Federal prisons, to serve terms of from one to eleven years [quotation marks original].[99]

Fewer pharmacists were prosecuted perhaps because of the difference in their respective roles, the apothecary being more protected than the

---

[99] Williams, Henry Smith. Drug Addicts are Human Beings: The Story of Our Billion-Dollar Drug Racket. Washington, DC: Shaw Publishing Company, 1938 AA, Book III *The Blackmail Code and the Doctors*, Chapter XV *25,000 Innocent Physicians Branded as Felons*, p. 113; Kolb, 1962, p. 146.

physician from entrapment operations, as he only sold drugs on prescription, usually only to his older customers.

Viewed from a distance, the law enforcement and the therapeutic estates were competing for a monopoly on the psychotropic medicines most in demand in that epoch. Whereas before, physicians competed with pharmacists and the diploma-less for prescribing privileges, now they competed with armed bureaucrats. In 1920 an editorial in a leading medical journal criticized "legislative doctoring" by which was meant

> the practice of medicine by legislative dictation instead of at the discretion of educated, experienced and responsible physicians. We mean ... the politicians and lawyers with the power to say what drugs shall or shall not be prescribed for sick people, and in what doses that shall be administered.[100]

By 1932 a Field Supervisor of the newly created Federal Bureau of Narcotics admitted to the "desire of some of our field men to build up a good record at the expense of the professional classes."[101] To this he added that sometimes their agents would contact these professionals and "black-jack them into line."[102]

The concerns of physicians did not go unrecognized by members of the legislature. Lester David Volk (1884 – 1962), a Republican congressman from New York, denounced the interference in the medical profession by narcotics agents as being part of

---

100 Unknown editor. *Harvey's Weekly*, Volume 3, No. 23, Week Ending June 5, 1920 BGU, p. 5.

101 Musto, 1999, p. 369, fn 9, citing H. T. Nugent from a stenographic typescript of Proceedings, located in box 31, American Pharmaceutical Association Archives, Washington D.C., pp. 86-87.

102 Musto, 1999, p. 369, fn 9.

an organized conspiracy ... to drive narcotic-drug addicts into established sanitaria purporting to treat and cure narcotic-drug addictions ... [while] making it impossible for the medical profession to treat narcotic-drug addicts without fear of arrest, indictment, and conviction, or interference and persecution by the criminal authorities. ... An undeniable effort is now being made whereby physicians are to be denied any discretion and power in the prescribing of narcotic drugs and to force all those addicted to the use of these drugs into hospitals exploiting questionable 'cures' [quotation marks original].[103]

Volk also denounced their interpretation of the *Harrison Act* as contrary to the US Constitution:

Obviously the ruling or regulation [from the Narcotic Division] ... nullify and negative the intent of the Harrison narcotic law .... If these new regulations or rulings squared with known medical facts they would still be open to challenge on the ground that they constitute an amendment to the law on our statute books without reference to or regard for the wishes of Congress in this matter. In fact they might be impeached upon the further ground that they invade the police power of the States of this Union in regulating the practice of medicine, which is entirely the purview of the Federal Constitution as at present interpreted.[104]

A hint of renewed concern in the judiciary appeared in a Supreme Court case in which a doctor was condemned for prescribing to a client "more than three thousand ordinary doses"[105] of morphine, cocaine and heroin. The judgment was handed down by a majority of

---

[103] Volk, Lester D. "Extension of Remarks of Hon. Lester D. Volk of New York in the House of Representatives, *Friday, January 13, 1922*," Appendix to the Congressional Record, Volume 62, Part 13. Washington, DC: Government Printing Office, 1922 [govinfo.gov, hereinafter GIG], pp. 13340, 13341.

[104] Volk, 1922, p. 13343.

[105] *United States v Behrman*, 258 US 280 (1922), at p. 289 [tile.loc.gov, hereinafter TLG].

six to three writing that the purpose of the so-called prescription was only to gratify a diseased appetite:

But the quantities named in the indictment are charged to have been entrusted to a person known by the physician to be an addict without restraint upon him in its administration or disposition by anything more than his own weakened and perverted will. Such so-called prescriptions could only result in the gratification of a diseased appetite for these pernicious drugs or result in an unlawful parting with them to others ....[106]

Only two judges joined Chief Justice Holmes in dissent, holding that the principle of good faith protected the accused physician, no matter how foolish his actions:

[I]t must be assumed that he gave them in the regular course of his practice and in good faith. ... It seems to me impossible to construe the statute as tacitly making such acts, however foolish, crimes, by saying that what is in form a prescription and is given honestly in the course of a doctor's practice, and therefore, so far as the words of the statute go, is allowed in terms, is not within the words, is not a prescription and is not given in the course of practice, if the Court deems the doctor's faith in his patient manifestly unwarranted.[107]

It is worth observing the unusual manner of answering a purely technical question, teaching the physician what constitutes a morbid appetite. On the one hand, the dissenting justices qualify the prescription as bad and foolish, on the other they recur to the principle of good faith of the professional, an elliptical form of recognizing his competence in a given field. To calibrate the depth of this intrusion, we can imagine a meeting of the AMA or APhA qualifying a judicial decision as misnamed and foolish, although protected by the principle

---

[106] *United States v Behrman*, 258 U. S. 280 (1922), at p. 289.

[107] *United States v Behrman*, 258 U. S. 280 (1922), at p. 290.

of good faith. One must take into account that the *Harrison Act* (and the other laws on narcotics) always spoke of medical use as an exception to the repressive legislation.

Three years later an alarm sounded at the Narcotics Division when the Supreme Court in *Linder* unanimously reversed the conviction of a doctor for prescribing a small quantity of cocaine and morphine to a police informant. The court was blunt in distinguishing the facts in the new case from those of *Behrman*:

> This opinion [*US v Behrman*] related to definitely alleged facts and must be so understood. The enormous quantity of drugs ordered, considered in connection with the recipient's character, without explanation, seemed enough to show prohibited sales and to exclude the idea of *bona fide* professional action in the ordinary course. The opinion cannot be accepted as authority for holding that a physician, who acts *bona fide* and according to fair medical standards, may never give an addict moderate amounts of drugs for self-administration in order to relieve conditions incident to addiction. Enforcement of the tax demands no such drastic rule, and if the Act had such scope it would certainly encounter grave constitutional difficulties [italics original].[108]

Figure 337. "*Narcotic* (1933)." Poster, IMDB.

[108] *Linder v United States*, 268 U. S. 5 (1925), at pp. 22, 23.

E. Militant Prohibitionists React

The gravity of this unanimous decision caused the Treasury to initiate procedures to obtain a constitutional amendment. The Narcotics Division submitted to Congress a six-point bill, of which the most important were:

1. To prevent physicians who are themselves addicts from registering under this act, and further forbidding physicians who have been convicted of violations of this act from registering for one year thereafter. ...
3. To forbid making the so-called 'ambulatory [outpatient] treatment' for narcotic drug addiction an excuse for providing drugs to addicts.
4. To place some responsibility upon the druggist to exercise reasonable precaution, before filling prescriptions, that the prescription has been written in good faith [quotation marks original].[109]

One of the underlying arguments urging the approval of this amendment was that the US was obligated to do so by the Hague Agreement. This argument was untenable. The Hague Agreement did not contain in any of its recommendations anything remotely similar to the policy in practice domestically in the US. In fact, it did not even accept that illegal possession was a punishable crime, saying only in Article 20 that the Powers should examine the possibility of enacting laws to punish possession of morphine, cocaine and heroin.[110] On the

---

[109] Green, William R., Chairman. Amendments to the Harrison Narcotic Act, Hearing before a Subcommittee of the Committee of the Ways and Means, House of Representatives, Sixty-Ninth Congress, First Session on H. R. 11612 ... May 21, 22 and 26, 1926. Washington, DC: Government Printing Office, 1926 BGU, letter from L. C. Andrews, Assistant Secretary of the Treasury, to the Hon. William R. Green, Chairman, House Ways and Means Committee, 29 March 1926, p. 2.

[110] Chapter V, Article 20: "The contracting Powers shall examine the possibility of enacting laws or regulations making it a penal offence to be in illegal possession of

other hand, to achieve the approval of an amendment in the middle of the 1920s, when the majority of Americans were against the *Volstead Act*, would not only be problematic but unthinkable, and it was the most prohibitionist sectors of Congress who recommended dropping the idea. If the initiative failed, the government's interpretation of the *Harrison Act* would be considered contrary to the Constitution in an unappealable manner, with the consequent loss of what had already been won. In the widespread deliberations and debates prior to the amendment, there would be publicity regarding the less than inspiring practical results of the statute so far, not only with regards to both dispensers and repressors, but to the black market as well. If this was not enough, the therapeutic estate would now be fully opposed, and substantive objections would be raised by the ABA. Thus, the second opportunity to openly illegalize certain drugs following a process of hearings and discussions analogous to any other amendment to the Constitution would remain unfulfilled. There would not be a third.

The rationale behind the government's interpretation of the *Harrison Act* was the active and passive belief in the dope fiend, maintained by a number of anti-drug organizations who supported the Treasury. Speaking of alcohol, Wayne Bidwell Wheeler (1869 – 1927) of the Anti-Saloon League admitted before Congress that the difficulties in enforcing the National Prohibition Law could not be overcome by enlarging the definition of intoxicating:

---

raw opium, prepared opium, morphine, cocaine, and their respective salts ..." (Bevans, Charles I., compiler. Treaties and Other International Agreements of the United States of America 1776 – 1949, Volume I Multilateral 1776 – 1917. Washington, DC: Department of State, Division of Publishing and Reproduction, 1968 LG, Suppression of Abuse of Opium and Other Drugs, p. 858; International Opium Convention, 1912, p. 201); see for further discussion, this volume, Chapter 23, 3. Details, p. 1580.

> The present one-half of 1 per cent definition in the law has been enforced for six years. ... The principal argument advanced for the modification of the law is the alleged difficulty in enforcing the present statute. These difficulties can not be lessened by amending the law so as to adopt a definition of intoxicating liquor which experience has shown to be unenforceable.[111]

Of course the same argument could be used against the *Harrison Act.*

Chief Nutt said the problem was clearly on the way to a solution and that the narcotics farms could without any difficulty rehabilitate even longterm addicts. The support of the hard line was manifest in the testimony of many organizations including The White Cross International Anti-Narcotic Society, the International Narcotic Education Society, the International Narcotic Association, the World Narcotic Defense Association, the National Drug League, the World Anti-Narcotic Union, the World Conference on Narcotic Education and the Federation of Women's Clubs.[112] Also in support of the government's position were the Knights of Columbus, the Loyal Order of Moose, The Grotto, the Mystic Order of the Veiled Prophets of the Enchanted Realm, the Benevolent and Protected Order of Elks and others; President Harding reputedly had been a member of the Grotto.[113]

The president of the World Anti-Narcotic Union, for example, "with its cooperating women's organizations, with memberships in

---

[111] Wheeler, Wayne B. "Statement of Wayne B. Wheeler on Bills Relating to Prohibition Enforcement," The National Prohibition Law, Hearings Before the Subcommittee of the Committee on the Judiciary, United States Senate, Sixty-Ninth Congress, First Session on ... Bills to Amend the National Prohibition Act, April 5 to 24, 1926, Volume 1. Washington, DC: Government Printing Office, 1926 BGU, Enforcement Can Not Be Improved by Weakening the Enforcing Statute, p. 856.

[112] Musto, 1999, pp. 190, 371 fn 31, 373, fn 38.

[113] Musto, 1999, pp. 193, 374 fn 43.

every State in the Union, and containing millions of the greatest mothers, wives and sisters in the Union" advocated for involuntary

> confinement of an addict relative or friend in a hospitalization institution, with the hopes of having him returned rehabilitated and his normal self ... to prevent his conviction as a criminal and his incarceration in a prison, from which he could only return with the brand of convict.[114]

She gave this testimony in spite of her own personal experience as "deputy commissioner of narcotic drug control for New York State" during which she "had official relations with 38,000 individual addicts" where she discovered only three who were no longer using: "The tragic truth, from my own personal acquaintance with several thousand addicts ... compels me to confess at the outset that these three cases ... are absolutely all to whom I can point as having been taken off and having stayed off the drug."[115]

Indeed, the member who had introduced the bill to establish the narcotic farms himself questioned the so-called cures available: "I have often been asked if drug addiction is curable. My reply has always been that we do not know, because we have never really tried it. The

---

[114] Mulhall, Sara Graham. "The World Antinarcotic Union Presents its Reasons for Supporting the Porter Narcotic Farms Bill to the House Judiciary Committee April 26, 1928. Statement of Mrs. Sarah Graham Mulhall, President New York City Federation of Women's Clubs," Establishment of Two Federal Narcotics Farms, Hearings Before the Committee on the Judiciary, House of Representatives Seventieth Congress, First Session on H. R. 12781 and H. R. 13645, April 26, 27, 28, Serial 29 (Revised Print). Washington, DC: US Government Printing Office, 1928 BGU, p. 90.

[115] Graham-Mulhall, Sara. Opium: The Demon Flower. NY: Harold Vinal, 1926 BGU, Chapter I America's Anathema on Opium, pp. 3-4, Chapter XIV The Few Lasting Cures, p. 117.

only place where we have had an opportunity to try to cure it is in a prison."[116]

The response of the Supreme Court to popular opinion and to pressures from the executive branch was a decision in *Nigro* in which a majority of six to three accepted both that persons meant all persons not simply those required to register, as well as that the *Harrison Act* was constitutional because the taxes had been increased:

> By the Revenue Act of 1918, the Anti-Narcotic Act was amended so as to increase the taxes under §1, making an occupation tax for a producer of narcotic drugs of $24 a year, for a wholesale dealer, $12, for a retail dealer, $6.00, and for a physician administering the narcotic, $3.00. The amendment also imposes an excise tax of one cent an ounce on the sale of the drug. Thus the income from the tax for the Government becomes substantial. Under the Narcotic Act, as now amended, the tax amounts to about one million dollars a year, and since the amendment in 1919 it has benefited the Treasury to the extent of nearly nine million dollars. If there was doubt as to the character of this Act – that it is not, as alleged, a subterfuge – it has been removed by the change whereby what was a nominal tax before was made a substantial one. It is certainly a taxing act now ....
>
> In this case, the qualification of the right of a resident of a State to buy and consume opium or other narcotic without restraint by the Federal Government, is subject to the power of Congress to lay a tax by way of excise on its sale. Congress does not exceed its power if the object is laying a tax and the interference with lawful purchasers and users of the drug is reasonably adapted to securing the payment of the tax. Nor does it render such qualification or interference with the original state right an invasion of it because it may incidentally discourage some in the harmful use of the thing taxed [section marks original].[117]

---

116 Porter, Stephen G. "Statement of Hon. Stephen G. Porter, a Representative in Congress from the State of Pennsylvania," Establishment, 1928, p. 13.

117 *Nigro v. United States*, 276 U. S. 332 (1928), at pp. 353, 354.

Along with this good news, which sank the fears of the dismantling of its bureaucratic apparatus, the Narcotics Bureau (formerly the Narcotic Division) closed out the year with a certain bitterness:

> The year 1929 brought havoc to the country and to the Narcotics Bureau. ... [A] federal grand jury investigated charges of misconduct against narcotics agents in New York City. ... The jury lacked any concrete proof of corruption but was of the opinion that circumstances suggested collusion between the agents and drug dealers. ... The deeper the jury probed, the more corruption and incompetence it uncovered; there seemed to be no bottom. ... The reputation and integrity of the Narcotics Division had been seriously impaired.[118]

The records of the Prohibition Unit [covering both alcohol and narcotics] reveal that from "the beginning of prohibition in January, 1920, to February 1, 1926, the separations of enforcement officers, agents, and inspectors for delinquency or misconduct numbered 752."[119] The numbers in the three largest categories separated for delinquency were 121 for "extortion, bribery, or soliciting money," 187 for "intoxication and misconduct," and 119 for "unsatisfactory service and insubordination."[120] This meant nearly thirty percent of the agents employed were dismissed for collusion, dereliction of duty, submitting false reports, perjury, illegal disposition of liquor, and embezzlement, and other charges.[121]

Chief Nutt fared little better with the grand jury:

---

[118] McWilliams, John C. The Protectors: Harry J. Anslinger and the Federal Bureau of Narcotics, 1930 – 1962. Newark, NJ: University of Delaware Press, 1990 AA, pp. 39, 40, 41.

[119] Schmeckebier, 1929, p. 51.

[120] Schmeckebier, 1929, p. 52.

[121] McWilliams, 1990, p. 34, citing Schemeckebier, *Bureau*, 53.

Added to his official problems as Narcotics Chief, Nutt was also embarrassed by the grand jury investigation of his son, Roland, and his son-in-law L. P. Mattingly who operated a law and accounting firm in New York City. Rolland Nutt ... handled tax matters and represented ... Arnold Rothstein ... [who] had extensive control of gambling activities, liquor distribution, and international narcotics traffic.[122]

The uneasiness and distrust surrounding the Narcotics Bureau was overcome by replacing its head and restructuring the demoralized organization. Following these scandals it was renamed the Federal Bureau of Narcotics and its new director Harry Jacob Anslinger (1892 – 1975), would remain in charge until 1962.

Figure 338. "Harry Jacob Anslinger (1892 – 1975), center, receiving an award, 1962." Cecil William Stoughton (1920 – 2008), White House photographer. JFK Presidential Library and Museum, Boston, MA [jfklibrary.org, hereinafter JFK].

[122] McWilliams, 1990, p. 41.

If Hamilton Wright was the soon disappeared father of prohibition, Anslinger would be its exemplary executive who preserved and expanded it over a reign of six decades. He had begun his career as a detective on the Pennsylvania Railroad, became an attaché with the State Department in Europe, Venezuela and the Bahamas, then joined the Prohibition Unit where he stood out among his colleagues as a staunch defender of repressive measures:

> Anslinger was a loyal prohibitionist. In spite of the mismanagement, incompetence, and corruption within the Prohibition Bureau, he believed Prohibition could work if it were more properly administered and enforced. ... He advocated extreme punishment for Volstead violators in 1928 just as he would for marijuana offenders a decade later.[123]

But he was certainly not alone in his strict policy toward opiate users:

> In the Federal Bureau of Narcotics, Anslinger's opinions on how best to put teeth into the law met with almost no objection. He rarely found himself curbed by the administrations under which he worked; he was in fact encouraged not to deviate from stringent enforcement. Early in Roosevelt's first administration Anslinger recalls a visit from the President's close adviser Louis Howe, who made it clear to Anslinger that should he ever forward to the White House a recommendation for clemency for a drug pusher, he could attach his resignation to it. That intelligence, Howe said, 'came from the Boss' [quotation marks original].[124]

However, the new chief commissioner, wishing to avoid controversy, recommended to his subordinates that they cease their inquiries at the corner drugstore and with the family doctor in order to pursue traffickers and smugglers, hoping

---

[123] McWilliams, 1990, pp. 28, 29, 31, 32, 33.

[124] Musto, 1999, p. 212.

that new rules for the agents would cut down on harassment of health professionals. ... Two months after assuming office, Anslinger issued orders that no agent should begin criminal investigation of professionals without written orders from the agent in charge, a copy of which was also sent to the commissioner's office.[125]

Of course, dispensing justice to traffickers, who paid generous bribes and were disposed to murder those who would not accept such, was much more inconvenient than arresting the druggist or physician.

The intimidation of physicians continued into the late twentieth century, according to the first-hand accounts of a rather famous junkie born the year of the passage of the *Harrison Act*:

All croakers [physicians] pack in sooner or later. One day when Roy came for his script, the doctor told him, 'This is positively the last, and you guys had better keep out of sight. The inspector was around to see me yesterday. He has all the R-xes I wrote for you guys. He told me I'll lose my license if I write any more, so I'm going to date this one back. ... For God's sake, cover up for me if they question you. This could mean my whole professional career. ... Here's the script and don't come back' [quotation marks original].[126]

---

[125] Musto, 1999, p. 369 fn 9, citing H. T. Nugent, Field Supervisor of the FBN, speaking at the Fourth Annual Conference of Pharmaceutical Law Enforcement Officials in Toronto on 25 August 1932, found in the stenographic typescript of Proceedings, located in box 31, American Pharmaceutical Association Archives, Washington D.C., pp. 86-87.

[126] Burroughs, William S. Junky. London: Penguin Books, 1977 AA, pp. 23-24.

Figure 339. "William Seward Burroughs (1914 – 1997)." Frontispiece photography by Peter Ross. Rub Out the Words: The Letters of William S. Burroughs, 1959 – 1974, ed. Bill Morgan. NY: Harper Collins Publishers, 2012 AA.

Cocaine Lil and Morphine Sue

Did you ever hear about Cocaine Lil?
She lived in Cocaine town on Cocaine hill,
She had a cocaine dog and a cocaine cat,
They fought all night with a cocaine rat. ...

Lil went to a snow party one cold night,
And the way she sniffed was sure a fright.
There was Hophead Mag with Dopey Slim,
Kankakee Liz and Yen Shee Jim.

There was Morphine Sue and the Poppy Face Kid,
Climbed up snow ladders and down they skid;
There was the Stepladder Kit, a good six feet,
And the Sleigh-riding Sister who were hard to beat.

Along in the morning about half past three
They were all lit up like a Christmas tree;
Lil got home and started for bed,
Took another sniff and it knocked her dead.

They laid her out in her cocaine clothes:
She wore a snowbird hat with a crimson rose;
On her headstone you'll find this refrain:
'She died as she lived, sniffing cocaine.'
-- Anonymous

Figure 340 (previous page). "Cocaine Lil." Protagonist of a popular jazz song from the 1930s. Lyrics from Auden, W. H., editor. The Oxford Book of Light Verse. Oxford, UK: At the Clarendon Press, 1938 AA, No. 280, p. 499.

25

The Crusade Begins (II)

The sway of alcohol over mankind is unquestionably due to its power to stimulate the faculties of human nature, usually crushed to earth by the cold facts and dry criticisms of the sober hour. Sobriety diminishes, discriminates, and says no; drunkenness expands, unites, and says yes.

-- William James (1842 – 1910)[1]

A. The Re-legalization of Alcohol

1. Possession and Trafficking

2. The European View

B. The Demonization of Cannabis

1. Opposing Viewpoints

2. The *Marihuana Tax Act* of 1937

C. International Agreements

1. The 1925 Geneva Conference

2. The 1931 Geneva Conference

3. The 1936 Geneva Conference

D. Spain

1. International Obligations

2. Social Reality

---

[1] The Varieties of Religious Experience: *A Study in Human Nature*, Being the Gifford Lectures on Natural Religion Delivered at Edinburgh in 1901-1902. NY: The Modern Library, 1902 [archive.org, hereinafter AO], pp. 377-378.

While the medical, judicial and repressive establishments in the United States were embroiled in these complex relationships, other parts of the world also began to accept the idea that a citizen's pharmacological diet was a matter for the state. The League of Nations created permanent bodies dedicated to the control of drug trafficking, and economically advanced countries became accustomed to legislate in this new field. Except in the US (where conflict still prevailed, especially with the repeal of the *Volstead Act*), in large parts of the world it could be said that legislating in the matter of psychoactive drugs was already a reality that was spreading without hurry and without pause, always at the urging of an international conference which in turn had adopted initiatives suggested by the American delegation. Decisively determining the outcome of World War One, the US is going to continue expanding slowly and steadily, recognized by the whole planet as a beacon of wealth, freedom and strength.

With regards to the chemistry, discoveries never cease to crown the experiments in the laboratories of the pharmaceutical companies, producing psychoactive drugs of great potential, both stimulants and sedatives. As yet, these are not linked to marginalized groups or colonized cultures but remain simple medicines. Because these drugs are available without legal complications, many of those who used to partake of the natural opiates and cocaine decide (more or less willingly) to sedate and stimulate themselves with the new products since they are unadulterated, cheap and nearly as effective for the basic necessities of peace and energy. From the 1930s onward, the widespread diffusion of these pharmacological alternatives means that the pharmacies have (for the client who seeks such remedies) as many mood-altering preparations as they had on their shelves at the end of the nineteenth century.

Figure 341. "Agents Pour Alcohol into Sewer." NYWT&S Collection, c. 1921. Library of Congress, Prints & Photographs Division [loc.gov, hereinafter LG].

Figure 342. "Liquor Raid at Luigi's, Greenwich Village, NYC, 24 Jan 1923." Cityana Collection, gift of Benjamin Blum, Museum of the City of New York [mcny.org, hereinafter MCNY].

A. The Re-legalization of Alcohol

A classic scholar on the genesis and application of the *Volstead Act* attributed the success of the Anti-Saloon League (its principal promoter) to a number of factors:

> The success of the prohibitionists is, in fact, easier to understand than their defeat would have been. For they had control of the best part of the communications of the time. They had organization, money, and a purpose. ... The foundation of the Woman's Christian Temperance Union and of the Anti-Saloon League before the close of the nineteenth century gave the prohibitionists a disciplined army, ready to exploit politics and the American people in the interests of their chosen reform. The refusal of the liquor trade to regulate the saloons of its own accord and the national psychology created by the First World War were sufficient to give victory to the prohibitionists. ... For the old America of the villages and farms distrusted the new America of the urban masses. ... [T]he Anti-Saloon League backed dry candidates for political office ... [and] weak politicians knuckled under to the prohibitionists for fear of losing the dry vote.[2]

The weakness of the political class is of course elections. Unwilling to yield a single vote to a competitor, both Democrats and Republicans consented to propaganda calculated to incite terror in the masses and make law an instrument of ethnic sectarianism, delivering the final decision to a demanding minority like the Prohibition Party. This can be clearly observed when alcohol becomes legal, and a large number of Congressmen can drink tranquilly in public again; even if organizations like the Anti-Saloon League contradicted their own internal values, not one had wanted to lose the abstemious vote.

---

[2] Sinclair, Andrew. Prohibition: The Era of Excess. Boston, MA: Little, Brown and Company, 1962 [annas-archive.org, hereinafter AA], Prologue to Prohibition, pp. 4-5, Chapter 7 Trimming for the White House, p. 142.

Neither did the therapeutic and religious estates protest. The *Volstead Act* declared that the "use of beverage alcohol was restricted to the patients of doctors, communicants at religious services, and makers of vinegar and cider."[3] Thanks to this loophole, doctors and pharmacists could prescribe wines and liquors, and priests could obtain wine for mass. As noted earlier, physicians writing prescriptions for medicinal alcohol made huge profits (almost as much as the Treasury had received in taxes prior to Prohibition), "40,000,000 in 1928," and "even sacramental wine reached the dinner table rather than the communion cup" due to the "loopholes in the Volstead Act."[4] While the doctors made money, the bootleggers made even more.

By 1930, after the crusade against drinking was a decade old, one American authority calculated that from every fifty liters of denatured industrial alcohol manufactured, five were diverted to make illegal liquor. In the late 1920s

> some forty people in every million were dying from bad liquor each year. Most of the slaughter was caused in the New York area by the sale of bootleg containing wood alcohol, a denaturing substance which could blind and kill. The wet press accused the Prohibition Bureau of conspiring to poison American citizens, because the Bureau knew that at least one gallon of industrial alcohol in ten would be diverted into the human stomach. ... But it was a nasty truth that the very same reformers who had supported the Hepburn Pure Food and Drug Bill twenty years before now wanted to put poisons into alcohol which they knew would be drunk by human beings.[5]

---

[3] Sinclair, 1962, Chapter 8 The Turncoat Congress, p. 168.

[4] See this volume, Chapter 23, Section 2 The Therapeutic Estate, p. 1639; Sinclair, 1962, p. 191.

[5] Sinclair, 1962, p. 201.

Prohibition agents were suspected of accepting bribes or allowing extortion:

> Graft, corruption, injustice, inconsistency, hypocrisy, violation of constitutional rights, and the creation of a new criminal class developed rapidly and accelerated until finally public pressure brought the demise of the act with the Twenty-first Amendment to the Constitution, which became law in 1933. Almost 45,000 people had received jail sentences for alcohol offenses in 1932 alone. In the first 11 years of the Prohibition Bureau, 17,972 people were appointed to the agency, 11,982 were terminated 'without prejudice,' and 1,604 were dismissed for bribery, extortion, theft, falsification of records, conspiracy, forgery, and perjury.[6]

Thirteen years of prohibition convinced the country that the only result was astonishing corruption, injustice, hypocrisy, the creation of huge numbers of new delinquents, and the foundation of organized crime; the same will be said forty years later of a different war on different drugs:

> Excessive reliance upon the criminal law to perform tasks for which it is ill-suited has created acute problems for the administration of criminal justice. The use of criminal law to enforce morals has tended both to be inefficient and to produce grave handicaps for enforcement of the criminal law against genuinely threatening conduct. It has served to reduce the criminal law's essential claim to legitimacy by inducing offensive and degrading police conduct, particularly against the poor and the subcultural, and by generating cynicism and indifference to the criminal law. It has also fostered organized criminality and has produced possibly more crime than it has suppressed.[7]

---

[6] Fort, Joel. The Pleasure Seekers: The Drug Crisis, Youth and Society. NY: Grove Press, Inc., 1969 AA, p. 69.

[7] Fort, 1981, pp. 232-233, citing "The President's Commission on Law Enforcement and Administration of Justice, 'Narcotics and Drug Abuse,' Task Force Report," United States Government Printing Office, 1967.

The Eighteenth Amendment was repealed by the Twenty-First. Almost half a million condemned as criminals became, from one day to the next, irreproachable citizens again under the law. No compensation was provided, not for them and not for the thousands of dead and wounded in gun battles, settling of accounts or similar practices resulting from the crusade. Neither was compensation extended to another quarter of a million poisoned with pernicious distillations, resulting in death or permanent disability. As happened in the crusade against the witches, no one was held responsible. Prohibition may have managed to reduce in its first year somewhere between ten and thirty percent of *per capita* alcohol drinking in the United States, though this is disputed. Considering that such a small, temporary reduction could not compensate for the direct and indirect harm caused to society in general, the country overturned the *Volstead Act* and returned to permitting the manufacture, sale and consumption of alcohol in public.

Figure 343. "Representative La Guardia pours beer in his congressional office to protest Prohibition, 1926." La Guardia and Wagner Archives, MCNY.

Figure 344. "Anti-prohibition parade, 5th Avenue, NYC."
Underwood & Underwood Photo Archives, 4 July 1921 MCNY.

Figure 345. "Parade for Repeal." Painting by Ben Shahn (1898 – 1969).
Courtesy Fine Arts Program, USGSA, New Deal Art Projects, 1934 MCNY.

CH. 25 THE CRUSADE BEGINS (II)

1. Possession and Trafficking

Although the *Harrison Act* punished trafficking much more severely than the *Volstead Act*, the 1914 statute was not criminal in the strict sense as technically it only punished indirectly infractions of rules concerning registration. The *Volstead Act*, in contrast, was recognized as a criminal statute, although it also did not incriminate the consumption and possession of alcohol, only its sale and manufacture. One might suppose therefore that it posed a danger only to those who sold or fabricated alcoholic beverages, and that the tens of thousands incarcerated each year were exclusively distillers and owners of speakeasies. But the system of penalizing trafficking in but not possession of alcohol was a contradiction in terms.

Since neither whiskey nor wine grew on trees, without invoking the supernatural it was impossible to access these beverages without engaging in an economic transaction. Consumption could be considered as evidence of trafficking, and whether it would be or not depended fundamentally on the prohibition agents themselves; a simple technique of infiltration among consumers could result (with patience, liquor and money) in the indictment of those persons or groups who for one reason or another deserved stigma or blackmail. In this way, those accused or extorted by prohibition agents for violating the *Volstead Act* were not only sellers and manufacturers, but also a much larger group of simple users and owners of businesses like restaurants, hotels, and casinos who, if they did not play by the rules of the game, would be at a ruinous disadvantage before less timorous colleagues, disposed to pay for impunity with liberal bribes. The incongruence of authorized consumption and castigated sales was evident in the fact that few large traffickers and manufacturers (with thugs and lawmen at their service, protected by solid political support) ended in prison for these kinds of charges. The cases brought against

Capone (incarcerated not for sales but for income tax fraud) is one example among many. Not only gangsters who have passed into memory as assassins, but members of great and respectable families as well made their fortunes from bootlegging.

The system of punishing traffic but not consumption achieved basically two things: a) reducing manufacturers and sellers to true scoundrels, who in addition to degrading alcohol and multiplying its toxicity also corrupted or killed as many of the forces of law and order as their less scrupulous competitors; and b) forcing ordinary citizens to confront the dilemma of abstinence or frequenting establishments dominated by criminal enterprises, backed by a colossal business syndicate. It's true that citizens could also pay for a consultation with a physician to obtain a prescription for whiskey, cognac or wine; but this was as expensive or more, and lacked the other attractions of the saloon.

Figure 346. "Speakeasy." Watercolor by Retta Ernestine Worcester, neé Scott (1916 – 1990). Exhibited at the Laguna Art Museum, 2016 [californiawatercolor.com, hereinafter CW].

2. The European View

A marvelous work by the great psychopharmacologist Louis Lewin (1850 – 1929), *Phantastica* was first published in German in 1924[8] and expresses the mixture of astonishment at and rejection of the puritan initiative in America. As with any other treatise on toxicology, it offers a very dark picture of alcoholism. However, it immediately clarifies that the subjective factor cannot be depreciated. It would be useless to attempt to fix the quantity of alcohol capable of marking a man with the stamp of an alcoholic because the gravity of consequences derived from drinking depends in large part on individual tolerance:

> To believe that the effects of ethyl alcohol on the psyche are the same in all individuals is a fundamental error. This assertion is without any foundation in the case of those who take, even daily, a moderate dose of alcohol, provided it is kept within the limits which their individual sensibility permits them to tolerate, and it is only of relative significance in the case of those who exceed these limits. Perusal of my work on the secondary effects of medicinal substances will show that on every page there are facts to prove that the influence of personality renders illusory every fixation or pre-conceived determination of the effects on the body of a chemical substance.[9]

---

[8] Holmstedt, Bo. "Foreword," in Lewis Lewin's Phantastica: Narcotic and Stimulating Drugs, Their Use and Abuse, tr. P. H. A. Wirth. NY: E. P. Dutton & Company, Inc, 1964 AA, p. ix; see photograph of Lewin in GHDV3P1, Chapter 15 Liberalism and its Repercussions, A. Pharmacological Progress, p. 1002.

[9] Lewin, Louis. Phantastica: Narcotic and Stimulating Drugs, Their Use and Abuse. NY: E. P. Dutton & Company, 1964 AA, Inebrantia, Alcohol, 2. Chronic Alcoholism, e) Temperance and Abstinence, p. 183; *Es ist der Grundirrtum ... auf den Menschen illusorich macht* (*Phantastica: Die Betäubenden und Erregenden Genussmittel, Für Ärzte und Nichtärtze*. Berlin, DE: Verlag von Georg Stilke, 1924 AO, Inebrantia, Berauschungsmittel, Der Alkohol, e) Maßigkeitsbestrebungen und Abstinententum,

His observations deserve to be cited at length:

> No period of history has been free from attempts to combat alcoholism on a larger or smaller scale. Individuals and groups addressed its devotees in the language of religion, common sense and reason, and by means of laws and regulations. They even attempted altogether to suppress alcohol for consumption. For the reasons which I set forth when dealing with morphia these efforts were of little or no avail, with the exception of those of Mohammedanism, which for several centuries kept its believers from alcohol but could not prevent the use of equivalent substances. ... At the present day the ancient and multiform combat against alcoholism shows itself in a new form. It is directed chiefly against alcohol in itself. By 'psycho-scientific' processes all its physiological effects are transformed into sins. Minute experiments prove that not only is drunkenness an evil, but that everyone who drinks alcohol in whatever quantity is a dangerous person. The band of abstainers, though as old as the world itself, was formerly not a very large one. At the present day it has become more important, and many of its members, convinced apostles of its principles, carry forth in speech and in writing the gospel of abstinence. ...
>
> [T]o whom does the world of to-day owe its form and its activity, to abstainers or to non-abstainers? To the latter alone, without doubt. They have been the creators and promoters of science. To them we owe the beautiful creations of art. They have supplied the wonderful feats of the poetic imagination, and the noble productions of music have been forthcoming from the profound depths of their sensibility. ... It is incomprehensible and indefensible that abstainers should consider a man who has a liking for wine as an inferior creature. ... In my opinion it is not possible to formulate a law applicable equally to the abuse of alcohol and the apparent consequences. Even the richest toxicological experience is bound to fail in seeking to prevent drunkenness. In the school and the home efforts must be made to prevent the development of alcoholism [quotation marks original].[10]

---

pp. 187-188).

[10] Lewin, 1964, e) Temperance and Abstinence, pp. 177-178, 179, 180, 181, 193; *Nun kenne ich keine Zeit der Welt ...* (Phantastica, 1924, p. 181 et seq).

An undisputed eminence in his day, this German toxicologist presents the additional interest of demonstrating the opinion of a European in the 1920s observing what was happening in the United States with regards to the prohibition of alcohol. But although in this period more than 10,000 (in good measure physicians and pharmacists) are incarcerated for violations of the *Harrison Act*, someone as learned and literate as Lewin simply has no opinion of the American prohibition of the opiates and cocaine. The scarce news that arrives concerning the difficulties of therapists and patients are interpreted as exceptional cases of abuse, falsification of prescription and theft. What he calls the brotherhood of the abstinent (tea and coffee drinkers)[11] is represented by the Prohibition Party, not the specific group of Brent, Crafts and Wright. Here he is ironical (without perceiving his error) on the fact that only wine and liquor are being persecuted:

> Why such an expenditure of efforts against alcohol alone, where there are other deeper cravings which well deserve some apostolic effort? Why is there no general crusade against morphia, cocaine, nicotine, caffeine, lust, gambling? The anti-alcoholic fight is based on no clear judgment; it is conducted with party-spirit.[12]

Lewin knows perfectly well the international legislation on opiates and cocaine. But he does not interpret these laws as a crusade against those substances, but only as an effort to keep such drugs under medical supervision, controlling their exportation as well. And

---

[11] Lewin, 1964, Excitantia, Coffee, 3. Effects of Coffee, p. 256; *Die Kaffee-schwestern und Teebrüder* ... (Lewin, 1924, Excitantia. Erregungsmittel, Der Kaffee, 3. Die Wirkungen des Kaffees, p. 270).

[12] Lewin, 1964, Inebrantia, Alcohol, 2. Chronic Alcoholism, e) Temperance and Abstinence, p. 179; *Und warum so unendlich ... er mit Partieleidenschaft geführt wird* (Lewin, 1924, e) Maßigkeitsbestrebungen und Abstinententum, p. 179).

indeed the international conventions adopted up to then did not call for anything else. Like almost all European doctors of his time, he was ignorant of the very existence of the *Harrison Act*, and he would have laughed with his colleagues if someone had told him that decades later the opiates would be declared without therapeutic value in the US, and, afterwards, in the rest of the planet. This is even more noteworthy as Lewin always distinguishes himself as an acerbic enemy of frivolous use.

But it was one thing to be warned against alcohol at home, in school and in the Faculty of Medicine, and quite another to join the bandwagon of the abstinent:

> I respect those who for one reason or another abstain from alcohol just as I do those who live in conformity with religious prescriptions .... It is a private matter for the individual, as is the abstinence from alcohol. ... In all times clear-sighted people have recognized that a reasonable and moderate consumption of wine is not harmful, but that drunkenness is an evil. ... Abstinence may be justified as an individual conviction, but not as a gospel.[13]

Figure 347. "Assassin of Youth." Chasin, Alexandra. A Kaleidoscopic History of Harry J. Anslinger's War on Drugs. Chicago, IL: University of Chicago Press, 2016 AA, p. 185, citing Anslinger, H. J. and C. R. Cooper. "Assassin of Youth," *The American Magazine*, Vol. 24, No. 1, July 1937, p. 48, Harry J. Anslinger Papers, Special Collections Library, The Pennsylvania State University Libraries.

---

[13] Lewin, 1964, pp. 178-179, 188-189, 190; *Ich habe für den ... aber nicht eines Evangeliums* (Lewin, 1924, pp. 182, 193).

B. The Demonization of Cannabis

In the 1920s the US experienced an influx of immigrants from Mexico, both documented and undocumented, in a wave that spread along a front from Louisiana to California, penetrating deep into Colorado and Utah; in Texas at least it was less emigration than a return to ancestral lands. In that decade the country maintained high rates of economic growth, and the Mexicans (as happened before with the Chinese) were welcomed by employers and detested by unions. But wherever they concentrated in large numbers, before long there was mention of cannabis (then *marihuana*). This remained at the level of a picaresque source of scandal in parish pulpits and women's clubs until the arrival of the Great Depression converted this unskilled labor into an undesirable excess of hungry mouths, scattered across a region devastated by unemployment.

By the early 1930s the end of Prohibition had created two opposing viewpoints. For the conservatives, the re-legalization of alcohol was a catastrophe of incalculable proportions, which required them not to be demoralized and to maintain a position of intransigence with regards to narcotics in the face of the predictable tidal wave of tolerance. For the liberals, with the end of the *Volstead Act* and the supply of new drugs available without a prescription at the pharmacies, the necessities of sedation and stimulation were completely covered. If to this, one adds that it was no longer necessary to deceitfully collude with the therapeutic establishment, the future for the enlightened consumer was bright indeed.

Not so for the Federal Bureau of Narcotics. As their fellow prohibitionists had lost the battle against wines and liquors, it could have recognized that the users of the natural opiates and cocaine being supplied by the *Cosa Nostra* were statistically insignificant common criminals, running the institutional risk of letting them now be surveilled by local constabularies instead. It could have created a new stigma around the synthetic drugs taking the place of the older natural ones, every day being consumed more liberally. Or, as Anslinger suggested, it could find new dope fiends to take the place of the opium-besotted Chinese and the cocaine-crazed Negroes of the past, the best defense being a good offense as soon as possible against new inanimate pharmacological threats not yet declared as such.

It chose the latter, turning its gaze to cannabis. Already at the turn of the century Reverend Crafts had highlighted the markedly pagan and even idolatrous aspects of the plant, denounced by missionaries in both Africa and Asia. One can add that the 1925 Geneva Convention had included it in the list of substances deserving of international control.

The initial unease can be detected in a contribution read before the Louisiana State Medical Society in 1931 making an equivalence between the criminal deviant and a drug that sexually stimulates and erases civilized inhibitions:

> The underworld was quick to realize that mariahuana [sic] was an ideal drug to quickly cut off the inhibition, especially in the type of inadequate personality. Under the influence of cannabis indica, these human derelicts are quickly subjugated by the will of the master mind. The moral principles or training inculcated in the mind from infancy deter from committing willful theft, murder or rape, but this inhibition for crime may be destroyed by the addiction to mariahuana [sic]. ... [I]n the suggestibility resulting from hashish intoxication, the last vestige of man's artificially acquired restraint is swept away.[14]

A threat from the criminal is a threat from the drug and vice versa.

---

[14] Fossier, A. E. "The Mariahuana [sic] Menace," *New Orleans Medical and Surgical Journal*, Volume 84, No. 4, October 1931 AA, p. 249.

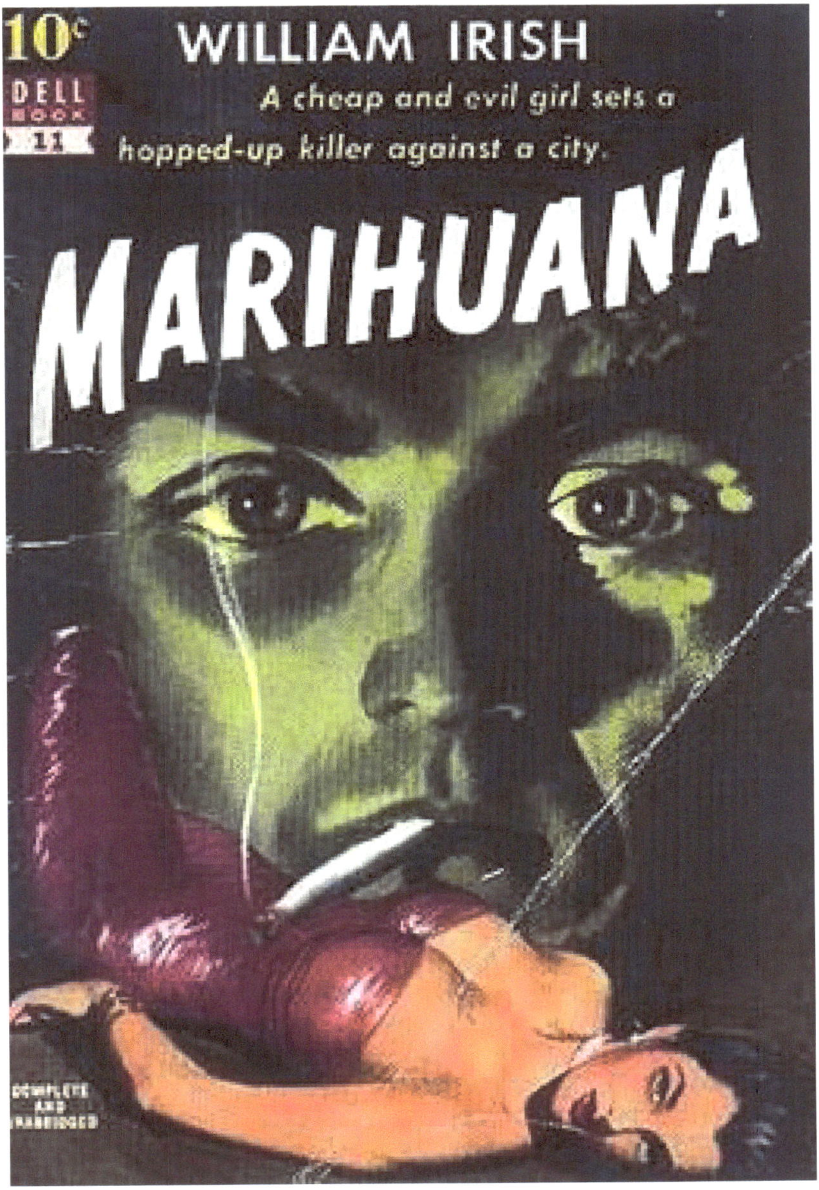

Figure 348. "Marihuana." Cover art for novel by William Irish, pen name of Cornell Woolrich. NY: Dell Publishing, 1941 LG.

Two or three years later groups like the Alliance of Patriotic Societies, the Key Men of America, and the American Coalition whose motto is 'Keep America American' appear. To their desire to maintain a morally pure nation was added a consideration of political economy:

> Marijuana, perhaps now the most insidious of our narcotics, is a direct by-product of unrestricted Mexican immigration. Easily grown, it has been asserted that it has recently been planted between rows in a California penitentiary garden. Mexican peddlers have been caught distributing sample marijuana cigarets to school children. Bills for our quota against Mexico have been blocked mysteriously in every Congress since the 1924 Quota Act. Our nation has more than enough laborers.[15]

Around the same time, alarming articles also began to appear in major US newspapers. The *Washington Post* reported that cannabis was addictive, caused absenteeism, crime and impotence:

> The use of cannabis, whether smoked or ingested in its various forms, undoubtedly gives rise to a form of addiction, which has serious social consequences (abandonment of work, propensity to theft and crime, disappearance of reproductive power).[16]

---

[15] Musto, David F. The American Disease: Origins of Narcotic Control, Third Edition. NY: Oxford University Press, 1999 AA, Chapter 9 Marihuana and the Federal Bureau of Narcotics, p. 220, citing an interview with eugenicist and real estate developer Charles Matthias Goethe (1875 – 1966), N. Y. *Times*, Section IV, 15 Sept. 1935, p. 9 (fn 21, p. 380).

[16] Doughton, Robert L., Chairman. Hearings Before the Committee on Ways and Means, House of Representatives, Seventy-Fifth Congress, First Session on H. R. 6385, April 27, 28, 29, 30, and May 4, 1937. Washington, DC: Government Printing Office, 1937 BGU, report by Dr. J. Bouquet, Tunis, to the League of Nations, citing the *Washington Post*, 23 November 1936, p. 21.

The author did not mention that cannabis arrived in America with the Europeans nor of the Vedic, Zoroastrian and Buddhist traditions connected with its use over many thousands of years.

The *Chicago Tribune* called it a dangerous intoxicant and compared it to cocaine and opium:

> As a stimulant to crime the drug is probably as important as cocaine, certainly far more so than opium or any of its derivatives, and narcotic-control agencies will be put to a severe test in rooting out the traffic. As a rule the addict passes into a dreamy state in which judgment is lost and imagination runs riot. Fantasies arise which are limitless and extravagant. ... Under relatively large doses consciousness does not leave entirely, even though actions and movements are out of control. ... [T]he thrill seeker finds inhibitions destroyed and, abandoning his normal sense of propriety, he may do and say things quite foreign to his make-up. ... [I]t is one of those dangerous drugs that should be known only to be shunned – an intoxicant with the most vicious propensities.[17]

The *St. Louis Star-Times* described how it drove a young man insane:

> A case in point is that of a young man, an intelligent high-school student, now confined to an institution for the mentally diseased. His experience is entirely the result of acquiring the habit of smoking marihuana cigarettes. ... He was a swell fellow until marihuana got him. Like the rest of us, he thought the weed wasn't habit-forming and had no idea of the possible consequences of smoking it. He smoked so many he couldn't quit. Finally he went crazy and his folks put him in a sanitarium.[18]

---

[17] Doughton, 1937, "Today's Health Talk (by Dr. Irving S. Cutter), A Dangerous Intoxicant," p. 22, citing the *Chicago Tribune – New York News* Syndicate, Inc., 1936.

[18] Doughton, 1937, "Marihuana – A More Alarming Menace Than All Other Habit-Forming Drugs," by Gomila, Frank R. and Madelaine C., p. 33, citing the *St. Louis Star-Times*, 18 Jan 1935, "Young Slaves to Dope Cigaret Pay Tragic Price for Their Folly," by Hulius Kleen.

A number of fawning, disingenuous letters and editorials were also published around the country, suggesting a campaign of astroturfing[19] by the Federal Bureau of Narcotics itself. One of them was written by the city editor of the Alamosa, Colorado *Daily Courier*:

Is there any assistance your Bureau can give us in handling this drug? Can you suggest campaigns? Can you enlarge your Department to deal with marijuana? Can you do anything to help us? ...

I wish I could show you what a small marijuana cigarette can do to one of our degenerate Spanish-speaking residents. That's why our problem is so great: the greatest percentage of our population is composed of Spanish-speaking persons, most of whom are low mentally, because of social and racial conditions. ... Through representatives of civic leaders and law officers of the San Luis Valley, I have been asked to write to you for help.[20]

Anslinger responded by comparing the leaves of the plant to rattlesnakes and the drug to a fictional monster:

As a matter of fact the staminate leaves are about as harmless as a rattlesnake. ... In medical schools the physician-to-be is taught that without opium medicine would be like a one-armed man. That is true, because you cannot get along without opium. But here we have a drug that is not like opium. Opium has all of the good of Dr. Jekyll and all the evil of Mr. Hyde. This drug is entirely the monster Hyde, the harmful effect of which cannot be measured.[21]

---

[19] "[O]n radio and at major forums ... I told the story of this evil weed .... I wrote articles for magazines .... In network broadcasts I reported on the growing list of crimes, including murder and rape." (Anslinger, Harry J. and Will Oursler. The Murderers: The Story of the Narcotic Gangs. NY: Farrar, Strauss and Cudahy, 1961 AA, p. 38).

[20] Doughton, 1937, letter from 'Baskette, Floyd K., city editor, Alamosa Daily Courier, Alamosa, Colorado,' p. 32; Musto, 1999, p. 223.

[21] Doughton, 1937, Statement of Dr. H. J. Anslinger, Commissioner of Narcotics, Department of the Treasury, p. 19.

CH. 25 THE CRUSADE BEGINS (II)

By 1936 Anslinger's Federal Bureau of Narcotics felt the time was ripe to submit to the Treasury a proposal for a repressive law on cannabis, with a view to getting it passed by Congress. His first idea was to get it approved in an international treaty that would be binding on the Senate. Specifically, Anslinger thought he had found legal support in a 1935 law on migratory birds, which though it restricted the rights of states had been declared constitutional as a consequence of treaties signed with Mexico and Canada:

> The Commissioner's recommendation for the marihuana legislation was to follow the example of the Migratory Bird Act, which had been declared constitutional, although it intruded into the police powers of the states, because it had been enacted as a requirement of treaties with Canada and Mexico (*Missouri* v. *Holland*, 252 U.S. 416). Anslinger suggested a similar treaty requiring the control of marihuana. Once the treaty was ratified by the Senate, a federal marihuana law would not meet the constitutional blocks he felt sure it would face if it were based on federal tax or commerce powers [italics original].[22]

Although restricting civil rights was not the same thing as protecting migratory bird waystations, Anslinger's proposal was agreed to by a representative of the Permanent Central [opium] Board of the League of Nations as well as by officials in the Treasury and State Departments.[23] Any legislative scruples would be quelled by alleging that the plant and its derivatives were already included under an international convention. The idea was rejected, however, at the 1936 Geneva Conference for the Suppression of Illicit Traffic in Dangerous Drugs.[24]

---

[22] Musto, 1999, The Marihuana Tax Act, p. 224.

[23] Musto, 1999, p. 224.

[24] Musto, 1999, p. 225.

Only domestic federal legislation was available. Naturally, in this post-*Volstead* era, any new proposal could not be framed as an amendment to the Constitution but instead would have to follow the path blazed by the *Harrison Act*, though here the emphasis was on the tax not the registration. Manufacturers, sellers and possessors of cannabis would have to declare this on certain forms and pay a transfer tax.

Figure 349. "Injecting Marihuana." Poster, c. 1936. American Institute of the History of Pharmacy [aihp.omeka.net, hereinafter AIHP].

1. Opposing Viewpoints

But in this era there were few studies of cannabis that would modify the conclusions established at the end of the nineteenth century in British India that cannabis was not addictive and did not lead to crime.[25] For example, in 1925 a committee appointed by the Governor of the Panama Canal Zone to "investigate the use of mariajuana [sic]" reported it to be neither habit-forming nor a deleterious influence and recommended no special legislative action:

> There is no evidence that mariahuana [sic] as grown here is a 'habit-forming' drug in the sense in which the term is applied to alcohol, opium, cocaine, etc., or that it has any appreciably deleterious influence on the individuals using it.
> The Committee recommended 'that no steps be taken by the Canal Zone authorities to prevent the sale or use of mariahuana [sic], and that no special legislation be asked for [quotation marks original].'[26]

A second inquiry concluded in 1929 found much the same: "The reports of the twelve months indicate that the use of the drug is not widespread and that its effects upon military efficiency and upon discipline are not great. There appears to be no reason for reviving the penalties formerly exacted for the possession and the use of the drug."[27] A third investigation observed 34 soldiers in a hospital setting, concluding:

---

[25] Again, for a more involved discussion see the GHDV3P1, Chapter 17 Visionary Drugs, 4. The Indian Hemp Drugs Commission, pp. 1149 et seq.

[26] Siler, J. F., et al. "Mariajuana [sic] smoking in Panama," *Military Surgeon*, Volume 73, 1933, pp. 269-280 [Schaeffer Drug Library, hereinafter SDL], unpaged.

[27] Siler, 1932, unpaged.

3. Mariajuana [sic] as grown and used on the Isthmus of Panama is a mild stimulant and intoxicant. It is not a 'habit forming' drug in the sense that the derivatives of opium and cocaine are such drugs, as there are no symptoms of deprivation following its withdrawal. ... Delinquencies due to mariajuana [sic] smoking which result in trial by military court are negligible in number when compared with delinquencies resulting from the use of alcoholic drinks which also may be classed as stimulants and intoxicants [quotation marks original].[28]

A 1933 clinical study by a senior psychiatrist at Bellevue Hospital in New York examined 2216 criminals convicted of felonies but found no correlation between cannabis and addiction or cannabis and crime:

[N]ot one case of confirmed marihuana addiction was noted, although one prisoner (a Porto Rican) had used it for three months steadily. ... Of the 361 individuals diagnosed as psychopathic personality in the routine psychiatric examination 32 (9 per cent) were drug addicts and of these only seven had smoked marihuana for any period of time. None of the assault cases could be said to have been committed under the drug's influence. No crimes were committed in this group during or immediately after the intoxication. Of the sexual crimes (rape, sodomy, impairing morals of a minor, etc.) there were likewise none due to marihuana intoxication.[29]

The author discovered this in spite of earlier reports from India where cannabis caused a quarter of the mental illness and from New Orleans where half the murderers were cannabis addicts.[30]

Other researchers would come to similar conclusions. Six years after it was made illegal, an editor of the *Military Surgeon* commented:

---

[28] Siler, 1932, Resume of Observed Cases, unpaged.

[29] Bromberg, Walter. "Marihuana Intoxication: A Clinical Study of Cannabis Sativa Intoxication," *The American Journal of Psychiatry*, Volume 91, September 1934 AA, p. 307.

[30] Bromberg, 1934, pp. 306-307.

> The smoking of the leaves, flowers and seeds of *Cannabis sativa* is no more harmful than the smoking of tobacco or mullein or sumac leaves. ... The legislation in relation to marihuana was ill-advised ... it branded as a menace and a crime a matter of trivial importance. ... It is hoped that no witch hunt will be instituted in the military service over a problem that does not exist [italics original].[31]

Two military officers in the Army Medical Corps authored a study of 35 (all but one, negro) "marihuana addicts" of "low or very low social and economic background" involuntarily confined in a military hospital in California in 1944 because of "difficulties which brought them to the attention of the military or medical authorities."[32] Yet this addiction was not physiological but only psychological, based on withdrawal symptoms in their already admittedly disturbed patients: "Previous studies have insisted that marihuana addicts show no physiologic [sic] withdrawal symptoms such as characterize morphine addicts. However, in our cases the psychologic [sic] aspect of the withdrawal seems of extreme importance."[33] These extremely important symptoms were transient:

> When they had been given sedatives for a period of weeks, when they had been permitted certain freedoms and given encouragement in various activities, it was found that frequently hostility diminished and they showed evidence of better rapport. A few spontaneously declared to the psychiatrist on his rounds of the ward that they were feeling much better and that they no longer needed sedatives.[34]

---

[31] Lindesmith, Alfred R. The Addict and the Law. Bloomington, IN: Indiana University Press, 1965 AA, Chapter 8 The Marihuana Problem – Myth or Reality, Mayor La Guardia's Committee on Marihuana, p. 234, citing 'The Marihuana Bugaboo,' *Military Surgeon*, Volume 93, July 1943, p. 94.

[32] Marcovitz, Eli and Henry J. Meyers. "The Marihuana Addict in the Army," *War Medicine*, Volume 6, December 1944 AA, originally pp. 382-394, reprinted p. 1.

[33] Marcovitz and Meyers, 1944, p. 7.

[34] Marcovitz and Meyers, 1944, p. 6.

The "extremely adverse socioeconomic factors of class and caste" of each soldier were noted but it was his cannabis addiction that caused him to reject and rebel against "the authority from which he really wants love and of which he wants to be a part."[35] Yet this addiction with its easily relieved withdrawal symptoms that caused so many behavioral problems was not the cause of crime: "We have found no case of a marihuana addict who committed an act of violence or aggression against a person in order to obtain marihuana."[36]

In 1944 New York City Mayor Fiorello Henry La Guardia (1882 – 1947) commissioned a study that also found no addiction:

> Practically all of our group of users stated that they could and often did voluntarily stop the smoking for a time without any undue disturbance from the deprivation. ... The evidence submitted here warrants the conclusion that as far as New York City is concerned true addiction to marihuana does not occur.[37]

The study also found no link between cannabis and crime:

> During our investigation many law enforcement officers, representing various federal, state and local police bureaus were interviewed and asked for a confidential expression of opinion on the general question of crime and marihuana. In most instances they unhesitatingly stated that there is no proof that major crimes are associated with the practice of smoking marihuana. They did state that many marihuana smokers are guilty of petty crimes, but that the criminal career usually existed prior to the time the individual smoked his first marihuana cigarette. These officers further stated that a criminal generally termed as a 'real' or 'professional'

---

[35] Marcovitz and Meyers, 1944, p. 6.

[36] Marcovitz and Meyers, 1944, p. 7.

[37] Wallace, George B., Chairman. The Marihuana Problem in the City of New York: Sociological, Medical, Psychological and Pharmacological Studies by the Mayor's Committee on Marihuana. Lancaster, PA: The Jacques Cattell Press, 1944 AA, Addiction and Tolerance, p. 144.

criminal will not associate with marihuana smokers. He considers such a person inferior and unreliable and will not allow him to participate in the commission of a major crime [quotation marks original].[38]

Anslinger predictably called the La Guardia study

a very unfortunate report released some years ago by the so-called La Guardia committee on marihuana. The Bureau immediately detected the superficiality and hollowness of its findings and denounced it. However it gave wide circulation to the idea that this drug is relatively innocuous. Now marihuana is found to be the introductory drug to much of the heroinism in young people in the United States. The La Guardia report is the favorite reference of the proselytor for narcotic-drugs use.[39]

Figure 350. "Beware!" Anti-Cannabis Placard, Inter-state Narcotic Association, 1940. Kremer's Reference Files, AIHP.

---

38 Wallace, 1944, I. Sociological Aspects, Crime, pp. 14-15.

39 Anslinger, H. J. and Tompkins, W. F. The Traffic in Narcotics. NY: Funk & Wagnalls Company, 1953 AA, Chapter *VIII* Narcotics and Modern Medical Science, p. 168.

Figure 351. "Dr. Walter Lewis Treadway (1886 – 1973)." Still image, photoprint, c. 1938. Walter Lewis Treadway Collections, National Library of Medicine, National Institute of Health [nlm.nih.gov, hereinafter NLM].

2. The *Marihuana Tax Act* of 1937

The *Marihuana Tax Act* was also a criminal statute masquerading as an administrative regulation. That had caused deep distrust and even the screeching of judicial brakes in the case of the *Harrison Act.* On this occasion, however, the new law would be saved by a complete consensus among the legislative, executive and judicial branches. The draft bill was heavily edited by Anslinger and introduced by the Treasury.

The House Ways and Means Committee did not invite the Public Health Service, then under the influence of Lawrence Kolb who would have opposed the project. Dr. Walter Lewis Treadway (1886 – 1973), director of the Mental Hygiene Division of the PHS had previously answered a questionnaire from the Committee about addiction and any supposed social or moral harm occurring from cannabis. He wrote that none of the psychoactive preparations of cannabis produced dependency or tolerance and that (if the available scientific literature was not entirely incorrect) moderate use predominated, without danger to either physical or mental health:

> *Cannabis indica* does not produce dependence as in opium addiction. ... There is no dependence or increased tolerance such as in opium addiction. As to the social or moral degradation associated with cannabis it probably belongs in the same category as alcohol [italics original].[40]

The Committee did not refer to his conclusions during the hearings.

---

[40] Musto, 1999, p. 226, citing in footnote 32 on page 380, Marihuana questionnaire filled out by Dr. Walter L. Treadway (AP, Box 6).

Figure 352. "Dr. William Creighton Woodward (1867 – 1949)." Glass negative, c. 1910. Bain News Service. Library of Congress, Prints & Photographs Division LG.

The only in-person opposition to the bill came from Dr. William Creighton Woodward (1867 – 1949), Legislative Counsel for the American Medical Association, whose testimony was both extensive and direct. He began by saying that the facts about cannabis in Anslinger's report were incomplete and debatable when not false. He pointedly asked why the Public Health Service, whose experience with the Lexington and Fort Worth clinics could be of the greatest interest, had not been consulted, as he "had no knowledge that such a bill as this was proposed until after it had been introduced."[41]

In part, his confusion was due to nomenclature:

> [M]arihuana is not the correct term. It was the use of the term 'marihuana' rather than the use of the term 'Cannabis' or the use of the term 'Indian hemp' that was responsible, as you realized, probably, a day or two ago, for the failure of the dealers in Indian hempseed to connect up this bill with their business until rather late in the day. So, if you will permit me, I shall use the word 'Cannabis,' and I should certainly suggest that if any legislation is enacted, the term used be 'Cannabis' and not the mongrel word 'marihuana' [quotation marks original].[42]

In part, it was because the bill had been prepared in secret: "We cannot understand yet, Mr. Chairman, why this bill should have been prepared in secret for 2 years without any intimation, even, to the profession, that it was being prepared."[43]

Lacking studies and statistical data from the Bureau of Prisons, Woodward asked, what factual basis was there to allege that cannabis caused unstopable tendencies to homicidal dementia, violence and lust:

---

[41] Doughton, 1937, Statement of Dr. William C. Woodward, Legislative Counsel, American Medical Association, Chicago, Ill., p. 88.

[42] Doughton, 1937, p. 90.

[43] Doughton, 1937, p. 116.

Figure 353. "The Sweet Pill." *Reefer Madness* film poster, c. 1936, NLM.

> We are told that the use of marihuana causes crime. But yet no one has been produced from the Bureau of Prisons to show the number of prisoners who have been found addicted to the marihuana habit. An informal inquiry shows that the Bureau of Prisons has no evidence on that point.[44]

No one from the Children's Bureau had been called to speak about the use of the drug by school children. If it were true that pushers were giving away joints at the doors to the school houses, could the FBN specify who had been indicted and convicted for such acts? And if no one had been found guilty of such a thing, why was it being alleged?

> You have been told that school children are great users of marihuana cigarettes. No one has been summoned from the Children's Bureau to show the nature and extent of the habit, among children. Inquiry of the Children's Bureau shows that they have had no occasion to investigate it and know nothing particularly of it. Inquiry of the Office of Education – and they certainly should know something of the prevalence of the habit among the school children of the country, if there is a prevalent habit – indicates that they have had no occasion to investigate and know nothing of it.[45]

Did the FBN give more credence to anti-Mexican letters to the editor than to scientific literature accumulated over centuries and to millennia of peaceful traditional use? In order to make a medicine illegal, he argued, not mere rumors or ethnic prejudice was needed but immediate and primary evidence:

---

[44] Doughton, 1937, p. 92.

[45] Doughton, 1937, p. 92.

The newspapers have called attention to it so prominently that there must be some grounds for their statements. It has surprised me, however, that the facts on which these statements have been based have not been brought before this committee by competent primary evidence. We are referred to newspaper publications concerning the prevalence of marihuana addiction.[46]

If cannabis was addictive why wasn't there any evidence of this on the government's own narcotic farms:

Moreover, there is in the Treasury Department itself, the Public Health Service, with its Division of Mental Hygiene. ... That particular Bureau has control at the present time of the narcotics farms that were created about 1929 or 1930 and came into operation a few years later. No one has been summoned from that Bureau to give evidence on that point. Informal inquiry by me indicates that they have had no record of any marihuana or Cannabis addicts who have ever been committed to those farms.[47]

The members of the Committee on Ways and Means attacked Dr. Woodward's testimony as being counter to a recent editorial in the *Journal* of the American Medical Association, contrary to Anslinger's report, differing from the recent position of the Supreme Court, and contradictory to his previous positions on popular legislation already passed.[48] His arguments that the bill was unnecessary and would not work were ignored.[49] Congress approved the new law which came into effect on 1 October 1937.[50]

From then until 1971 there will be dozens of such bills which will be quickly approved, demonstrating that any deviation from the

[46] Doughton, 1937, p. 92.

[47] Doughton, 1937, p. 92.

[48] Doughton, 1937, pp. 97 et seq.

[49] Doughton, 1937, pp. 94 et seq.

[50] Musto, 1999, p. 228.

most severe orthodoxy would be for the senators and representatives an act of electoral suicide. Even more clearly (if that is possible) than with the passage of the *Harrison Act*, the *Marihuana Tax Act* demonstrated that performative morality and political convenience overshadowed a dispassionate factual and pharmacological discussion of the phenomenon. Anslinger's bill, laced with legal inconsistencies and based on fundamentally false data, was rapidly approved by the Committee. The users and sellers of cannabis were equated to the users and traffickers of the opiates and cocaine. All these drugs were denominated narcotics.

In a curious twist of history (not infrequent in this field) beginning in the 1970s the United States will become the largest consumer and one of the largest cultivators of this plant. Given the lack of seriousness with which Congress had debated the criminalization of cannabis, one can understand that the La Guardia report would be relegated to a dusty basement file cabinet, together with other old fashioned and useless items of only historical curiosity. Even if the testimony of doctors Woodward and Treadway had been fairly examined, the opinions of the committee members would not have been changed.

Within less than a decade after it became illegal, an editorial in the *Journal* of the AMA wrote exactly what Anslinger had been hoping to hear, in that the La Guardia report

> states unqualifiedly to the public that the use of this narcotic does not lead to physical, mental or moral degeneration and that permanent deleterious effects from its continued use were not observed on 77 prisoners. This statement has already done great damage to the cause of law enforcement. Public officials will do well to disregard this unscientific, uncritical study, and continue to regard marihuana as a menace wherever it is purveyed.[51]

---

[51] Unknown Editor. "Marihuana Problems," *The Journal of the American Medical*

C. International Agreements

In the 1920s and 1930s the League of Nations sponsored three different international conferences on drugs before its demise. The United States was not a party to the League but attempted to influence the discussions. The results were mixed at best.

Specifically, the Americans were already anticipating what would later come to fruition: a policy of dispossessing farmers, destroying harvests and defoliating inaccessible jungles and mountainsides. Of course, other countries found the fact that the United States was in the middle of a full-blown prohibition on alcohol in the 1920s and early 1930s somewhat astonishing, its position on this issue paradoxically resembling that of a number of Islamic regimes. Moreover, the US wanted to be able to dictate to other countries which plants they could cultivate and how much, regardless of their own traditions. The alleged motive for this extended control was that such plantations represented a threat to people thousands of miles away. Yet, at the time for most nations interference in national sovereignty for the purpose of international drug prohibition was still unthinkable.

Association, Volume 127, Number 17, Saturday, April 28, 1945 AA, p. 1129.

CH. 25 THE CRUSADE BEGINS (II)

1. The 1925 Geneva Conference

Although the US had been the principal supporter of increasing restrictions on drugs, the American delegation to the 1925 Geneva Conference on the Restriction of the Traffic in Opium, Morphine and Cocaine marched out the door before it was ended. While the Americans[52] put forth a proposal to limit internal production (not simply external importation), the other delegations only wanted to discuss problems of drug manufacture, without considering a quota on the production of raw opium in each country:

> Such a suggestion took the scope of the meeting way beyond the original subject of the Conference. The key objective of the international meetings to that date had been to ensure that the nations involved would agree not to supply the people of another country with opium or cocaine where the government of that country had banned or limited access to the drugs. It had urged countries to combat the demand of their peoples for the substances but had never attempted to force governments to impose regulations on their own peoples. The American motion implied an unprecedented intervention by the League of Nations to stamp its will on populations over and above the national sovereignty of their own governments. ... The focus would have shifted from regulating international trade between governments to forcing domestic policies on them. ... [I]t was the eventual rejection of this American proposal that caused them to storm out halfway through its proceedings.[53]

---

52 Including the Honorable Stephen Geyer Porter (1869 – 1930), the Reverend Charles Henry Brent (1862 – 1929) and Mrs. Elizabeth Hamilton Wright neé Washburne (1874 – 1952), who had taken up her late husband's mantle.

53 Mills, James H. Cannabis Britannica: Empire, Trade, and Prohibition 1800 – 1928. Oxford, UK: Oxford University Press, 2003 AA, Chapter 7 'An allusion was made to hemp in the notes appended to the Hague Opium Convention': The League of Nations and British Legislation, 1912 – 1928, p. 166.

The result of the conference then was a pact that referred exclusively to inspection of certain manufacturing facilities without establishing limits on cultivation. Otherwise, the attendees reiterated the principles in the Hague Agreement of 1912, in which the parties would limit production and sale to scientific and medical use:

The Contracting Parties shall enact effective laws or regulations to limit exclusively to medical and scientific purposes the manufacture, import, sale, distribution, export and use of the substances to which this Chapter applies. They shall co-operate with one another to prevent the use of these substances for any other purposes.[54]

This article was not to be understood as restrictive but only textual since only a corresponding medical or scientific authority could decide in each case. Neither was the conference restrictive in other areas, contemplating for example direct dispensation of a number of opiate preparations:

Any contracting Party may authorise the supply to the public by chemists, at their own discretion, as medicines, for immediate use in urgent cases, of the following opiate officinal preparations: tincture of opium, Sydenham laudanum and Dover powder. The maximum dose, however, which may be supplied in such cases must not contain more than 25 centigrammes of officinal opium, and the chemist must enter in his books the quantities supplied, as provided in Article 6 *(c)* [italics original].[55]

The Hague Convention of 1912 had closed with a compromise by the signers to consider the possibility of laws to punish possession.

---

[54] No. 1845. – International Opium Convention, Adopted by the Second Opium Conference (League of Nations). Signed at Geneva, February, 1925. League of Nations Treaty Series, 1928-1929 [worldlii.org, hereinafter WLO], Chapter III Internal Control of Manufactured Drugs, Article 5, p. 329.

[55] No. 1845, 1925, Article 9, p. 331.

The 1925 Geneva Convention ignored possession and punished trafficking instead, by confiscation if necessary:

> Each of the Contracting Parties agrees that breaches of its laws or regulations by which the provisions of the present Convention are enforced shall be punishable by adequate penalties including in appropriate cases the confiscation of the substances concerned.[56]

Confiscation was not an especially terrible punishment, and in this (like excluding simple possession) one sees the lack of influence of the Americans. Like the 1912 Hague Agreement, what was finally agreed to in 1925 at Geneva was to not export to a country forbidding importation, and to reserve the listed drugs to medical and scientific purposes.

Yet there were also a number of novelties. The first was to create a Permanent Central Board, a body composed in the beginning "of eight persons who, by their technical competence, impartiality and disinterestedness, will command general confidence."[57] The United States would appoint one member of the Board and Germany another, with the other six appointed by the Council of the League of Nations to represent equitably the manufacturing and consuming countries:

> The members of the Central Board shall be appointed by the Council of the League of Nations. The United States of America and Germany shall be invited each to nominate one person to participate in these appointments. In making the appointments, consideration shall be given to the importance of including on the Central Board, in equitable proportion, persons possessing a knowledge of the drug situation, both in the producing and manufacturing countries on the one hand and in the consuming countries on the other hand, and connected with such countries.[58]

---

[56] No. 1845, 1925, Chapter VII General Provisions, Article 28, p. 345.

[57] No. 1845, 1925, Chapter VI Permanent Central Board, Article 19, p. 339.

[58] No. 1845, 1925, Article 19, p. 339.

This consulting body is the first enduring international institution concerned with drugs. It was required to "continuously watch the course of the international trade."[59] Annual reports from each signing country detailing the quantities of imports, production, manufacture, inventory, consumption and confiscation were required to be sent to the Board.[60] It will be the seed of a vast network of similar permanent consultative organizations.

The second novelty was to expand the list of controlled substances from six (raw, prepared and medicinal opium, morphine, cocaine and heroin)[61] in the 1912 Hague Agreement to nine (raw and medicinal opium, morphine, heroin, coca leaf, crude cocaine, cocaine, ecgonine [a precursor of cocaine], and Indian Hemp).[62]

The latter was defined as:

> *Indian Hemp*. – "Indian hemp" means the dried flowering or fruiting tops of the pistillate plant *Cannabis sativa L.* from which the resin has not been extracted, under whatever name they may be designated in commerce [italics, quotation marks original].[63]

It received its own special chapter in the agreement whereby the Contracting Parties were to undertake:

---

[59] No. 1845, 1925, Article 24, p. 343.

[60] No. 1845, 1925, Articles 21 and 22, pp. 339, 341.

[61] No. 222. The International Opium Convention signed at The Hague, January 23, 1912, and subsequent relative papers. League of Nations Treaty Series, 1922, pp. 193, 195, 197.

[62] No. 1845, 1925, pp. 327, 329.

[63] No. 1845, 1925, Chapter I Definitions, Article 1, pp. 327, 329.

(a) To prohibit the export of the resin obtained from Indian hemp and the ordinary preparations of which the resin forms the base (such as hashish, esrar, chiras, djamba) to countries which have prohibited their use, and, in cases where export is permitted, to require the production of a special import certificate issued by the Government of the importing country stating that the importation is approved for the purposes specified in the certificate and that the resin or preparations will not be re-exported [italics original] ....[64]

The British delegation proposed incorporating cannabis resin (hashish) into the list of controlled substances, even though

no significant change in the patterns of use of cannabis in British society or British medicine. It remained largely unknown as an intoxicant and was infrequently used in medical practice. It was not therefore developments in domestic drug consumption that had inspired these new restrictions.[65]

This appeared to be incompatible with the general opinion of English physicians and pharmacologists at the end of the nineteenth century as well as with the monumental study prepared by its army in India in 1894.[66] What those investigators had had in common was astonishment at the lack of toxicity and multitude of possible uses combined with a certain depreciation of what seemed to be a typical primitive drug compared to the refined alkaloids. Until the middle of the twentieth century, no one will manage to isolate its so-called active principle (tetrahydrocannabinol, a nonalkaloidal natural compound), so the plant will remain chemically mysterious.

Why Britain decided to mention cannabis is also somewhat mysterious. Italy had expressed at the 1912 Hague conference a desire to include cannabis among the drugs restricted to medical and

---

[64] No. 1845, 1925, Chapter IV Indian Hemp, Article 11, p. 333.

[65] Mills, 2003, Chapter 7, p. 152.

[66] See GHDV3P1, Chapter 17, 4. The Indian Hemp Drugs Commission, p. 1149.

scientific use, as noted earlier,[67] but this was not acted upon. In a 1923 letter, the Prime Minister of the Union of South Africa asked to place 'Dagga [cannabis]' on the international list.[68] The head of the British delegation then

> made reference to the letter from South Africa in order to draw attention to the cannabis issue. ... He told his colleagues that it had been informed of the South African communication and that it had acted promptly to consult the various administrations in India so as to discover whether it would be possible to prohibit the export of Indian hemp. He suggested leaving a full consideration of the subject for future sessions in order to allow time for information to be collected.[69]

At the conference, however, it was the head of the Egyptian delegation who introduced the proposal, blaming the drug for causing insanity:

> There is, however, another product which is at least as harmful as opium, if not more so, and which my Government would be glad to see included in the same category as the other narcotics already mentioned. I refer to hashish, the product of the Cannabis indica or sativa. ... I cannot sufficiently emphasise the importance of including this product in the list of narcotics .... The illicit use of hashish is the principal cause of most of the cases of insanity occurring in Egypt. ... Generally speaking, the proportion of cases of insanity caused by the use of hashish varies from 30 to 60 per cent of the total number of cases occurring in Egypt.[70]

---

[67] See this volume, Chapter 23 Junkies and Juicers, 2. Other Drugs, pp. 1577-1578.

[68] Mills, 2003, pp. 160-161.

[69] Mills, 2003, p. 161.

[70] Zahle, Herluf, President. Records of the Second Opium Conference Geneva, November 17th, 1924 – February 25th, 1925, Volume I Plenary Meetings, Text of the Debates. Geneva, Switzerland: League of Nations, 1925 [digitallibrary.un.org, hereinafter DLU], Fifth Meeting *Held at Geneva on Thursday, November 20th, 1924 at 10:30 a.m.*, p. 39, Sixteenth Meeting *Held at Geneva on Saturday, December 13th, 1924, at 4:30 p.m.*, p. 134.

CH. 25 THE CRUSADE BEGINS (II)

Other motivations have been proposed such as that hashish had become a symbol of subversive activities (anything opposed to colonialism) which had been gaining strength in Egypt and especially in Cairo where the drug was the "centre of a subversive sub-culture."[71] Many well off Egyptians joined campaigns against whiskey and gin, against cigarettes and generally against anything that represented colonialism, even while accepting the tropes of the occupiers:

> The Egyptian elite of the time ... came to see social tidiness and physical cleanliness as the country's fundamental political requirement. As Western commentators were describing non-Western societies in terms of indolence, ... personal discipline and the ability to utilize unfilled moments of the day [were] ... equivalent with collective progress. Disorder, the inability to discipline time, space and mobility rationally, was becoming a political issue. In this context, the idleness of the hashish smoker and his inability to control his mind and his time were emblematic of those traits that Egyptian society, and particularly its lower orders, needed to abandon to serve collective progress.[72]

As well the Egyptian war on the plant was faring poorly:

> 'In 1884 the cultivation of this plant was forbidden. The cafes (or mashhashas) in which hashish was consumed by smoking in special hookahs were closed and are still mercilessly sought out by the police.' In 1924 the Egyptian customs service alone had seized 3,262,227 kg of hashish, so it was clear that the demand for the drugs was being met by illegal supplies from abroad [quotation marks original].[73]

---

[71] Laurie, Peter. Drugs: Medical, Psychological and Social Facts. Baltimore, MD: Penguin Books, 1967 AA, Chapter 1 The Meaning of Drug, p. 16.

[72] Kozma, Liat. "Cannabis Prohibition in Egypt, 1880 – 1939: From Local Ban to League of Nations Diplomacy," *Middle Eastern Studies*, Volume 47, No. 3, May 2011 AA, p. 446.

[73] Mills, 2003, p. 171.

Hence, the Egyptians could use some international help.

Two countries that could have objected to the English provision were Afghanistan (which was not represented at Geneva) and Persia which sent a representative but did not ratify. Spain did not send a representative but did ratify in that same year, pointedly excluding Morocco, since one of the most tenacious centers of opposition and resistance was in Ketama, a traditional area of hashish fabrication. France showed real interest in supporting the initiative, but added reservations with regards to "the colonies, protectorates and mandated territories under its authority"[74] not only because the drug was widely used in Algeria, Tunisia and Libya, but also by virtue of its own colonial history in Egypt where Napoleon had prohibited the drug albeit briefly; as well the memory of the artificial paradises denounced by Baudelaire suggested an attitude of vigilence. Indeed, it was the men of Europe (where cannabis was practically unknown as a psychopharmaceutical) who decided to classify cannabis with the opiates and cocaine.

A third novelty was to substantially expand the list of prohibited substances. Article 14 *(d)* of the 1912 Hague Agreement required the contracting powers to apply laws and regulations not only to opium, morphine, cocaine and heroin but also to

> all new derivatives of morphine, of cocaine, or of their respective salts, and to every other alkaloid of opium, which may be shown by scientific research, generally recognised, to be liable to similar abuse and productive of like ill-effects.[75]

Article 10 of the 1925 Geneva Agreement went further, recommending such regulations to "any narcotic drug ... [that] is liable

[74] No. 1845, 1925, p. 352: *les Colonies, Protectorats et Pays sous mandat, dépendant de son autorité.*

[75] No. 222, 1922, p. 199.

to similar abuse and productive of similar ill-effects."[76] The second international opium convention had now truly become an international drug convention.

Most of the European powers by 1929 had signed and ratified the convention. Also appointing plenipotentiaries or filing accessions were a few countries from Central and South America (Cuba, Dominican Republic, Venezuela, Salvador, Nicaragua, Brazil, Chile, Uruguay).[77] In Asia and Africa the plant was not only linked to medicine but also to traditional religious rites and recreational use. However, Asia and Africa were hardly represented as independent countries. Britain ratified the convention for India, Australia, New Zealand and South Africa, the Netherlands for the Netherlands Indies, Surinam and Curaçao, and Spain for its colonies excluding Morocco.[78] Only Sudan and Siam (which had little influence) represented autonomously their continents. Moreover, it was clear that the drug was not threatening in itself for the Europeans but was simply inconvenient for the British in Egypt. By including it in the convention, they were assured that they could prohibit it anew as had Napoleon and could be sure that no other country would take advantage of them as they had taken advantage of the intransigence of the Chinese emperors.

But notable are the countries who did not sign, including almost all the largest and medium-sized countries then producing opium such as China, the Soviet Union, Afghanistan, Turkey and Persia (which sent a representative), the largest producers of coca including Peru and Bolivia (which refused to prohibit coca leaves to the native population), as well as other growers of coca (Paraguay and

---

[76] No. 1845, 1925, p. 331.

[77] No. 1845, 1925, pp. 319, 321, 323, 325, 327.

[78] No. 1845, 1925, p. 319, footnote 1, Deposit of Ratifications.

Ecuador).[79] Britain excluded Sarawak and the Bahamas, Belgium excluded the Belgian Congo and Ruanda Urundi, Spain as noted Morocco, and Bolivia the places of Villazon, Yacuiba, Antofagasta, Arica and Mollendo.[80] The United States, for whom such timid compromises and obvious loopholes were a betrayal of the spirit of the 1912 Hague conference, walked away and did not sign.

2. The 1931 Geneva Conference

With ten more countries sending plenipotentiaries than the previous 1925 conference[81] (among which the important producers of raw materials such as China, the Soviet Union, Turkey and Afghanistan remained absent) but with the presence of representatives from the United States, Persia, Bolivia and Paraguay, the 1931 conference for Limiting the Manufacture and Regulating the Distribution of Narcotic Drugs aimed to put into practice the directives of 1925 and hopefully "curtail the illegitimate trade which has succeeded in getting around the 1912 and 1925 conventions."[82] This meant making so-called evaluations of the quantities needed for medical and scientific use, which each country was obligated to present to the Permanent Central Board. These evaluations were linked to the condition considered

---

[79] No. 1845, 1925, pp. 319-327.

[80] No. 1845, 1925, pp. 319, 321.

[81] No. 1845, 1925, pp. 321, 323, 325, 327; Bevans, Charles I., compiler. "Convention for Limiting the Manufacture and Regulating the Distribution of Narcotic Drugs," Treaties and Other International Agreements of the United States of America 1776 – 1949, Volume 3, Multilateral 1931-1945. Washington, DC: Department of State Publications, 1968 [loc.gov, hereinafter LG], pp. 2, 3, 4, 5, 6.

[82] Wright, Quincey. "The Narcotics Convention of 1931," *American Journal of International Law*, Volume 28, No. 3, July 1934, p. 478.

essential by the American delegation, which was the acceptance of a limit of production for each country.

On top of the energy exhibited by its representatives, it is important not to forget that by then the US was the largest financial contributor to the League of Nations. This gave its proposals not only moral but practical force. To be certain, all the invitees knew that from the beginning the survival of their organization depended directly on preserving the pleasure of the Americans. However, the question of limiting production needed the votes of the rest of the nations attending, and faced with the impossibility of arriving at an agreement without mutual concessions, each state required subtle, even pharasaical forms of calculating the total quantity for its legitimate needs. Under Article 6 the following were admissible:

(a) The quantity required within the limits of the estimates for that country or territory for that year for use as such for its medical and scientific needs including the quantity required for the manufacture of preparations for the export of which export authorisations are not required, whether such preparations are intended for domestic consumption or for export;
(b) The quantity required within the limits of the estimates for that country or territory for that year for conversion, whether for domestic consumption or for export;
(c) Such quantity as may be required by that country or territory for the execution during the year of orders for export in accordance with the provisions of this Convention;
(d) The quantity, if any, required by that country or territory for the purpose of maintaining the reserve stocks at the level specified in the estimates for that year;
(e) The quantity, if any, required for the purpose of maintaining the Government stocks at the level specified in the estimates for that year.[83]

[83] Bevans, 1968, Volume III, Chapter III Limitation of Manufacture, Article 6, p. 11.

To verify the details of the submissions from every country and every territory would require a complex oversight mechanism at the Permanent Central Board, capable of analyzing and evaluating every year the detailed statistics submitted. This led to the idea of a spiritually analogous institution to the American Federal Bureau of Narcotics (though only consultative) within the bosom of the League of Nations, whose basic mission would be to organize the struggle against toxicomania, taking all available measures to stop its spread and to combat illicit trafficking under Article 15:

> The High Contracting Parties shall, if they have not already done so, create a special administration for the purpose of:
> (a) Applying the provisions of the present Convention;
> (b) Regulating, supervising and controlling the trade in the drugs;
> (c) Organising the campaign against drug addiction, by taking all useful steps to prevent its development and to suppress the illicit traffic.[84]

The creation of this international prohibitionist organization (which would eventually spawn both the Commission on Narcotic Drugs and the Narcotics Control Board, both based in Vienna) along with the compromise on evaluations was already a great triumph for the United States. As a result Congress deigned to ratify this convention (as it had not done with the previous conventions at The Hague, Versailles and Geneva) and authorize a generous increase in the budget to put in practice the international accords.

The most scandalous part of the convention, apart from the absences and the convoluted manner of calculating the quantities authorized for each country, was that under Article 26 the colonial powers assumed no obligation in whole or in part for the territories under their control:

---

[84] Bevans, 1968, Volume III, Chapter VI Administrative Provisions, Article 15, p. 16

Any High Contracting Party may, at the time of signature, ratification, or accession, declare that, in accepting the present Convention, he does not assume any obligation in respect of all or any of his colonies, protectorates and overseas territories or territories under suzerainty or mandate, and the present Convention shall not apply to any territories named in such declaration.[85]

Japan, for example, signed the treaty but formulated a reservation incorporated into Section II of the Protocol of Signature that raw morphine produced in Formosa would not be subject to these limitations:

Crude morphine resulting from the manufacture of prepared opium in the factory of the Government-General of Formosa and held in stock by that Government shall not be subjected to the limitation measures provided for in this Convention.

Such stocks of crude morphine will only be released from time to time in such quantities as may be required for the manufacture of refined morphine in factories licensed by the Japanese Government in accordance with the provisions of the present Convention.[86]

Japan was presently in the process of conquering China and its armies were distributing large quantities of morphine and heroin in the occupied parts of the continent.

The US, in contrast, was now firmly on board at least with the spirit of the previous agreements:

In September, 1933, the United States announced its willingness to submit the names of candidates for membership in the Permanent Central Opium Board set up by the Opium Convention of 1925, and to act with the Council of the League of Nations in the selection of that board. It was explained that although the board was set up

85 Bevans, 1968, Volume III, Chapter VII General Provisions, Article 26, p. 19.

86 Bevans, 1968, Volume III, Protocol of Signature, pp. 23-24.

under a treaty to which the United States was not a party (1925), it is entrusted with important functions under a treaty which the United States has ratified (1931), and that the United States had obligated itself to coöperate and had coöperated wholeheartedly with the board since its establishment in 1928.[87]

3. The 1936 Geneva Conference

Forty governments sent accredited delegations to the Convention for the Suppression of the Illicit Traffic in Dangerous Drugs held in Geneva in the summer of 1936 but only twenty-six signed the final document.[88] China, the Union of Soviet Socialist Republics, Afghanistan, Turkey and Peru sent delegations, though the last two did not sign. Persia and Bolivia were not represented. The US delegation (including H. J. Anslinger) also did not sign.

One immediately notices that the subject of these periodic conferences has morphed from opium to narcotics to the much broader and undefined concept of the dangerous drug. In spite of its title, the treaty obligated its signers to "severely" punish not only the traffic in but any involvement whatsoever with such poorly denominated substances, demanding in Article 2 that each country alter its own national laws for this purpose:

---

[87] Wright, 1934, p. 478.

[88] Limburg, M., President. Records of the Conference for the Suppression of the Illicit Traffic in Dangerous Drugs (Geneva, June 8th to 26th, 1936), Text of the Debates. Geneva, Switzerland: Members of the League, 1936 AO, List of Members, pp. 7-11 (Finland and Latvia sent observers); Kohona, Palitha T. B., Chief, Treaty Section, Office of Legal Affairs. Convention of 1936 for the Suppression of Illicit Traffic in Dangerous Drugs. Geneva, Switzerland: League of Nations, 1936 [treaties.un.org, hereinafter TUN], pp. 6-10.

Each of the High Contracting Parties agrees to make the necessary legislative provisions for severely punishing, particularly by imprisonment or other penalties of deprivation of liberty, the following acts – namely:

(a) The manufacture, conversion, extraction, preparation, possession, offering, offering for sale, distribution, purchase, sale, delivery on any terms whatsoever, brokage, despatch, despatch in transit, transport, importation and exportation of narcotic drugs, contrary to the provisions of the said Conventions;

(b) Intentional participation in the offences specified in this Article;

(c) Conspiracy to commit any of the above-mentioned offences;

(d) Attempts and, subject to the conditions prescribed by national law, preparatory acts.[89]

Notice that possession is now a criminal act.

Under Article 11, each signing party agreed to create a "central office" to prevent and prosecute any offences:

1. Each of the High Contracting Parties shall set up, within the framework of its domestic law, a central office for the supervision and co-ordination of all operations necessary to prevent the offences specified in Article 2, and for ensuring that steps are taken to prosecute persons guilty of such offences.

2. This central office:

(a) Shall be in close contact with other official institutions or bodies dealing with narcotic drugs;

(b) Shall centralise all information of a nature to facilitate the investigation and prevention of the offences specified in Article 2;

(c) Shall be in close contact with and may correspond direct with the central offices of other countries.[90]

Nominally at least, the American crusade was interfering in not only the laws but the institutions of other nations, as it becomes a more intrusive and organized world crusade.

---

[89] Convention, 1936, p. 2.

[90] Convention, 1936, p. 3.

Figure 354. "Alfonso XIII (1886 – 1941)." Portrait (c. 1916) by Antonio Canovas Castillo y Vallejo (Kaulak, 1862 – 1933). Museu Nacional d'Art de Catalunya, Barcelona.

D. Spain

There are few firm figures on the production, importation and sale of drugs in Spain during the nineteenth century perhaps because much of the commerce was unregulated. A doctor in 1858 calculated that the country consumed two tons of raw opium annually,[91] but had no data on morphine, codeine or other products that were increasingly supplanting the ancient remedy.

In 1860 a *Real Decreto* [Royal Decree] approved *Ordenanzas de Farmacia* [Pharmacy Regulations] on 18 April prohibiting the sale of drugs, chemical products and medicines in groceries and spice shops.[92] Once in force, the elaboration and sale of medicines became the prerogative of diplomaed pharmacists, although the sale of drugs, wholesale or retail, could continue by herbalists, druggists and perfumeries. Commerce in medicines by those without this license could be punished publicly or privately, in aggravated cases by incarceration from 1 to 15 days.[93] Which medicines were unspecified.

The *Codigo Penal* [Penal Code] of 1870 (which was not modified until 1928) did not distinguish between the harm caused by psychoactive drugs from that caused by many other chemical substances.[94] Article 351 punishes those not competently authorized

---

91 Marqués, R. "Opio," *La Actualidad. Seman. de Med., Farm. y Ciencias Aux., Valencia*, enero 1859, pp. 8-10.

92 *las Ordenanzas de Farmacia de 18 de abril de 1860, prohibiendo la venta de «drogas, productos químicos y medicinales» en los «comercios de Especias, Abacerías, Coloniales y Ultramarinos»* (Usó Arnal, Joan Carles. "*Sobre los orígenes del «problema de la droga» en España*," *Ateneo de Castellón*, No. 4, Octubre, 1991 [repositori.uji.es, hereinafter RIU], 5 de julio de 1921, p. 130).

93 *Real Decreto*, 10-4-1860, art. 75.

94 *substancias nocivas á la salud* (Usó Arnal, 1991, p. 160, footnote 139, discussing articles 351, 352 and 354 of the code).

to elaborate substances harmful to one's health or chemical products which can cause great devastation with detention and a fine of from 250 to 2,500 *pesetas*.[95] Article 352 punishes with detention and a fine of from 125 to 1,250 pesetas those authorized to traffic in substances harmful to one's health without fulfilling the formalities prescribed by the respective rules of their profession.[96] The discussion that accompanies this article specifies no particular drug but only poisonous substances or, again, chemical products that can cause great devastation; those authorized are pharmacists, druggists, makers of chemical products and herbalists.[97] Pharmacists who sell deteriorated medicines or substitutes are fined and can receive fines and prison time by Article 353.[98] Article 354 applies the previous two articles to those who work for the pharmacists.[99]

Neither do we know, even approximately, what number of persons were consuming psychopharmaceuticals chronically or sporadically. It appears there was a system of self-control, conditioned only by the price of each product. Around 1910, for example, a pamphlet from Bayer in Spain recommended heroin due to its ability to combat a wide variety of symptoms from cough, bronchitis and pulmonary catarrh to states of confusion, depression and

---

95 *El que sin hallarse ... 2.500 pesetas* (Salvador Viada y Vilaseca, D. Código Penal Reformado de 1870, Libro Primero. Barcelona: Establecimiento Tipográfico de Luis Tasso, 1874 AO, Capítulo II De los delitos contra la salud pública, Art. 351. p. 477).

96 *El que hallándose ... multa de 125 á 1.250 pesetas* (Salvador Viada y Vilaseca, 1874, Art. 352, p. 478).

97 *sustancias venenosas ... yerberos* (Salvador Viada y Vilaseca, 1874, Art. 352, p. 478).

98 *Los farmacéuticos que ... 2.500 pesetas* (Salvador Viada y Vilaseca, 1874, Art. 353, p. 479).

99 *Las disposiciones ... cuando fueron los culpables* (Salvador Viada y Vilaseca, 1874, Art. 354, p. 480).

neurasthenia.[100] In 1907 Bonald Laboratories announced not only heroin pills (soothing, calming, cough suppressing), but also other remedies containing morphine, codeine and cocaine. Merck's cocaine, advertised under the sobriquet '*La Insuperable* [The Unbeatable]' was perhaps the most charismatic, even mentioned by name in a police report from 1926.[101] No prescription was needed, and neither in the specialized literature nor in the press or novels is there any reference to street sales of the drug. Neither was there a drug problem, at least to judge from the annual reports presented by prosecutors to the *Tribunal Supremo* [Supreme Court].

Figure 355. "Advertisement for Bonald Laboratories." *Gaceta* de Madrid, April 1907.

---

100 *una especie de panaceas universales, indicadas para todo tipo de males y enfermedades. Cfr. Productos Farmacéuticos de las Farbenfabriken vorm. Friedr. Bayer & Ca. Leverkusen* (Usó Arnal, 1991, footnote 138, p. 160).

101 *cocaína pura, de la 'insuperable,' de la marca 'Merck'* [quotation marks original] (Usó Arnal, 1991, 13 de mayo de 1926, p. 135).

1. International Obligations

Though not represented at the 1912 Hague Conference,[102] Spain signed the protocol in 1912, ratified the treaty in 1919 and brought it into force in 1921.[103] The signing led to the *Real Decreto* of 31 July 1918, which set out rules for the importation, registration, inspection, re-export, possession, sale and dispensing of a number of specific substances.[104] It says a lot about the country at the time that Article 11 punished the possession without a prescription of opium, coca, cocaine, narcotics, antipyretics, anaesthetics, contraceptives and abortifacients for nonmedical use with fines of from 50 to 500 pesetas.[105]

Indeed, the 1918 *Real Decreto* demonstrates eloquently the values underlying the chemistry of the day, and to what degree family planning was as scandalous in Spain as intoxication with non-alcoholic substances. On the one hand, the legislator wanted to fulfill the obligations signed onto with the Hague Agreement, essentially to restrict the use of opium, morphine and cocaine to medical and scientific purposes, and to prohibit the export of these substances to

---

[102] No. 222, 1922, pp. 189, 191, 193.

[103] International Opium Convention, League of Nations *Treaty Series*, Volume 8. Geneva, 1922 [treaties.un.org, hereinafter TU], Schedule containing the signatures of the Convention ..., p. 187.

[104] *Real decreto por el que se aprueba el Reglamento para el comercio y dispensación de substancias tóxicas y en especial de las que ejercen acción narcótica, antitérrnica o anestésica* (Usó Arnal, 1991, 31 de julio de 1918, p. 129).

[105] *La possession del opio ... asi como ... antigenésicos y abortivos ... segán la importancia del caso* (*Real Decreto de 31 de julio de 1.918, por el que se aprueba el reglamento para el comercio y dispensación de las sustancias tóxicas y en especial de las que ejercen acción narcótica, antitérmica o anestésica*. Legislación española sobre drogas, I. Normativa de ámbito estatal, 1918 [pnsd.sanidad.gob.es, hereinafter PSG], Artíclulo 11, pp. 2-3).

the other signers of the convention which had prohibited them.[106] But the stereotypical addict and pusher were absent from Spain; thus, whoever sold these products outside a pharmacy would be denounced before a subcommittee on medicine or pharmacy as an illegal seller of medicines.[107] At the same time, in the US a similar person was not simply an unlicensed vendor, subject to a government fine, but a corrupter of souls, more dangerous than a murderer, requiring years of incarceration in a penitentiary.

An analysis of the text and the motives of the legislator suggests that one of his preoccupations was ether (retailed only in the pharmacies, demanding a prescription when the repetition and frequency would suspect abuse),[108] and that he was attentive to the conflict with druggists, perfumists and other establishments.[109] Only pharmacists could import opiates and cocaine.[110] Sales at the pharmacy required a medical prescription.[111] Taking the side of physicians and pharmacists, demanding a prescription from someone with a diploma supposes the consolidation of a monopoly by the therapeutic estate on

---

106 *para asegurar la eficacia de la intervención acordada con la mencionada Convención* (Real Decreto de 31 de julio de 1.918, Artíclulo 10, p. 2).

107 *denunciándose por los Subdelegados de Medicina y de Farmacia, como expendedor ilegal de medicamentos* (Real Decreto de 31 de julio de 1.918, Artíclulo 14, p. 3).

108 *El comercio del éter etílico ... un empleo abusivo* (Real Decreto de 31 de julio de 1.918, Artíclulo 22, p. 4).

109 *Las droguerías, perfumerias y otros establecimientos ... para impedir que continúe el comercio ilegal de estos medicamentos peligrosos* (Real Decreto de 31 de julio de 1.918, Artíclulo 16, p. 3).

110 *únicamente a los agentes representantes de los Colegios de Farmacéuticos, a personas notoriamente reconocidas y matriculadas* (Real Decreto de 31 de julio de 1.918, Artíclulo 7°, p. 2).

111 *será requisito indispensable la prescripción facultativa, escrita y firmada por el Médico quedando la fórmula en poder del farmacéutico* (Real Decreto de 31 de julio de 1.918, Artíclulo 15, p. 3).

a wide range of medicinal products, something the Colleges of Medicine and Pharmacy accepted with undisguised pleasure.

The changing social situation and the need to ratify the Geneva Convention of 1925 required a more practical statute,[112] still preoccupied with the illegal use of ether but which equated possession with trafficking. Mere illicit possession would be evidence of guilt in the absence of proof to the contrary,[113] considered to be seriously unethical conduct on the part of pharmacists or their assistants. The range of economic sanctions was severe. Each person involved in the production, importation, sale or distribution would be fined from 50 to 100 pesetas for each gram of substance seized. For a second offense, the fine was increased to 500 pesetas .... The same fines would be imposed upon those responsible for mere possession or illicit consumption.[114]

The spirit of this norm will be incorporated in the new *Codigo Penal* of 1928, whose novelty is to separate toxic drugs or stupefacients from substances harmful to the health or chemical products that can cause great damage.[115] It articulated the previous generic punishment of incarceration (up to a maximum of three years) for production and illicit trafficking. The organization responsible for overseeing the new policy was the *Junta de Servicio de Restriccion de Estupefacientes*, of whose twelve members only one belonged to the police, clearly in contrast to

---

112 *El Real Decreto – Ley* [Royal Decree – Law] of 30 April 1928 approving grounds for state restrictions on the distribution and sale of stupefacients; *bases para la Restricción del Estado en la distribución y venta de estupefacientes* (Usó Arnal, 1991, 30 de abril de 1928, p. 144).

113 *Base* 40.

114 *Base* 43. The salary for an assistant pharmacist then was around 100 pesetas a month.

115 *drogas tóxicas o estupefacientes ... substancias nocivas para la salud o productos químicos que puedan causar grandes estragos* (Usó Arnal, 1991, p. 145).

he situation in Northamerica; the statute also evidenced a notable lifference in orientation by leaving it up to the medical faculty to decide what was medical use, including indefinite maintenance therapy for addicts.

Figure 356. "Juan Carlos Usó Arnal (b. 1959)." Photograph, 28 March 2018. Biblioteca del Museo Valenciana de Etnologia.

2. Social Reality

Although this legislation could be considered benevolent, and even permissive if compared with the Northamerican statutes, the possession and consumption of certain drugs (previously left to the discretion of the adult) now became something that fell within the jurisdiction of the state. This is a decisive change, which will very soon unleash unexpected consequences. Thanks to a pioneering and exhaustive work by the historian, writer and professor Juan Carlos Usó Arnal (b. 1959) which examined articles related to this theme appearing in Spanish newspapers between 1920 and 1930, we are able to follow closely those consequences.

The first effect of the 1918 *Decreto* was a quick rise in the prices of medicine. Now it was necessary to pay for a consultation with a physician, and pharmaceutical laboratories took advantage of their monopoly to double or triple their profits. In 1922 the protagonist of a well-known novel (a professional accountant with a monthly salary of 200 pesetas) could not afford without great sacrifice the morphine treatment prescribed for his wife, suffering from uterine cancer:

> He loved her. ... Her illness ate up his savings. ... After a period of acute poverty Sanchiz found employment in an office as an accountant at two hundred pesetas a month. What were two hundred pesetas to him who had a sick wife in need of daily morphine injections?[116]

---

[116] Barea, Arturo. The Forging of a Rebel, tr. Ilsa Barea. NY: Reynal & Hitchkock, 1946 AA, Book Two, Part II, 4. Dictator in the Making, p. 363; *A quien él quería era a ella. ... Pero ¿qué eran doscientas pesetas para quien tenía una mujer enferma que necesitaba diariamente una inyección de morfina?* (La forja de un rebelde II La ruta. Arturo Barea y Herederos de Arturo Barea, 1951 AA, Segunda Parte, Capítulo V El embrión de dictador, p. 246).

Another novelist relates how in that era a local doctor removed a bullet from the hand of a ten year old without a local anaesthetic: "The boy seems brave, but without an anaesthetic it will hurt him. And I don't want to give him a general anaesthetic. If I had an ampule of cocaine, that would do nicely."[117]

Naturally, the response from the people was a flourishing black market. In 1919 cocaine was on sale in all the public establishments along the Barcelona *Rambla*: "The promenade is impressive, with its lights, traffic, people and money. Almost every establishment offers cocaine. Many foreigners [tr. gwr]."[118] In 1921 the president of the *Colegio Médico de Valencia* [College of Medicine of Valencia] denounced the use of cocaine and morphine in cabarets and music halls in the province.[119]

This black market was fed by diversions from the pharmaceutical suppliers, but also from ever increasing imports from outside the country, where manufacturers do not block the sale of products destined for export. The illegal traffic can be verified especially passing through Irún, and between the autumn of 1924 and the summer of 1925 almost five kilos of cocaine were seized along with five kilos of opium, quantities never before seen outside the

---

117 Sender, Ramón J. Chronicle of Dawn, tr. W. R. Trask. London: Jonathan Cape, 1945 AA, Section III, p. 66; *El chico parece valiente, pero sin anestesia voy a hacerle daño. Si tuviera una ampolla de cocaína, con eso me bastaría* (Cronica del alba. NY: Las Américas Publishing Company, 1963 AA, Tomo I, Crónica del alba, p. 59).

118 *La Rambla está imponente de luces, de tráfico, de gente y de dinero. Os ofrecen cocaína en casi todos los establecimientos. Muchos extranjeros* (Pla, Josep. El cuaderno gris, tr. Dionisio Rodruejo et al., orig. El quadern gris, 1966 Epublibre, 25 de mayo, 1919, p. 465/635); Usó Arnal, 1991, pp. 130 et seq.

119 *denunciando el abuso que se hace de la morfina y la cocaína en los cabarets y music-halls valencianos* (Usó Arnal, 1991, 5 de julio de 1921, p. 130, citing "Una carta del presidente del Colegio Médico," en *Las Provincias*, Valencia, 9 de julio de 1921, p. 1).

traditional supply chain.[120] It is curious to observe that the three persons found with the 4,820 grams of contraband cocaine were condemned by the civil governor of San Sebastián to pay a fine of 500 pesetas each and were later absolved.[121] In effect, the judicial climate still was not favorable to criminalization, and in a 1921 Report of the Prosecutor to the Supreme Court there is not a single allusion to the consumption of cocaine, morphine or ether; on the contrary, it highlights alcoholism as one of the principal causes of *delito de sangre* [blood felony, literally a crime that sheds blood], proposing taverns should close at the same time as other shops, and measures to repress the adulteration of alcoholic beverages.[122]

But the crusade is also underway, led by moral entrepreneurs very similar to those in Northamerica a decade earlier. This is clearly evident in a campaign launched in *Las Provincias*, a very conservative daily newspaper in Valencia, which on its front page published articles demanding a hard line on the consumption of cocaine and morphine in places of recreation. The response was not long in coming, and in a Republican daily of Valencia, *El Pueblo*, there appear various articles signed by the Republican journalist Carlos Esplá Rizo (1895 – 1971), secretary to the journalist, novelist and politician Vicente Blasco Ibáñez (1867 – 1928), and a future minister of propaganda in the short-lived government (1936 – 1937) of Francisco

---

120 Usó Arnal, 1991, 29 de abril de 1925, 4 de julio de 1925, p. 133.

121 Usó Arnal, 1991, Octubre de 1924, 29 de abril de 1925, p. 133, citing the *Gaceta de Madrid* of 9 de agosto de 1927, pp. 39-40, and of 11 de agosto de 1927 as well as *Jurisprudencia criminal*, Madrid, Editorial Reus, 1931, t. LV, pp. 106-109.

122 *no hace ningún tipo de alusión al consumo de cocaína, morfina éter ... clausurando los establecimientos donde se expendan* (Usó Arnal, 1991, 15 de septiembre de 1921, p. 131 citing Covian y Junco, Victor. "Memoria elevada al Gobierno de S. M. en la solemne apertura de los Tribunales el día 15 de septiembre de 1921 par el Fiscal del Tribunal Supremo...," Madrid, Editorial Reus, 1921, pp. 19-21 y 59).

Figure 357. "Carlos Esplá Rizo (1895 – 1971)." Cervantes Virtual [cervantesvirtual.com, hereinafter CV].

Largo Caballero (1869 – 1946). Esplá issued a warning against this moralizing which masked the troops of order and cassock arrayed against morphine and cocaine, calling for a greater respect for the decisions and free will of the consumers of these drugs.[123]

The balance decidedly inclined to repression when the civil governorship of Valencia was occupied by the young and energetic José Calvo Sotelo (1893 – 1936). In fact, Calvo Sotelo solemnly threatens doctors and pharmacists who dispense these drugs in cases not absolutely necessary, promising to close *sine die* [indefinitely] any local establishment where they were consumed.[124] His position was crystallized soon after in an *Asociation contra la Toxicomanía* [Association against Drug Abuse], headquartered in Barcelona, presided over by the civil governor of the region, Lieutenant General Joaquín Milans del Bosch y Carrió (1854 – 1936).[125] King Alfonso XIII (1886 – 1941) himself joined the indignant clamor against drug abuse and issued on 17 January 1927 an order to severely punish any infractions.[126] Two

---

[123] *la finalidad moralizante que enmascara la campaña iniciada por «la tropa de orden y sotana» contra la morfina y la cocaína, al tiempo que reclama un mayor respeto para la condición y el libre albedrío de los consumidores de drogas* (Usó Arnal, 1991, 13 y 14 de julio de 1921, p. 131, citing "No es un peligro muy grande," in *El Pueblo*, Valencia, 13 de julio de 1921, p. 1 and "Otra dosis de cocaína," in *El Pueblo*, Valencia, 14 de julio de 1921, p. 1).

[124] *sólo se recete opio, morfina y cocaína en los casos absolutamente precisos ... pudieran venderse clandestinamente estas substancias* (Usó Arnal, 1991, Diciembre de 1921, p. 131, citing "Contra el abuso de la morfina," in *Las Provincias*, Valencia, 8 de diciembre de 1921, p. 3; "Noticias del gobierno civil," in *Las Provincias*, Valencia, 9 de diciembre de 1921, p. 4; and "Noticias del gobierno civil," in *Las Provincias*, Valencia, 23 de diciembre de 1921, p. 1).

[125] *Se funda en Barcelona la 'Asociación contra la toxicomanía' .... Preside dicha asociación el Gobernador civil, general Joaquín Milans del Bosch y Carrió* [quotation marks original] (Usó Arnal, 1991, 20 de mayo de 1926, p. 135).

[126] *Real orden ... venta y suministro de tóxicos estupefacientes* (Usó Arnal, 1991, 17 de enero de 1927, p. 137, citing *Gaceta de Madrid*, 18 de enero de 1927, pp. 404-405.

lays afterwards, the new prosecutor of the Supreme Court directed to all the prosecutors of the Audience a circular ordering

> a holy war against a form of refined criminality in which the most cold and pitiless egoism foments a morbid vice, destructive of the energy of the race, exploiting a pathological tendency of the poor and degenerate, before a public consciousness experiencing a growing alarm [tr. gwr].[127]

It could be said that, finally, there was in Spain a drug problem, or more exactly an alarmed conscience of such. From this moment one can detect the same phenomenon as seen in the United States: an increase in the trials against therapists and non-therapists, an increase in the prices of drugs, and the appearance of adulteration. No legal authority however establishes a connection between the presence of adulterants and new cases of overintoxication.

The vocabulary of the Spanish crusade is practically identical to that of the Northamerican. The Spanish police adapt to the new state of things and use the same methods as the prohibition agents in the US; almost all the pharmacists and doctors arrested are the objects of entrapment, where agents pretend to be patients needing medicine. At the same time, what grows up and consolidates its power is a new criminal class that lacks toxicological training and lives from trafficking powders. By 1928 the American crusade had even spread to Argentina where cocaine could be bought on the street often mixed with baking soda: "In Buenos Aires I became a general supplier of cocaine for altruistic reasons. ... I mixed cocaine hydrochloride with baking soda .... In this way I prevented those who wished to be intoxicated from committing suicide."[128] Two years later the same adulteration is recorded in Spain.[129]

---

127 *dar sañuda batalla ... conciencia pública experimentaviva alarma* (Usó Arnal, 1991, p. 138).

128 *En Buenos Aires ... su suicidio* (Gómez de la Serna, Ramón. El caballero del hongo gris.

Figure 358. "Severiano Martinez Anido (1862 – 1938)." Photograph, 1 December 1925. *Narodowe Archiwum Cyfrowe* (Polish National Digital Archive) [nac.gov.pl, hereinafter NAC].

Epub, Agencia Mundial de Librería, 1928 AA, p. 66/165).

129 *encontrado tres papelinas de cocaína pura y doce más en las que 'ya estaba mezclada con bicarbonato'* [quotation marks original] (Usó Arnal, 1991, 12 de octubre de 1930, p. 147).

Inflamed with alarm, General Severiano Martínez Anido (1862 – 1938), a minister in the government of the dictator Miguel Primo de Rivera y Orbaneja (1870 – 1930), declares before the *Asamblea Nacional* [National Assembly] that a single druggist had introduced five thousand kilos of cocaine for sale, causing the disgrace of countless others.[130] Ironically, Primo de Rivera himself was severely criticized for offering unconditional protection to a beautiful and dangerous Andalusian prostitute nicknamed *La Caoba* [Mahogany], accused of collaborating in drug trafficking.[131] The political affair resulted in the dismissal of the president of the Supreme Court Buenaventura Muñoz Rodríguez (1853 – 1925), who had dared to defend the local judge who had ordered her arrest. It also led to the closure of the *Ateneo de Madrid* [Scientific and Literary Athenaeum, founded 1835] between 1923 and 1930 and a number of banishments, among them that of essayist, novelist, poet, playwright and philosopher Miguel de Unamuno y Jugo (1864 – 1936) to the island of Fuerteventura.[132] General Martínez Anido is said to have exclaimed: "I would cut off the heads of all these intellectuals so they cannot bother us anymore. If I had my way, Unamuno would never arrive alive at Fuerteventura."[133] Around 1925

---

130 *hay farmacéutico que ha introducido cinco mil kilos de cocaína para la venta, que han podido ser causa de la desgracia de otros tantos hombres* (Usó Arnal, 1991, 18 de febrero de 1928, p. 144, citing "Asamblea Nacional ... El proyecto sobre la venta de estupefacientes," in *Diario de Castellón*, 18 de febrero de 1928, p. 5).

131 *una bellísima andaluza de vida muy azarosa ... (dedicada) por entonces al tráfico de drogas* (Usó Arnal, 1991, Febrero de 1924, p. 132 citing Cierva, Ricardo de la. *Francisco Franco: un siglo de España*. Madrid: Editara Nacional, 1973, t. 1, p. 234).

132 *El affaire se salda con la destitución de Buenaventura ... y el destierro ... de Miguel de Unamuno, por haber censurado el abuso de poder cometido por Primo de Rivera* (Usó Arnal, 1991, Febrero de 1924, p. 132, citing Garcia Queipo De Llano, Genoveva. *Los intelectuales y la dictadura de Primo de Rivera*. Madrid: Alianza, 1987).

133 *Yo cortaría varias cabezas de 'intelectuales' para que no molesten más. Si yo pudiera realizar*

when the sensational weekly *El Escándalo* appears, drug abuse is a theme of rabid topicality.[134]

When the military dictatorship disappears in 1930, it's clear that twelve years of progressively more severe laws have not managed to keep down the consumption of cocaine and the opiates, although they have managed to change in part the demography of the users and completely the access to these products. Now they are incomparably more expensive and adulterated, while being supplied by a criminal underworld ranging from the lumpenproletariate and the pimp to shady business owners with espionage and arms trafficking on the side. The fascination for artificial paradises does not wane even a bit, and in reality one can be affirmed that it increases considerably. Against this, it is thought that the prior consumer of cocaine and the opiates (the client of the herbalist, drugstore and boutique) uses much less, although this is disputed; in effect, these drugs were very accessible for the therapeutic estate, and it is reasonable to suppose that physicians, pharmacists and other healthcare personnel continued to dispense them as usual to their very appreciative regular clients, though now in a more discrete manner.

If between 1924 and 1925 five kilos of cocaine and five of opium were confiscated, in 1928 (three years after judges began handing down not just fines but jail sentences for drug crimes), the amounts seized rise to 32 and 20 kilos,[135] or an increase of 600 and 400 percent respectively. These quantities (and those not confiscated) are

---

mi programa, Unamuno no llegaría vivo a Fuerteventura [quotation marks original] (Ouimette, Victor. "*El destierro de unamuno y el ataque a la inteligencia,*" *Ediciones Universidad Salamanca*, Volume 27, 1982 [revistas.usal.es, hereinafter RUE], p. 40).

134 Usó Arnal, 1991, 22 de octubre 1925, p. 134, citing Madrid, Francisco. "*La tragedia de los paraísos artificiales. Cocaína, morfina, opio ...,*" in *El Escándalo*, Barcelona, 10 de diciembre de 1925, pp. 4-5 and ten more similarly titled articles.

135 Usó Arnal, 1991, 12 de febrero de 1928, p. 144, 24 de julio de 1928, p. 145.

destined for the salons of good society, along with nightclubs, cafes and slums. Although less than a decade earlier they were freely sold without a prescription regardless of the quantity, now the necessity to legally obtain said drugs is a medical prescription.

Altogether, in order to evaluate the harm caused to Spanish society by this campaign against cocaine and the opiates, it is fundamental to take into account the proportion of overdose deaths to the number of incarcerated. From the spring of 1920 to the spring of 1930, Usó Arnal (who had been tabulating reports in the Spanish press) only mentions six cases of death due to overdose, with another possible. The doubtful case is that of a woman, whose cardiac arrest could have been provoked by heroin. There are three deaths with morphine, and one of a man and a woman together by cocaine, though a different source mentions heroin.[136] The only case that might be clearly due to an overdose of cocaine corresponds to that of a woman from 1927, when this substance was frequently being adulterated.[137] One should remember that prior to 1921 overdose was so rare it was almost never even recorded as a cause of mortality on a death certificate.[138] Against this ultimate reality, complemented by a dozen overintoxications that did not result in death, one can compare the widespread fear campaign and the thousands of fines and jail sentences handed down throughout the same decade.

One way of understanding this index of mortality (if one compares it with the fifty or sixty thousand cases recorded during the 1980s), is to take into account that Spain had not taken the crusade to

---

136 Usó Arnal, 1991, pp. 129-148.

137 Usó Arnal, 1991, 6 de enero de 1927, p. 137 citing "Diligencia judicial," *Diario de Castellón*, 14 de enero de 1927, p. 4.

138 *la mortalidad por toxicomanía casi nunca se hace constar en los certificados de defunción* (Usó Arnal, 1991, 9 de julio de 1921, p. 130).

the popular level, and that neither in its institutions nor in its collective imagination was there planted the concept of a war on vice. For all the emphasis put on drugs by Calvo Sotelo (the monarchical president of the *Colegio Médico de Valencia*), Generals Milans del Bosch and Martínez Anido, and even Alfonso XIII, all these were railing against ancient things already assimilated in a country with many more urgent problems. Opium had been used for millennia, morphine for a century, and cocaine for half a century. To pretend such things were malignant powers only worked with the ignorant.

But perhaps because some of the ignorant were attracted to them (in search of artificial paradises, apocalyptic punishment or pure profit) these seeds did not fall on barren ground. Other ignorant ones were opposed to this, and from this mutual suspicion grew a lasting hatred. Truly, an inchoate fear that demanded the government act would now demand it act ever more imperiously.

Figure 359. "Miguel de Unamuno (1864 – 1936)." Agence de Presse Meurisse, 1921 [Gallicia Digital Library, hereinafter GDL].

BIBLIOGRAPHY

Ahlborn, Maurice B. "Heroine in the Morphine Habit," The New York Medical Journal, Volume LXXIV, July to December, 1901, Inclusive. NY: A. R. Elliott Publishing Company, 1901

Andersen, Lisa M. F. The Politics of Prohibition: American Governance and the Prohibition Party, 1869 – 1933. NY: Cambridge University Press, 2013

Anslinger, H. J. and C. R. Cooper. "Assassin of Youth," *The American Magazine*, Vol. 124, No. 1, July 1937

____________ and Tompkins, W. F. The Traffic in Narcotics. NY: Funk & Wagnalls Company, 1953

____________ and Will Oursler. The Murderers: The Story of the Narcotic Gangs. NY: Farrar, Strauss and Cudahy, 1961

A. P. writer. "U. S. Liquor Poison Blamed in 25 Deaths from Rum," *The Washington Post*, No. 18,457, Tuesday, December 28, 1926

Auden, W. H., editor. The Oxford Book of Light Verse. Oxford, UK: At the Clarendon Press, 1938

Barbier, Georges Augustin. *Le Bonheur du Jour, ou Les Graces à la Mode* [The Happiness of the Day, or Fashionable Graces], engraving by Henri Reidel. Paris: Chez Jules Meynial, 1924

Barea, Arturo. The Forging of a Rebel, tr. Ilsa Barea. NY: Reynal & Hitchkock, 1946

____________ *La forja de un rebelde II La ruta*. Arturo Barea y Herederos de Arturo Barea, 1951

Baum, Dan. "Annals of Epidemiology, "Jake Leg: *How the blues diagnosed a medical mystery*," *The New Yorker*, September 15, 2003

Beal, James H., editor. "Of General Interest, Proceedings Relating to the Organization of the National Drug Trade Conference, First Session," The Journal of the American Pharmaceutical Association, Volume II. Columbus, OH: Published by the Association, 1913

____________________ "The Senate Amendments to the Harrison Bill," The Journal of the American Pharmaceutical Association, Volume III, No. 4, April. Columbus, OH: Published by the Association, 1914

____________________ "The Editor's Reply to Mr. Freericks," The Journal of the American Pharmaceutical Association, Volume III. Columbus, OH: Published by the Association, 1914

Beale, Howard K. Theodore Roosevelt and the Rise of America to World Power. Baltimore, MD: The Johns Hopkins University Press, 1956

Bevans, Charles I., compiler. Treaties and Other International Agreements of the United States of America 1776 – 1949, Volume I Multilateral 1776 – 1917. Washington, DC: Department of State, Division of Publishing and Reproduction, 1968

____________________ Treaties and Other International Agreements of the United States of America 1776 – 1949, Volume II Multilateral 1918 – 1930. Washington, DC: Department of State, Division of Publishing and Reproduction, 1969

____________________ "Convention for Limiting the Manufacture and Regulating the Distribution of Narcotic Drugs," Treaties and Other International Agreements of the United States of America 1776 – 1949, Volume 3, Multilateral 1931-1945. Washington, DC: Department of State Publications, 1968

Bishop, Ernest S. The Narcotic Drug Problem. NY: The MacMillan Company, 1920

____________________"Morphinism and its Treatment," *Journal of the American Medical Association*, Volume LVIII, No. 20, 18 May 1912

BIBLIOGRAPHY

______________ "An Analysis of Narcotic Drug Addiction," New York Medical Journal, Volume CI, *January to June ... Inclusive*, NY: A. R. Elliott Publishing Company, 1915

______________ "Some Fundamental Considerations of the Problem of Narcotic Drug Addiction," American Medicine, Volume XXI, Complete Series, Volume X, New Series, January – December 1915

______________ "The Narcotic Addict, the Physician and the Law," The Medical Economist, Volume IV. Brooklyn, NY: The Physicians' Economist Publishing Company, Inc., 1916

Blair, Emma Helen and James Alexander Robertson, trs., eds. The Philippine Islands, 1493-1898, Vol. 52: 1841-1898. Cleveland, OH: Arthur Clark Co., 1907

Blount, James M. The American Occupation of the Philippines 1898-1912. NY: G. P. Putnam's Sons, 1913

Brain, Russell, chair. The Report of the Second Interdepartmental Committee on Drug Addiction. London: Her Majesty's Stationery Office, 1961

Brent, Charles H., President. Report of the International Opium Commission, Shanghai, China, February 1 to February 26, 1909, Volume I. Report of the Proceedings. Shanghai: North-China Daily News & Herald Ltd., 1909

Brewster, Sidney W. "Actual Trend of Drug Addiction and its Relation to Crime," *Narcotic Education Bulletin of the World Conference on Narcotic Education and the International Narcotic Education Association*, Volume 1, No. 1, July, 1927

Bromberg, Walter. "Marihuana Intoxication: A Clinical Study of Cannabis Sativa Intoxication," *The American Journal of Psychiatry*, Volume 91, September 1934

Bureau of Narcotics. Narcotic Clinics in the United States. Washington, DC: Government Printing Office, 1953

Burgess, J. W. "Germany, Great Britain and the United States," *Political Science Quarterly*, Volume XIX, No. 1, March 1904

Burroughs, William S. Junky. London: Penguin Books, 1977

________________ Rub Out the Words: The Letters of William S. Burroughs, 1959 – 1974, ed. Bill Morgan. NY: Harper Collins Publishers, 2012

Butler, Willis P. "How One American City is Meeting the Public Health Problems of Narcotic Drug Addiction," American Medicine, Volume XXVIII, Complete Series, Volume XVII, New Series, January-December. Burlington, VT: American Medical Publishing Company, 1922

Buzeta, E. Manuel and Fr. Felipe Bravo. *Diccionario geografico, estadistico e historico de las Islas Filipinas*, Vol. 2 D-Z. Madrid: Imp. de D. José C. de la Peña, 1850-1851

Campbell, Harry. "The Pathology and Treatment of Morphia Addiction," The British Journal of Inebriety, Volume XX [found together with Volume XIX], 1922-23. London: Baillière, Tindall and Cox, 1923

Carr, Charles Mylert, editor and director. "Legislative Organization: Have a Laugh with Us," The Journal of the National Association of Retail Druggists (Formerly N. A. R. D. Notes), Volume XVII, October 9, 1913 to April 2, 1914. Chicago, IL: Published by the National Association of Retail Druggists, 1914

Carter, Edward C., Chairman, et al. Report of the Committee Appointed by the Philippine Commission to Investigate the Use of Opium and the Traffic Therein. Washington, DC: Bureau of Insular Affairs, War Department, 1905

BIBLIOGRAPHY

Cherrington, Ernest Hurst, editor. The Anti-Saloon League Year Book 1916. Westerville, OH: Published by the Anti-Saloon League of America, 1916

________________________, editor. The Anti-Saloon League Year Book 1917. Westerville, OH: Published by the Anti-Saloon League of America, 1917

________________________, editor. The Anti-Saloon League Year Book 1918. Westerville, OH: Published by the Anti-Saloon League of America, 1918

Ching-hong, Wu. A Study of References to the Philippines in Chinese Sources from Earliest Times to the Ming Dynasty. Quezon City, PI: University of the Philippines, 1959

Coleridge, Samuel Taylor. Table Talk of Samuel Taylor Coleridge. London: George Routledge and Sons, 1884

Colvin, D. Leigh. Prohibition in the United States: A History of the Prohibition Party and of the Prohibition Movement. NY: George H. Doran Company 1926

Courtwright, David et al. Addicts Who Survived: An Oral History of Narcotic Use in America before 1965. Knoxville, TN: University of Tennessee Press, 2012

Crafts, W. F. Memorandum concerning Concerted International Restraint of the Traffic in Intoxicants and Opium Among Aboriginal Races. NY: Press of the Reliance Trading Company, 1906

____________ Opium Cures, Third Abridged Edition. Washington, DC: International Reform Bureau, 1908

____________ & Mrs. Wilbur F. and Misses Mary & Margaret W. Leitch. Intoxicating Drinks & Drugs in All Lands and Times: A Twentieth Century Survey of Intemperance, Based on a Symposium of Testimony from One Hundred Missionaries and

Travelers, Revised Eleventh Edition. Washington, DC: The International Reform Bureau, 1911

Dalyrmple, Louis. "The Age of Drugs," *Puck*, Volume XLVIII, No. 1231, 10 October 1900

Detwiler, Justice B., ed. Who's Who in California A Biographical Directory 1928-1929. San Francisco, CA: Who's Who Publishing Company, 1929

Doughton, Robert L., Chairman. Hearings Before the Committee on Ways and Means, House of Representatives, Seventy-Fifth Congress, First Session on H. R. 6385, April 27, 28, 29, 30, and May 4, 1937. Washington, DC: Government Printing Office, 1937

Dugdale, Richard L. "The Jukes" A Study in Crime, Pauperism, Disease and Heredity, Third Edition, Revised. NY: G. P. Putnam's Sons 1877

Duvall, Henrietta J., et al. "Followup Study of Narcotic Drug Addicts Five Years After Hospitalization," *Public Health Reports*, Volume 78, No. 3, March 1963

Eberle, E. G., chairman and Frederick T. Gordon. "Report of the Committee on the Acquirement of Drug Habits," Proceedings of the American Pharmaceutical Association. Baltimore, MD: Published by the American Pharmaceutical Association, 1903

Ellinger, Tage U. H., translator. Hippocrates On Intercourse and Pregnancy. NY: Henry Schuman, Inc., 1952

Estabrook, Arthur H. The Jukes in 1915. Washington, DC: Published by the Carnegie Institute of Washington, 1916

Ferrero, Gina Lombroso. Criminal Man, According to the Classification of Cesare Lombroso. NY: G. P. Putnam's Sons, 1911

Fiske, John. "Manifest Destiny," *Harper's New Monthly Magazine*, Volume LXX, No. CCCCXVIII, March 1885

Fort, Joel. The Pleasure Seekers: The Drug Crisis, Youth and Society. NY: Grove Press, Inc., 1969

Fossier, A. E. "The Mariahuana [sic] Menace," *New Orleans Medical and Surgical Journal*, Volume 84, No. 4, October 1931

Freericks, Frank H. "More About the Harrison Bill," The Journal of the American Pharmaceutical Association, Volume III. Columbus, OH: Published by the Association, 1914

Galenus, Claudius. How to be Healthy: An Ancient Guide to Wellness, tr. Katherine D. Van Schaik. Princeton, NJ: Princeton University Press, 2024

Gamella, Juan F. and Elisa Martin. "*Las Rentas de Anfion: El Monopolio Español del Opio en Filipinas (1844 – 1898) y su Rechazo por la Administracion Norteamericana* [The Profits of Opium: The Spanish Opium Monopoly in the Philippines (1844 – 1898) and its Rejection by the Northamerican Administration]," *Revista de Indias*, Volumen LII, número 194, 1992

Garfield, James Rudolph, Secretary of the Interior. Eighth Annual Report of the Philippine Commission to the Secretary of War, Part 2. Washington, DC: Government Printing Office, 1908

Gieringer, Dale H. "The Forgotten Origins of Cannabis Prohibition in California," *Contemporary Drug Problems*, Volume 26, Number 2, Summer 1999

Gómez de la Serna, Ramón. *El caballero del hongo gris*. Epub, Agencia Mundial de Librería, 1928

Gracián y Morales, Balthasar. The Art of Worldly Wisdom, tr. Joseph Jacobs. London: Macmillan and Co., 1892

________________________ *Oráculo Manual y Arte de Prudencia*. Huesca, ES: Juan Nogues, 1647

Graham-Mulhall, Sara. Opium: The Demon Flower. NY: Harold Vinal, 1926 [see also Mulhall, Sara Graham]

Graves, M. L., Chairman of the Reference Committee. Journal of the American Medical Association, Volume LXVIII, Number 24, Saturday, 16 June 1917

Greeley, Arthur P. The Pure Food and Drugs Act, June 30, 1906, A Study. Washington, DC: John Byrne & Company, 1907

Grinspoon, Lester and James B. Bakalar. Cocaine: A Drug and its Social Evolution, revised edition. NY: Basic Books, 1985

Hadley, Lindley H., Chairman Committee on Ways and Means. Sixty-Seventh Congress, Second Session, December 5, 1921 – September 22, 1922, House Reports (Public), Volume 2. Washington, DC: Government Printing Office, 1922

Hamilton, Niall and Lutz Beckert. "Dr Nathan Tucker's Asthma Specific: a treatment for asthma preceding inhaled steroids and beta-agonists," *The New Zealand Medical Journal*, Volume 123, No. 1323, 24 September 2010

Herrick, Walter R., Commissioner. Second Annual Report of the Narcotic Drug Control Commission. Albany, NY: J. B. Lyon Company, 1920

Hobson, Richmond Pearson. The Sinking of the Merrimac: A Personal Narrative. NY: The Century Co., 1899

Howard, Sidney. "The Inside Story of Dope in this Country," *Hearst's International*, Volume XLIII, No. 2, February 1923

Hubbard, S. Dana. "Some Fallacies Regarding Narcotic Drug Addiction," *The Journal of the American Medical Association*, Volume 74, No. 21, 22 May 1920

Hynson, Henry B. "Report of the Committee on Acquirement of the Drug Habit," *Proceedings of the American Pharmaceutical Association at the Fiftieth Annual Meeting held at Philadelphia, PA, September, 1902*

International Opium Convention, League of Nations *Treaty Series*, Volume 8. Geneva, 1922

Iorizzo, Luciano. *Al Capone: A Biography*. Westport, CT: Greenwood Press, 2003

Irish, William (Cornell Woolrich). *Marihuana*. NY: Dell Publishing, 1941

Jagor, Andreas Fedor. *Reisen in den Philippinen* [Travels in the Philippines]. Berlin: Weidmannsche Buchhandlung, 1873

James, William. *The Varieties of Religious Experience: A Study in Human Nature, Being the Gifford Lectures on Natural Religion Delivered at Edinburgh in 1901-1902*. NY: The Modern Library, 1902

Jefferson, Thomas to James Monroe, 24 October 1823, Monticello, Oct. 24. 23. Papers of James Monroe

Jones, W. H. S., tr. *Hippocrates*, Volume I. Cambridge, MA: Harvard University Press, 1984

Kidd, John G. and Orthello R. Langworthy. "Jake Paralysis: Paralysis Following the Ingestion of Jamaica Ginger Extract Adulterated with Tri-Ortho-Cresyl Phosphate," *Bulletin of the Johns Hopkins Hospital*, Volume LII, Number 1, January 1933

Knox, Philander Chase, Director. The Statutes at Large of the United States from March, 1909, to March, 1911, Volume XXXVI, Part I. Washington, DC: Government Printing Office, 1911

Kobler, John. Ardent Spirits: The Rise and Fall of Prohibition. NY: G. P. Putnam's Sons, 1973

Kohona, Palitha T. B., Chief, Treaty Section, Office of Legal Affairs. Convention of 1936 for the Suppression of Illicit Traffic in Dangerous Drugs. Geneva, Switzerland: League of Nations, 1936

Kolb, Lawrence. "Drug Addiction: A Study of Some Medical Cases," Archives of Neurology and Psychiatry, Volume 20. Chicago, IL: American Medical Association, 1928

______________ and C. K. Himmelsbach. "Clinical Studies of Drug Addiction, III. A Critical Review of the Withdrawal Treatments with Method of Evaluating Abstinence Syndromes," Supplement 128 to *Public Health Reports*, January 1938

Kozma, Liat. "Cannabis Prohibition in Egypt, 1880 – 1939: From Local Ban to League of Nations Diplomacy," *Middle Eastern Studies*, Volume 47, No. 3, May 2011

Kremers, Edward and George Urdang. History of Pharmacy: *A Guide and a Survey*. Philadelphia, PA: J. B. Lippincott Company, 1940

Lambert, Alexander. "Care and Control of the Alcoholic," *The Boston Medical and Surgical Journal*, Volume CLXVI, January – June. Boston, MA: W. M. Leonard, 1912

________________ "Address of the President Elect," The Journal of the American Medical Association, Volume 72, No. 24, June 14. Chicago, IL: The American Medical Association, 1919

Laurie, Peter. Drugs: Medical, Psychological and Social Facts. Baltimore, MD: Penguin Books, 1967

BIBLIOGRAPHY

Lessing, Ephraim Gotthold. Laocoön: An Essay on the Limits of Painting and Poetry, tr. Edward Allen McCormick. Indianapolis, IN: The Bobbs-Merrill Company, Inc., 1962

Lewin, Louis. *Phantastica: die betäubenden und Erregenden Genussmittel Für Ärzte und Nichtärzte*. Berlin: Verlag Von Georg Stilke, 1924

__________ Phantastica: Narcotic and Stimulating Drugs, Their Use and Abuse, tr. P. H. A. Wirth. NY: E. P. Dutton & Company, 1964

Lewis, H. Edwin, ed. American Medicine, Volume XXVIII, Complete Series, Volume XVII, New Series, January – December. Burlington, VT: American Medical Publishing Company, 1922

Light, Arthur B. and Edward G. Torrance. "Opium Addiction," Archives of Internal Medicine, Volume 43. Chicago, IL: American Medical Association, 1929

Limburg, M., President. Records of the Conference for the Suppression of the Illicit Traffic in Dangerous Drugs (Geneva, June 8th to 26th, 1936), Text of the Debates. Geneva, Switzerland: Members of the League, 1936

Linder v United States, 268 U. S. 5 (1925)

Lindesmith, Alfred R. The Addict and the Law. Bloomington, IN: Indiana University Press, 1965

__________________ and John H. Gagnon. "Anomie and Drug Addiction," Anomie and Deviant Behavior: A Discussion and Critique, ed. Marshall B. Clinard. NY: The Free Press, 1964

Lombroso, Cesare. *L'uomo Delinquente*. Milano, IT: Ulrico Hoepli, Libraio-Editore, 1876

Mahan, A. T. The Problem of Asia and Its Effect upon International Policies. Boston, MA: Little, Brown, and Company, 1900

Marcovitz, Eli and Henry J. Meyers. "The Marihuana Addict in the Army," *War Medicine*, Volume 6, December 1944

Marqués, R. "Opio," *La Actualidad. Seman. de Med., Farm. y Ciencias Aux., Valencia*, enero 1859

McCormack, Arthur T., Chairman. "Report of Reference Committee on Hygiene and Public Health," JAMA, 16 June 1917

McCoy, Alfred W. Policing America's Empire: The United States, the Philippines, and the Rise of the Surveillance State. Madison, WI: University of Wisconsin Press, 2009

McWilliams, John C. The Protectors: Harry J. Anslinger and the Federal Bureau of Narcotics, 1930 – 1962. Newark, NJ: University of Delaware Press, 1990

Mills, James H. Cannabis Britannica: Empire, Trade, and Prohibition 1800 – 1928. Oxford, UK: Oxford University Press, 2003

Monroe, James. "Message to Congress," December 1823, Annals of Congress, 18th Congress, 1st Session, Senate Journal

Moses, George H., Chairman. Hearing Before the Committee on Printing United States Senate, Sixty-Eighth Congress, First Session on S. Con. Res. 10. Washington, DC: Government Printing Office, 1924

Mulhall, Sara Graham. "The World Antinarcotic Union Presents its Reasons for Supporting the Porter Narcotic Farms Bill to the House Judiciary Committee April 26, 1928. Statement of Mrs. Sarah Graham Mulhall, President New York City Federation of Women's Clubs," Establishment of Two Federal Narcotics Farms, Hearings Before the Committee on the Judiciary, House of Representatives Seventieth Congress, First Session on H. R. 12781 and H. R. 13645, April 26, 27, 28, Serial 29 (Revised Print). Washington, DC: US Government Printing Office, 1928 [see also Graham-Mulhall, Sara]

Munsey, Cecil. "Paralysis in a Bottle (The 'Jake Walk' Story)," *Bottles and Extras*, Volume 17, No. 1, Winter 2006

Musto, David F. The American Disease: Origins of Narcotic Control, Third Edition. NY: Oxford University Press, 1999

Nast, Thomas. "Columbia – Hands off, gentlemen! America means Fair Play for All Men." *Harper's Weekly*, Volume XV, No. 738, 18 February 1871

___________ "The Usual Irish Way of Doing Things." *Harper's Weekly*, Volume XV, No. 766, Saturday, 2 September 1871

No. 222. The International Opium Convention, signed at The Hague, January 23, 1912, and subsequent papers. League of Nations Treaty Series, 1922

No. 1845. – International Opium Convention, Adopted by the Second Opium Conference (League of Nations). Signed at Geneva, February, 1925. League of Nations Treaty Series, 1928-1929

Okrent, Daniel. "The Man Who Turned Off the Taps," *Smithsonian Magazine*, May 2010

Osborn, W. H., Commissioner of Internal Revenue. Annual Report of the Commissioner of Internal Revenue for the Fiscal Year Ended June 30 1915. Washington, DC: Government Printing Office, 1915

____________, Commissioner of Internal Revenue. Annual Report of the Commissioner of Internal Revenue for the Fiscal Year Ended June 30 1916. Washington, DC: Government Printing Office, 1916

Ouimette, Victor. "*El destierro de unamuno y el ataque a la inteligencia,*" *Ediciones Universidad Salamanca*, Volume 27, 1982

Owens, Clarence J., Jr., Secretary. Report of the First Annual Conference of Committees of the World Conference on Narcotic Education and International Narcotic Education Association. Washington, DC: World Conference on Narcotic Education, 1927

Paisley, Fred D. Al Capone: *The Biography of a Self-Made Man*. Garden City, NY: Garden City Publishing Company, 1930

Peters, Gerhard and John T. Woolley, editors. William Howard Taft, Special Message Online, 21 February 1910, The American Presidency Project, University of California, Santa Barbara

Pilat, Oliver and Jo Ranson. Sodom by the Sea: An Affectionate History of Coney Island. NY: Garden City Publishing Co., Inc., 1943

Pla, Josep. *El cuaderno gris*, tr. Dionisio Rodruejo et al., orig. *El quadern gris*, 1966

Pomeroy, William J. The Philippines: Colonialism, Collaboration, and Resistance! NY: International Publishers, 1992

Porter, Stephen G. Remarks of Hon. Stephen G. Porter, Chairman, Committee on Foreign Affairs in the House of Representatives February 26, 1923. Washington, DC: Government Printing Office, 1923

________________ "Statement of Hon. Stephen G. Porter, a Representative in Congress from the State of Pennsylvania," Establishment of Two Federal Narcotics Farms, Hearings Before the Committee on the Judiciary, House of Representatives Seventieth Congress, First Session on H. R. 12781 and H. R. 13645, April 26, 27, 28, Serial 29 (Revised Print). Washington, DC: US Government Printing Office, 1928

Pound, Nathan Roscoe. "The Limits of Effective Legal Action," The American Bar Association Journal, Volume III. Baltimore, MD: Published by the American Bar Association, 1917

Powell, Lyman P. and Gertrude W. The Spirit of Democracy. New York: Rand McNally and Company, 1918

Prentice, Alfred C. "The Problem of the Narcotic Drug Addict," *The Journal of the American Medical Association*, Volume 76, Number 23, 4 June 1921

Rainey, Henry T., Chair, et al. Traffic in Narcotic Drugs: Report of the Special Committee of Investigation Appointed March 25, 1918 by the Secretary of the Treasury. Washington, DC: Government Printing Office, 1919

Real Decreto de 31 de julio de 1.918, por el que se aprueba el reglamento para el comercio y dispensación de las sustancias tóxicas y en especial de las que ejercen acción narcótica, antitérmica o anestésica. Legislación española sobre drogas, I. Normativa de ámbito estatal, 1918

Richardson, Frank, Commissioner. First Annual Report of the Narcotic Drug Control Commission. Albany, NY: J. B. Lyon Company, 1919

Rolleston, Humphry, chair. Report of the Departmental Committee on Morphine and Heroin Addiction. London: His Majesty's Stationery Office, 1926

Roosevelt, Theodore. "Theodore Roosevelt's Annual Message to Congress for 1904," Records of the U.S. House of Representatives, National Archives

________________ "Policy toward other nations of western hemisphere," Congressional Record, Senate, 6 Dec 1904

Rowell, Earl Albert. Battling the Wolves of Society: the Narcotic Evil. Mountain View, CA: Pacific Press Publishing Association, 1929

Sacco, Lisa N. "Drug Enforcement in the United States: History, Policy, and Trends," Congressional Research Service Report, October 2, 2014

Sajous, Charles E. de M., et al, editors. New York Medical Journal, Volume CIV, July to December, Inclusive New York: A. R. Elliott Publishing Co., 1916

Salvador Viada y Vilaseca, D. *Código Penal Reformado de 1870*, Libro Primero. Barcelona: Establecimiento Tipográfico de Luis Tasso, 1874

Schaff, Philip, ed. A Select Library of the Nicene and Post-Nicene Fathers of the Christian Church, Volume X: Saint Chrysostom: Homilies on the Gospel of Saint Matthew. NY: The Christian Literature Company, 1888

Schless, Robert A. "The Drug Addict," The American Mercury, Volume IV, No. 4, February 1925

Schmeckebier, L. F. The Bureau of Prohibition: Its History, Activities, and Organization. Washington, DC: Lord Baltimore Press, 1929

Schoell, Frank A. *Histoire des États-Unis*. Paris, FR: Payot, 1985

Schrad, Mark Lawrence. "The Forgotten History of Black Prohibitionism," *Politico Magazine*, 02/06/2021

Secretary of State, Director. The Statutes at Large of the United States of America from March, 1913, to March, 1915, Volume XXXVIII. Washington, DC: Government Printing Office, 1915

______________, Director. The Statutes at Large of the United States of America from April 1917, to March, 1919, Volume XL. Washington, DC: Government Printing Office, 1919

______________, director. The Statutes at Large of the United States of America from May, 1919, to March, 1921, Volume XLI, Part 1. Washington, DC: Government Printing Office, 1921

Sender, Ramón J. Chronicle of Dawn, tr. W. R. Trask. London: Jonathan Cape, 1945

_______________ *Cronica del alba*. NY: Las Américas Publishing Company, 1963

Seneca, Lucius Annaeus. L. Annaeus Seneca Minor Dialogues Together with the Dialogue On Clemency, tr. Aubrey Stewart. London: George Bell and Sons, 1889

______________________ Seneca Moral Essays, Volume II, tr. John W. Basore. Cambridge, MA: Harvard University Press, 1932

Shaw, Albert, ed. The American Review of Reviews, Vol. 53, Jan – June. NY: The Review of Review Co., 1916

Siler, J. F., et al. "Mariajuana [sic] smoking in Panama," *Military Surgeon*, Volume 73, 1933

Sinclair, Andrew. Prohibition: the Era of Excess. Boston, MA: Little, Brown and Company, 1962

Smith, Cecil Clementi, et al. Report of the British Delegates to the International Opium Conference held at The Hague, December 1911 – January 1912. London: His Majesty's Stationery Office, 1912

Spinoza, Benedict de. Improvement of the Understanding, Ethics and Correspondence, tr. R. H. M. Elwes. London: L. Beling Tetens, 1901

______, Benedicti de. *Opera*, Vol. I. Lipsiae: Typis et Sumtibus Bernh. Tauchnitz Jun., 1843

Stedman, Thomas L., ed. "The Growing Enslavement of the Medical Profession," Medical Record, Volume 99, January 1, 1921 – June 25, 1921. NY: William Wood and Company, 1921

Strong, Josiah. Our Country: Its Possible Future and its Present Crisis. NY: The American Home Missionary Society, 1885

Stuntz, Homer C. The Philippines and the Far East. Cincinnati, OH: Jennings and Pye, 1904

Szasz, Thomas. Ceremonial Chemistry: The Ritual Persecution of Drugs, Addicts, and Pushers. Garden City, NY: Anchor Press/Doubleday, 1974

Taft, W. H. "The Baccalaureate Oration Delivered on the Occasion of the Eighty-first Annual Commencement of Miami University at Oxford, Ohio," *The Miami Bulletin*, Series IV, Number 9, November. Miami, OH: Published by Miami University, 1905

Taylor, Arnold H. American Diplomacy and the Narcotics Traffic, 1900 – 1939: A Study in International Humanitarian Reform. Durham, NC: Duke University Press, 1969

Towns, Charles B. Habits that Handicap: the Menace of Opium, Alcohol, Tobacco, and the Remedy. New York: The Century Co., 1916

Underwood, O. W. Congressional Record: Containing the Proceedings and Debates of the Sixty-Third Congress, Third Session, Volume LII, Part I. Washington, DC: Government Printing Office, 1915

United States v Behrman, 258 US 280 (1922)

United States v. Doremus, 249 United States Reports 86 (1919)

United States v. Friedman, 224 Federal Reporter 276 (1915)

United States v. Jin Fuey Moy, 225 Federal Reporter 1003 (1915)

United States v. Woods (and five like cases), 224 Federal Reporter 278 (1915)

Unknown author. International Opium Conference The Hague december 1, 1911 – january 23, 1912, Summary of the Minutes (Unofficial). The Hague, NL: National Printing Office, 1912

Unknown compiler. *Importation and Use of Opium Hearings before the Committee on Ways and Means of the House of Representatives, 61st Congress, 3d Session.* Washington, DC: Government Printing Office, 1911

Unknown compiler. *Congressional Record: Containing the Proceedings and Debates of the Sixty-Second Congress, Second Session*, Volume XLVIII, Part I. Washington, DC: Government Printing Office, 1912

Unknown compiler. *Congressional Record: Proceedings and Debates of the Sixty-Third Congress*, Third Session, Volume 52, Part I – Bound Edition. Washington, DC: Government Printing Office, 1915

Unknown compiler. *Congressional Record Proceedings and Debates of the First Session of the Seventieth Congress*, Volume LXIX – Part 2, January 9 to January 31, 1928. Washington, DC: Government Printing Office, 1928

Unknown contributor. "The Proceedings of the International Opium Conference at The Hague," *The British Medical Journal*, Volume II, 14 September 1912

Unknown copywriter. "Advertisement for Chamberlain's Cough Remedy," Brisbane *Telegraph*, Saturday 9 May 1903

Unknown copywriter. "Directions for Using Chamberlain's Colic, Cholera and Diarrhoea Remedy." Des Moines, Iowa: Chamberlain's Medicine Company, 1910-1915

Unknown editor. *Harvey's Weekly*, Volume 3, No. 23, Week Ending June 5, 1920

Unknown editor. "Marihuana Problems," *The Journal of the American Medical Association*, Volume 127, Number 17, Saturday, April 28, 1945

Unknown writer. "Cross-Country Kissing Record," *St. Louis Post-Dispatch*, Volume 50, No. 127, Wednesday, 21 December 1898

Unknown writer. "J. J. Hill for Reciprocity: Too many Americans going to Canada – Chinese boycott serious," *New York Times*, Wednesday 10 January 1906

Unknown writer. "Copeland to Resign Soon, He Intimates," *The New York Times*, Volume LXVIII, No. 22,346, Monday 31 Mar 1919

Unknown writer. "Billy Sunday Speeds Barleycorn to Grave," *The New York Times*, Volume LXIX, No. 22638, Saturday, 17 January 1920

Unknown writer. "'Dry Act' Licenses Now Exceed 57,000," *The New York Times*, Volume LXVIIII, Issue 22,807, Sunday, 4 July 1920

Usó Arnal, Joan Carles. "*Sobre los orígenes del «problema de la droga» en España*," *Ateneo de Castellón*, No. 4, Octubre, 1991

Vaillant, George E. "A Twelve-Year Follow-Up of New York Narcotic Addicts: I. The Relation of Treatment to Outcome," *American Journal of Psychiatry*, Volume 122, Issue 7, January 1966

_________________ "A 20-Year Follow-Up of New York Narcotic Addicts," Archives of General Psychiatry, Volume 29, Number 2, August 1973

Volk, Lester D. "Extension of Remarks of Hon. Lester D. Volk of New York in the House of Representatives, *Friday, January 13, 1922*," Appendix to the Congressional Record, Volume 62, Part 13. Washington, DC: Government Printing Office, 1922

Wallace, George B., Chairman. The Marihuana Problem in the City of New York: Sociological, Medical, Psychological and Pharmacological Studies by the Mayor's Committee on Marihuana. Lancaster, PA: The Jacques Cattell Press, 1944

Wannamaker, John. Book News: A Monthly Survey of General Literature, Volume XI, September 1892 to August 1893. Philadelphia, PA: John Wannamaker, 1893

Washington, Booker. "Prohibition and the Negro," *The Outlook*, Volume 88, No. 11, Saturday, 14 March 1908

Webb et al. v. United States, 249 United States Reports 96 (1919)

Weicker, Theodore, President. Squibb's Materia Medica, Part II. NY: E. R. Squibb & Sons, 1906

Wheeler, Wayne B. "The Meaning of the Supreme Court Decision on National Prohibition," *The Christian Advocate*, Volume XCV, No. 22, 1 July 1920

_______________ "Statement of Wayne B. Wheeler on Bills Relating to Prohibition Enforcement," The National Prohibition Law, Hearings Before the Subcommittee of the Committee on the Judiciary, United States Senate, Sixty-Ninth Congress, First Session on ... Bills to Amend the National Prohibition Act, April 5 to 24, 1926, Volume 1. Washington, DC: Government Printing Office, 1926

Williams, Henry Smith. Drug Addicts are Human Beings: The Story of Our Billion-Dollar Drug Racket. Washington, DC: Shaw Publishing Company, 1938

Wolff, Leon. Little Brown Brother: How the United States Purchased and Pacified the Philippine Islands at the Century's Turn. NY: History Book Club, 2006

Wright, Hamilton. "The International Opium Commission (Part 1)" The American Journal of International Law, Volume 3. New York: Baker, Voorhis & Company, 1909

_______________ "The International Opium Conference," The American Journal of International Law, Volume 6. New York: Baker, Voorhis & Company, 1912

________________ "The International Opium Conference. Part II," The American Journal of International Law, Volume 7. New York: Baker, Voorhis & Company, 1913

________________ "Report to the Secretary of State on the Second International Opium Conference by the American delegates: Hamilton Wright, Lloyd Bryce, Gerrit John Kollen (31 July 1913)," Papers Relating to the Foreign Relations of the United States, with the address of the President to Congress December 2, 1913

Wright, Quincey. "The Narcotics Convention of 1931," *American Journal of International Law*, Volume 28, No. 3, July 1934

Zabriskie, Alexander C. Bishop Brent: Crusader for Christian Unity. Philadelphia, PA: The Westminster Press, 1948

Zahle, Herluf, President. Records of the Second Opium Conference Geneva, November 17th, 1924 – February 25th, 1925, Volume I Plenary Meetings, Text of the Debates. Geneva, Switzerland: League of Nations, 1925

INDEX

Adulteration of alcohol 1641

Alfonso XIII, portrait 1770

against drug abuse 1782

American Association of Pharmaceutical Chemists 1590

American Medical Association

early conflicts with APhA 1513

cooperation with government 1517

established 1587

decries drug addiction 1614

decries alcohol 1636

promotes sexual continence 1637

wine as medicine 1637

medicinal alcohol 1638

maintenance doses as exploitation 1664

cannabis as problem 1753

American Pharmaceutical Association

drugs destroy the soul 1515

against the Chinaman 1678

Anido, Severiano Martínez

photograph 1784

disgrace of cocaine 1785

threatens Unamuno 1785

Anslinger, Harry J.

photograph 1713

versus alcohol 1714

"Assassin of Youth" 1732

cannabis as monster 1738

migratory bird law 1739

reaction to La Guardia study 1745

Ateneo de Madrid 1785

Atropa belladonna 1560
in Town's concoction 1603

Bishop, Ernest S. 1613
photograph 1654
at Bellevue 1655
on maintenance doses 1656
supported by fellow doctors 1659
Bosch y Carrió, Joaquín Milans del, photograph 1782
Boutell, Henry Sherman 1557
Brent, Charles Henry
arrives in Philippines 1530
on opium as social vice 1535
on colonialism 1537
photograph 1541
useless historical questions 1550
at Hague Conference 1568
Bryan, William Jennings 1583
fires Wright 1583
Burgess, John William 1521
Burroughs, William Seward, photograph 1716
Butler, Willis Pollard
photograph 1660
on maintenance doses 1661
photograph, and wife 1663
starting the clinics 1677
denounced by undercover agent 1687
morphine not heroin 1689
older not younger 1689
economics 1691

Cannabis
as threat to civilization 1734
lurid movie poster 1735
as stimulant to crime 1737
as cause of insanity 1737
as drug of degenerate Mexicans 1738
as Mr. Hyde 1738
injecting cannabis 1740
Canal Zone study 1741
Bellevue study 1742
Army study 1743
La Guardia study 1744
in 1925 Geneva Agreement 1758
Egyptian proposes ban 1760
Capone, Alphonse Gabriel 1644
photograph 1648
Chamberlain's Colic, Cholera and Diarrhoea Remedy 1564
Chamberlain's Cough Remedy 1563
Chinese
attacks on, cartoon by Nast 1519
Chinese Exclusion Act 1542
Clark, James Beauchamp "Champ" 1558
Cocaine Lil, lyrics 1718
Coleridge, Samuel Taylor 1651
Crafts, Wilbur F.
director of the International Reform Bureau 1524
and *child races* 1525
derails Tafts opium proposal 1534
ethical-theological argument 1583

Daugherty, Harry Micajah 1640
Dewey, George A. 1527
Diamond, Jack "Legs" 1644
Doctors boiled in oil 1617
Dry zones 1626
DuMez, Andrew Grover 1666

E*l Escándalo* 1786
Estimating the number of drug addicts 1518

Fall, Albert Bacon 1640
Finger, Henry James 1568
    photograph 1569
Foster, David Johnson
    photograph 1551
    presents bills to Congress 1553
    forerunner to *Harrison Act* 1585
Francis Burton Harrison 1556

Galenus, Claudius 1657
German saloons unpatriotic 1626

Hague Conference 1568
    England and morphine, cocaine 1575
    morphine replacing opium in China 1576
    Italy proposes adding cannabis 1577

medical or legitimate 1579
expanded to other drugs 1579
heroin 1580
possession 1580
lack of signatures 1581
inserted into Treaty of Versailles 1582
Harding, Warren Gamaliel 1640
Harrison Act 1585
amendments 1591
seen as taxing measure 1596
as criminal law 1596
versus *Volstead Act* 1597
possession as crime 1606
burden of proof shifted to defendant 1606
probatio diabolica 1607
duty to register lacking 1607
punishment not fitting 1608
possession not presumptive 1609
patients not required to register 1610
law needs recasting 1612
upheld as constitutional 1615
prescription not in good faith 1616
penalties vs *Volstead Act* 1698
violations 1699
arraignments and convictions 1702
Harrison, Francis Burton 1585
photograph 1586
Hill, James J. 1542
on Chinese boycott 1543
Hippocratic Oath 1637

Hobson, Richmond Pearson
 Father of American Prohibition 1601
 photograph 1602
 heroin addicts as lepers 1603
 International Narcotics Education Association 1617
 on white, black and red 1621
 apocalypse 1622
 scuttling the *Merrimac* 1625
Holmes, Oliver Wendell, Jr.
 dissent in *Behrman* 1705
Hosie, Alexander 1546
Hyoscyamus niger 1560
 in Town's recipe 1603

Ibáñez, Vicente Blasco 1780
International Opium Commission of 1909 1544
 recommendations 1549
International Narcotics Education Association 1617
Irish, as drunks, cartoon by Nast 1516
Italy
 proposes cannabis be added 1577

Jamaica Ginger 1642
James, William, quote 1719
Jefferson, Thomas
 letters to James Monroe 1523
John Chrysostom 1559
Jukes 1633

Kolb, Lawrence
photograph 1598
opium and crime 1599
estimates addicts 1618
PHS study 1673
follow up study 1674
on uselessness of so-called cures 1700

***L**a Caoba* 1785
Lansky, Meyer 1644
photograph 1646
Largo Caballero, Francisco 1782
Lessing, Ephraim Gotthold 1651
Lewin, Lewis
on prohibition of alcohol 1729
comparing to other prohibitions 1731
Lexington, Kentucky farm
five year follow up study 1667
twelve year follow up study 1667
twenty year follow up study 1668
aerial photograph 1669
Liquor taxes as percentage of internal revenue 1627
Lombroso, Ezechia Marco 1634
Luciano, Charles "Lucky" 1644
photograph 1647

Mahan, Alfred Thayer 1521
Manifest Destiny

article in *Harper's*, 1885 1520
Mann Act (White-Slave Traffic Act of 1910) 1552
Mann, James Robert 1552
forerunner to *Harrison Act* 1585
Mas y Sanz, Sinibaldo de 1532
McKinley, William 1521
Mellon, Andrew W.
photograph 1693
increased smuggling of narcotics 1694
increased smuggling of alcohol 1696
Missionaries
and Far East policy 1520
Monroe Doctrine
influence of Thomas Jefferson 1523
text 1524
Monroe, James
letters from Thomas Jefferson 1523
Morphine
blessing and curse, Lewin 1517
Muir, William Edward 1559

National Association of Manufacturers
of Medicinal Products 1590
National Association of Retail Druggists 1588
versus government interference 1589
National Prohibition Act 1629
National Wholesale Druggists' Association 1556
kills Foster bill 1562
at National Drug Trade Conference 1589
Nutt, Levi G. 1696

photograph 1697
few addicts 1697
on narcotic farms 1709
scandal of son and son-in-law 1713

Opium den on Manila Street 1536
Opium
substitution policy in Philippines 1539
1909 International Commission 1544

Payne, Sereno E. 1557
Philippines
war with Spain, 1898 1527
proportion of dead to wounded 1528
opium in the Chinese colony 1529
Spanish policy on opium 1531
Spanish opium commission 1532
opium monopoly established 1533
Philippine Opium Investigation Committee 1537
recommendations of committee 1538
Plaut, Albert 1561
Porter, Stephen Geyer
photograph 1680
exaggerating the number of addicts 1681
Pound, Roscoe
photograph 1592
law as ethical minimum 1593
Pure Food and Drug Act 1510

Racial prejudice and drugs 1518
Rivera y Orbaneja, Miguel Primo de 1785
Rizo, Carlos Esplá 1780
    photograph 1781
Rodríguez, Buenaventura Muñoz 1785
Rolleston, Humphry Davy
    portrait 1670
    committee 1671
    recommendations 1672
    forty year follow up study 1673
Root, Elihu 1535
Roosevelt, Theodore
    becomes president after McKinley 1521
    corollary to Monroe Doctrine 1523
    Big Stick 1524
    portrait 1526
    on Chinese boycott 1542
Rothstein, Arnold 1644

Schless, Robert A. 1662
Schlieffelin, William Jay 1557
Schultz, Dutch
    photograph 1639
    one of many mobsters 1644
Scientific Temperance Federation of Boston 1626
Seneca 1567
Sotelo, José Calvo 1782

Spain
policy on opium in the Philippines 1531
opium commission 1532
opium monopoly established 1533
annual import of opium 1771
Codigo Penal of 1870 1771
Bonald Labs heroin, cocaine 1773
Real Decreto of 31 July 1918 1774
Codigo Penal of 1928 1776
price of morphine 1778
black market 1779
adulteration of cocaine 1783
Strong, Josiah
WASP ideals and racial dreams 1520
Portrait 1522
Stunz, Homer Clyde 1530
thirty millions oppose Taft opium policy 1535
petition 1536
Sunday, William Ashley "Billy" 1630
mock funeral 1630
photograph 1631

Taft, William Howard
governor of Philippines 1530
portrait 1507
proposes opium monopoly 1534
exclude labor not trade 1543
on Foster bills 1554
backlash 1574

Teapot Dome 1640
Tenney, Charles Daniel 1544
Torrio, Johnny 1643
Towns, Charles Barnes 1560
  recipe of cure 1561
  on cannabis and addiction 1562
  on cigarettes 1585
  concoction 1603
  diarrhea, delirium and damnation 1604
  lack of results 1604
  vomiting 1665
  irreproducible results 1667
Treadway, Walter Lewis
  photograph 1746
  and *Marihuana Tax Act* hearings 1747
Treaty of Nanking 1531
Treaty of Versailles
  incorporates Hague Agreement 1582
Tuan Fang 1545

Unamuno y Jugo, Miguel de 1785
  photograph 1788
Underwood, Oscar Wilder 1593
Usó, Juan Carlos
  photograph 1777

Volk, Lester David
  photograph 1701
  denounces government interference 1703

denounces legal interpretation 1704
Volstead Act 1620
six million petitioners 1620
passes 1621
penalties vs *Harrison Act* 1698
success due to 1722
loopholes 1723
adulteration 1723
corruption 1724
anti-prohibition parades 1726
possession not criminalized 1727
Volstead, Andrew John
photograph 1619

Washington, Booker Taliaferro 1622
photograph 1624
Wheeler, Wayne Bidwell 1620
Wiley, Harvey Washington 1510
photograph, working in lab 1511
Woodruff, Charles Marius 1558
Woodward, William Creighton
photograph 1748
cannabis not marihuana 1749
no evidence of crime 1751
no evidence of addiction 1752
Wright, Hamilton 1544
photograph 1547
rewriting history 1551
on Foster bills 1555
on cocaine, rape and Negroes 1555

at Hague Conference 1568
on Portugal 1571
on Persia 1571
on Holland 1572
on France 1572
on Russia, Siam, Japan, Formosa 1573
on Germany 1576

Zanthoxylum americanum 1560
in Town's recipe 1603

www.ingramcontent.com/pod-product-compliance
Lightning Source LLC
La Vergne TN
LVHW051157210926
848486LV00021B/412/J
9781735787879